D0760814

William Blake's Illustrations to
the Poetry of Milton

Paradise Lost VI: The Expulsion of the Rebel Angels. Huntington Library, San Marino, California

PAMELA DUNBAR

William Blake's Illustrations to the Poetry of Milton

CLARENDON PRESS · OXFORD
1980

Oxford University Press, Walton Street, Oxford OX2 6DP

OXFORD   LONDON   GLASGOW

NEW YORK   TORONTO   MELBOURNE   WELLINGTON

KUALA LUMPUR   SINGAPORE   HONG KONG   TOKYO

DELHI   BOMBAY   CALCUTTA   MADRAS   KARACHI

NAIROBI   DAR ES SALAAM   CAPE TOWN

Published in the United States
by Oxford University Press, New York

© *Pamela Dunbar 1980*

British Library Cataloguing in Publication Data
Dunbar, Pamela
  William Blake's illustrations to the poetry of Milton.
  1. Blake, William
  2. Milton, John—Illustrations
  I. Title
  759.2   ND1942.B55   79-41155
  ISBN 0-19-817345-8

Printed in Great Britain by
Butler & Tanner Ltd, Frome and London

To Keith

PREFACE

This work offers a detailed study of Blake's Milton illustrations. It examines their relationship with their texts, their design and symbolic detail, Blake's attitudes towards Milton, and the artist's cosmological and metaphysical 'system' as it reveals itself in the illustrations. In addition it endeavours to assess the artistic merits of the Milton plates and, where relevant, to suggest pictorial sources for them.

As it is the illustrations themselves that form the basis of the study, it has not been possible for me to provide a detailed explication of Blake's 'system', its complexities and inconsistencies, and the way in which it develops from the period of the shorter Prophetic books to the time of the late masterpieces—*Jerusalem*, and the *Job* and Dante illustrations. However, I have tried to provide enough detail to give the general reader a working knowledge of those aspects of the 'system' which are directly relevant to the Milton illustrations.

Those drawings which may have been based either on Milton's writings or on the Bible, or which serve primarily as illustrations to other works, like Edward Young's *Night Thoughts*, are not accorded a separate place in my discussion although many are mentioned in passing. This applies also to pictures which are associated with Milton's writings but which are in some fundamental way inconsistent with them—for example 'God Creating the World', which depicts not Christ but the Urizenic god in the act of creation, and which therefore must have Proverbs 8: 27 as its primary source.

It gives me great pleasure to acknowledge the debts which I have incurred while writing this study: to Sir Geoffrey Keynes, elder statesman of Blake scholars; to Miss Kathleen Raine, poet and author of several monographs on Blake; and to Professor J. B. Trapp, Director of the Warburg Institute. The greatest of my debts is to Professor Ian Jack of Pembroke College, Cambridge, who was associated with the project since its inception and whose tactful guidance, scholarly rigour, and general encouragement have been unfailing.

I am most grateful to the Council of Girton College, Cambridge, for a grant towards a publication subvention, and to the Trustees of the Worts Travelling Scholars' Fund (Cambridge University) for a grant towards the cost of a visit to the United States, during which I examined the many Milton Blakes which are now in that country. I am particularly indebted to Mr. George Watson of St. John's College, Cambridge, whose exceptional generosity in endowing a Fund in Support of Academic Publications, of which I am proud to be one of the first beneficiaries, has been instrumental in enabling this volume to be produced. I am also grateful to the Publications Committee of the British Academy, which administers the Fund.

PAMELA DUNBAR

CONTENTS

LIST OF PLATES

TEXTUAL NOTE

Quotations from Blake's writings are taken from *The Complete Writings of William Blake*, ed. Geoffrey Keynes, 1966. In citation this edition is referred to as 'K', followed directly by the page number then by the number of the plate (preceded by the abbreviation 'pl.') and, in the case of the poetry, the lines in which the quotation occurs. Extracts from the poetry of Milton are taken from *The Poems of John Milton*, ed. John Carey and Alastair Fowler, 1968. References to quotations from Blake and Milton are placed in the text; other references are cited in footnotes.

For convenience I have sometimes referred to the illustrations which form part of a series by citing the name of the poem illustrated followed by a Roman numeral indicating the order of the picture in its series: for example, the first illustration of the *Comus* series becomes *Comus* I. Illustrations are frequently identified by reference to their present ownership: for example, 'the Huntington (or Boston) *Paradise Lost* series'.

I INTRODUCTION

Milton's influence is apparent almost everywhere in Blake's works. It begins with his first volume of verses and some of his early sketches, and it only concludes on his deathbed, where he was said to have been working up a print of his celebrated design 'God Creating the World'[1] only a few days before he died. It informs almost all of his poetry and many of his drawings—either directly in subject-matter and style, or indirectly in the sense that they would not have been conceived as they were without a knowledge of Milton's interpretation of the Christian story. It far exceeds that of any of his other artistic mentors.

Blake's relationship with Milton never became a slavish, one-sided affair, and neither was it a purely 'literary' connection. It was a lively, stimulating, intimate, intense, and provocative kinship of mind and spirit that on the part of Blake, the 'active' partner, combined deep affection and admiration with elements of profound disapprobation, and which had at its core the later poet's capacity readily to evoke the spirit of Milton and to engage in 'discourse' with it. With this spirit Blake must have attained as nearly reciprocal a relationship as it can be possible to attain with the dead. Something of its individual flavour is caught in the following anecdote from the *Reminiscences* of the literary socialite and diarist Henry Crabb Robinson:

As he (Blake) spoke of frequently Seeing Milton, I ventured to ask, half ashamed at the time, which of the three or four portraits in *Hollis's* Memoirs ... is the most like(.)—He answd (')They are all like, At different Ages(.)—I have seen him as a youth And as an old man with a long flowing beard(.) He came lately as an old man(.)—He said he came to ask a favor of me(.)—He said he had committed an error in his Paradise Lost, which he wanted me to correct, in a poem or picture; but I declined(.) I said I had my own duties to perform(.)—It is a presumptuous question(.') ... He wished me to expose the falsehood of his doctrine, taught in the Paradise Lost—That Sexual intercourse arouse [*sic*] out of the Fall(.)—Now that cannot be, for no good can spring out of Evil(.')[2]

[1] Also known as 'The Ancient of Days'—a design partly inspired by the account in *Paradise Lost* of Christ reaching down with his golden compasses to inscribe the world upon the deep (vii, 225–31). For the anecdote about Blake on his deathbed, see John Thomas Smith, *Nollekens and his Times*, 1828, ii, 479.

[2] 26.2.52; reproduced in *Blake Records*, ed. G. E. Bentley, Jr., 1969, pp. 543–4. It is difficult to believe

This preoccupation with the spirit of Milton extends naturally to an interest in his life and personality and the influence which these may have had upon his works. Blake's Milton portrait for instance, which was executed in 1800 as one of a series of 'Poets' Heads' for William Hayley's new library, stresses the Puritan poet's unique combination of visionary insight and 'corporeal' error and the way in which these elements pervade his works.

The head, which was almost certainly modelled on William Faithorne's portrait from the life, completed when Milton was sixty-two, is almost frontal. It has wavy, shoulder-length hair and the blank eyes of an antique statue—here doubtless intended to suggest Milton's blindness. The head emerges from a stiff white collar and is set within a wreath of interwoven leaves. An apple hangs from the lower right-hand section of the wreath and the Serpent, with another apple clamped between its jaws, disports its sinuous body along the lower edge of the plate, thus forming a grimly decorative base for the picture. Palm trees are shown at the left and right-hand extremities of the plate. A harp leans against the tree on the left and a set of pan-pipes is hanging from that on the right. These musical instruments suggest the main types of poetry with which Milton was associated—the pastoral and, through the harp of David, the lyrical and the scriptual-Prophetic.

In the poet's wreath oak-leaves mingle conspicuously with those of the celebratory, and more conventional, laurel. The oak is for Blake a negative emblem associated in particular with the sacrificial murders of the ancient Druids and in general with the whole of the fallen world. The apple of biblical discord which dangles from the wreath seems to accuse the poet himself, and the Serpent, which appears in earlier Milton portraits merely as an ornament or else as a commemorative tribute to the poet's greatest work, here emerges, through its pre-eminence in size and in placement, through the realism of its portrayal, and through the duplication of the apple, to threaten the poet's own composure. So the Milton of Blake's portrait is himself presented as a victim of the errors that he exposes in his greatest work.

On the other hand, because he told the redemptive story in his poetry, particularly in *Paradise Lost* and *Paradise Regained*, and because he manifested in his own nature the supreme genius of man as well as some of his basest 'errors', Milton also serves for Blake both as an epitome of human nature and as an agent of the salvation of mankind—in short, as an avatar of Christ. In the Prophetic book *Milton* Blake has the titular hero return to earth after death in order to expurgate his 'errors'—his

---

that a careful and sympathetic reader like Blake could have overlooked the 'bower' scene in Book IV of *Paradise Lost*, in which the sexuality of Milton's Paradise is unambiguously asserted. This must cast some doubt on the accuracy of Crabb Robinson's account.

support of a tyrannical political establishment and his own puritanical and rationalizing habits of mind. As an indirect result of this saving gesture he eventually combines with other divine beings to form the body of 'One Man, Jesus the Saviour, wonderful!' (K 534; pl. 42, 11) The illustrations to *L'Allegro* and *Il Penseroso* are a visual record of Milton's 'first' life and end with a prophecy of his redemptive return and regeneration similar to that expounded in the Prophetic book. It seems that for Blake the mission of Milton the artist can only be fully realized with the regeneration of Milton the individual.

In a celebrated passage from *The Marriage of Heaven and Hell* Blake again shows irritation with the superficial import of Milton's writings, together with faith in the integrity of his 'true', or subconscious, personality and attitudes:

Those who restrain desire, do so because theirs is weak enough to be restrained; and the restrainer or reason usurps its place & governs the unwilling.

And being restrain'd it by degrees becomes passive, till it is only the shadow of desire.

The history of this is written in Paradise Lost, & the Governor or Reason is call'd Messiah.

And the original Archangel, or possessor of the command of the heavenly host, is call'd the Devil or Satan, and his children are call'd Sin & Death. ...

It indeed appear'd to Reason as if Desire was cast out; but the Devil's account is, that the Messiah fell, & formed a heaven of what he stole from the Abyss. ...

... in Milton, the Father is Destiny, the Son a Ratio of the five senses, & the Holy-ghost Vacuum!

Note: The reason Milton wrote in fetters when he wrote of Angels & God, and at liberty when of Devils & Hell, is because he was a true Poet and of the Devil's party without knowing it.

(K 149–50; pls. 5–6)

It is not always possible to distinguish clearly between influence and affinity, and what may be regarded as Blake's indebtedness to Milton might also be ascribed—indeed was so ascribed by Blake—to an ideal affinity of minds between the two men, to their mutual devotion to the Christian-Platonist tradition of fall and redemption, and to a humanist vision according to which man's grandeur and uniqueness derive from the conjunction within him of body and spirit, mortality and divinity.

The scholar, poet, and bibliophile William Hayley appears considerably to have strengthened Blake's interest in Milton, for it was not until after 1800, when Blake moved to the Sussex village of Felpham to work under Hayley's patronage, that he embarked on the two projects which were to become his most significant tributes to the Puritan poet—the illuminated Prophetic book *Milton* (1804–8) and the eight sets of illustrations to Milton's poetry (c. 1801–16). Hayley himself was an enthusiastic admirer of Milton's works, the owner of many editions of his poetry, and the author of a celebratory *Life*.[3] Later he also took over the editorship of Cowper's translations of Milton's Latin and Italian poems. His part in stimulating Blake's interest in Milton must have been largely indirect, however, for—apart from the portrait for the frieze of poets' heads in his new library—the only Milton-related project for which he commissioned Blake came to nothing.

This commission was to design and engrave some plates for the Cowper venture, originally conceived as a complete edition of Milton's writings. In fact all of the project except the foreign-language poems fell victim to Cowper's final illness, and when these were eventually published under the editorship of Hayley as the *Latin and Italian Poems of Milton* (1808), the volume contained no art works at all from Blake's hand: the only two plates in it were engraved by Raimbach after Flaxman.

Blake's major Milton projects, the Prophetic book and the sets of illustrations, differ from the earlier Milton-influenced poetry and paintings—the *Poetical Sketches*, the opening stanzas of the 'Prophecy' to *Europe*, the *Book of Urizen*, parts of *Vala*, and isolated paintings and sketches—in their scale, their preoccupation with the life and personality of Milton as well as with his works, and the lively criticism which they combine with their evident admiration for their subject.

Although the Milton illustrations have never been among Blake's best-known works, the seventy-six plates of the sets, and the dozen or so paintings related to them, are of considerable artistic merit and supply a perceptive visual analogue to their texts. They also provide a detailed record of Blake's literary and philosophical views—particularly of his attitudes towards Milton—during the sixteen or seventeen years over which they were executed, as well as a kind of gloss on Blake's own poetry.

Blake's choice of poems for illustration—*Paradise Lost, Paradise Regained*, the *Nativity Ode, L'Allegro* and *Il Penseroso*, and *Comus*—needs no justification, for it includes most of Milton's best-known and most-loved works. All of the first three poems which he tackled, *Comus, Paradise Lost*, and the *Nativity Ode*, generated not one but two complete sets of illustrations (and a third *Paradise Lost* set was begun)—something which may suggest the existence of ready buyers as much as the artist's possible dissatisfaction with first attempts.

One version of each of the duplicated sets, and all the *L'Allegro* and *Il Penseroso* pictures, were bought from Blake by Thomas Butts, a clerk in the Office of the Muster-Master General and one of the artist's most loyal patrons. The other *Comus* series was executed for the Rev. Joseph Thomas of Epsom, and it has been argued

[3] *Poetical Works of John Milton with a Life of the author by William Hayley*, 1794.

that the second *Paradise Lost* and *Nativity Ode* sets were also bought by him.[4] The first owner of the *Paradise Regained* plates and of the uncompleted *Paradise Lost* series, for which only three illustrations were produced, was the artist John Linnell. The duplicated sets differ to some degree in detail and in style but their subjects and general conception remain largely the same.

The eight sets of Milton drawings form a cohesive group. Most of the plates are intricately organized and of considerable beauty, all are executed in pen and delicate shades of water-colour, and all stress the gentler and more optimistic aspects of Milton's vision. They differ strikingly from the early colour-print 'The House of Death', which is thought to have been executed under the influence of Fuseli and which is comparatively dark in colouring and unrelievedly sombre in conception. All the sets emphasize the 'universal' themes that dominate Blake's mature works—the lapse from grace, the spiritual, physiological, intellectual, and social consequences of this lapse, and the promise of redemption; the nature of 'error' and of 'truth' (to Blake any belief in 'sin' and 'virtue' was abhorrent); the connections between matter and spirit, between externality and inwardness; and the relations between man and woman, between man and his 'negative' self, and between man and God.

Emphatically held beliefs and a strong creative personality inevitably led Blake in his designs for the works of others to 'correct' those works in the light of his own acquaintance with the one Truth. Yet such was his belief in Milton's visionary insight—even though an insight marred in part by the 'errors' of repressiveness and puritanism—that instead of making any radical restatement of his texts he confined himself to releasing the insights which he considered to lie hidden beneath them. This he did through the unobtrusive omission or addition of 'minute particulars', the subtle alteration of emphases, and the intermittent interpolation of another 'layer' of significance that brings a detail or a whole passage into harmony with his own 'system'. This approach contrasts markedly with his method in the earlier Young and Gray designs, where he had concentrated simply on exposing the 'errors' of his authors by altering or directly contradicting their message.

Blake's respect for the Milton texts is also shown in his fidelity to their mood, their detail, their complex narrative structures (particularly in the case of *Paradise*

[4] By Leslie Parris in 'William Blake's Mr. Thomas' (*Times Literary Supplement*, 5.12.68, p. 1390), on the basis of the common appearance of all three sets at Sotheby's sale of 2 August 1872, probably as part of a single collection, and of notes by W. M. Rossetti attributing previous ownership of the *Comus* and *Paradise Lost* drawings to Thomas's grandson, Drummond Percy Chase, who is known to have been the indirect beneficiary of at least one of his grandfather's artistic and literary treasures, a Second Folio Shakespeare that had been extra-illustrated by, among others, Blake.

Lost), and in the fact that all of the subjects which he selects for illustration depict incidents central to the main concerns of the poems, even though many of them are new to the Miltonic illustrative tradition.

With an artist as technically versatile as Blake, the choice of medium is often significant. The Milton illustrations are executed in water-colour, and the delicacy of their tints—to which reproductions rarely do justice—is in keeping with their generally optimistic message. The ink outlinings of the pictures serve to emphasize that 'Line of Beauty' (K 603) which Blake had learned both as an engraver and as a Neoplatonist to adore: 'The want of this determinate and bounding form evidences the want of idea in the artist's mind ... Leave out this line, and you leave out life itself; all is chaos again, and the line of the almighty must be drawn out upon it before man or beast can exist' (*A Descriptive Catalogue*, K 585).

The intricate textures and miniaturist effects of the Milton pictures differ radically from the succinct and vigorous impressionism of the Young drawings—where there was of course an unusual technical challenge to be met: how to expand the designs so that they would surround the inset pages of text—but they render to perfection that 'Definite & Determinate Identity' in which, to Blake, 'The Infinite alone resides' (*Jerusalem*, K 687; pl. 55, 64), that particularization and clarity of execution which he aspired to in his own works and which he recognized in those of Milton and the other 'immortals': 'Nor can an Original Invention Exist without Execution, Organized & minutely delineated & Articulated ... Drawn with a firm & decided hand at once, like Fuseli & Michael Angelo, Shakespeare & Milton' (*Public Address*, K 595).

Jean H. Hagstrum points out in *The Sister Arts*[5] that Milton's poetry is not on the whole pictorial, although it does contain pictorial elements:

Milton's visual touches ... remain [touches and strokes], serving other larger aims. The iconic and pictorialist conventions do appear, but they are soon absorbed in intellectual conceits, musical resonances, or sublime epic movements. ... One of the most characteristic motions of his imagination is to approach the pictorialist conventions and then to withdraw into other forms of expression.

Blake's task as an illustrator of Milton's works was therefore to organize such visual detail as he found into fully realized landscapes and characters, and to extend the potentially pictorial aspects of the writing. He also exploits fully those areas in which Milton was not pictorial and in which he, Blake, was therefore freed from any obligation of fidelity. For *Comus* he draws upon elements characteristic of the masque

[5] 1958, p. 127.

form—scenic transformations and visual detail offering symbolic resonance; for *Paradise Lost* he concentrates upon symbolic detail, gesture, and design; for the *Nativity Ode* he devotes himself to separate renderings of the wide-ranging effects of Christ's descent, indicating common causality by representing the Nativity stable in almost all the plates; for *L'Allegro* and *Il Penseroso*, probably in any event the most pictorial of all Milton's poems, he personifies allegorical abstractions and transforms hints of thumbnail scenes into complex, visionary land- and sky-scapes; and for *Paradise Regained* he concentrates attention on the duel between Christ and Satan by rendering it in an austerely literal manner and by reducing background detail to a minimum.

Blake's artistic debts in the Milton illustrations are far-reaching. They include classical statuary, the figure-drawing of Michelangelo and Raphael, medieval manuscript illumination, and the Miltonic paintings and drawings of his friends and contemporaries—notably Henry Fuseli, whose 'Milton Gallery' was first opened to the public in May 1799. Blake's conceptions share with Fuseli's a preoccupation with the heroic potential of the human form and an emphasis—expressionist in Fuseli—on its capacity to convey mental and spiritual states. Fuseli is said to have remarked that Blake was 'damned good to steal from': that the debt was reciprocal can be ascertained from a comparison of some of Blake's *Paradise Lost* pictures—particularly his pen-and-wash 'House of Death' and his 'Satan, Sin, and Death'—with their equivalents in the Milton Gallery.

In all Blake executed around 1,200 illustrations to the works of other writers, and illuminated 375 pages of his own poetry:[6] only his juvenile volume *Poetical Sketches* was produced without 'illumination' or illustration.[7] This predilection for complementing the written word with design springs from a determination to temper with the defining and redeeming image those elements of generalization and abstraction which are inherent in the nature of the word and which for Blake spell death to the Divine Vision. It also arises from a conviction of his that, if the Divine Vision is to prevail, truth must appeal to the whole man, and hence must be mediated to him by all of the 'three Powers ... of conversing with Paradise which the flood did not Sweep away' (*A Vision of the Last Judgment*, K 609)—the 'Powers' that is of poetry, painting, and music.[8]

[6] The figures are Jean H. Hagstrum's: see *William Blake: Poet and Painter*, 1964, p. 119.

[7] It was also his only volume of poetry to be brought out under a commercial publisher's imprint: all of his other poetic works were produced by his own hand.

[8] Although Blake never became a serious musician, Allan Cunningham records in his *Lives of the Most Eminent British Painters, Sculptors, and Architects*, 1830 (in G. E. Bentley, Jr., *Blake Records*, p. 482) that 'As he drew the figure he meditated the song which was to accompany it, and the music to which

The beauty of Blake's 'illuminated' works—so called because of their similarity to the illuminated manuscripts of the Middle Ages—suggests that their creator was attempting to restore to the written word that visual dimension which it has lacked since the invention of printing. The integration of word and design in these works— their texts are handwritten in the attractive 'copperplate' style, their illustrations penetrate deeply into the territory of the texts, and a single process of production governs them both—further indicates Blake's interest in the close association of the two arts. But despite their intimacy with their texts, the 'illuminations' often remain thematically independent of them, presenting a different aspect of the subject and sometimes even developing a complete narrative or thematic sequence of their own. This independence is as we have seen characteristic of his designs for the poetry of others.

Illustrations to the works of other writers generally present a different order of potential relationship and conflict from that which arises when an artist elects to become his own illustrator; but with Blake's illustrations to the works of Milton we experience the same combination of harmonious integration and creative tension that we derive from Blake's own 'illuminated' works. For in the Milton illustrations he has managed neither to 'efface himself behind his author (nor to) assert himself at the expense of the author',[9] but triumphantly to serve the interests of the Puritan poet—the visionary and 'unperverted' elements of his poet, at least—at the same time as he asserts his own significant vision.

---

the verse was to be sung, was the offspring too of the same moment.' Musical subjects and details play a prominent part in Blake's works, including those which have been influenced by Milton.

[9] The two ways in which, according to David Bland (*The Illustration of Books*, 1951, p. 14), an illustrator may 'approach his task'. Bland goes on: 'If he effaces himself too successfully there is always the risk that his work may lack character. But if he is determined to assert his individuality at all costs the danger is that his contribution may not be an illustration at all.'

II COMUS

Both of Blake's sets of illustrations to *Comus*[1] comprise eight plates, and the same eight subjects recur in each. All the corresponding plates are of similar design though they differ somewhat in detail, in style, and in size. The smaller set on the whole follows the detail of the text more closely than the larger, and its designs are generally balanced and symmetrical whereas those of the larger set are more natural and its figures more highly individualized.

The larger set was bought from Blake by the Rev. Joseph Thomas, and is now in the Huntington Library, San Marino, California. A note in a letter from Blake to John Flaxman, dated 19 October 1801, suggests that it was executed towards the end of 1801: 'Mr Thomas, your friend to whom you was so kind as to make honourable mention of me, has been at Felpham & did me the favor to call on me. I have promis'd him to send my designs for Comus when I have done them, directed to you' (K 810). The other set, which was bought from the artist by Thomas Butts, is today the property of the Museum of Fine Arts, Boston, Massachusetts. Its date of composition is not known.

The *Comus* illustrations provide an appropriate visual accompaniment to Milton's masque. Their elegant and engaging figurines are an admirable visual projection of the proto-allegorical ciphers of the text, and the statuesque poses and gestures of the figures—which in many cases correspond both within and between illustrations—counterbalance each other with masque-like formality:

> every one the dance
> Knows in its intricate mazes of delight artful to weave:
> Each one to sound his instruments of music in the dance,
> To touch each other & recede, to cross & change & return
> (*Milton*, K 512; pl. 26, 3–6)

[1] *A Masque presented at Ludlow Castle* will be referred to throughout as *Comus*, the short title by which it is usually known.

Similarly, Blake's evocative but curiously insubstantial backdrops are a fitting analogue to the allegorical and fairytale settings of the masque.

The illustrations also reflect the mood of *Comus*—a mixture of doctrinal earnestness
and lighthearted caprice—and its flirtations with the Platonist philosophy and with
the pastoral mode. In addition they share its preoccupation with the tension between
moral or philosophical evanescence and an unchanging ultimate reality, and its perception of the link (as well as the divorce) between the human and natural, and
the human and spiritual, worlds. Finally Blake has taken advantage of the pictorial
medium in order to emphasize the spectacular devices of the masque—notably its
scenic transformations and the stage-by-stage disenchantment of the Lady. The
sequential arrangement of an illustrative series is of course particularly well suited
to convey such a progression.

But despite their evident sympathy for *Comus* and the apparent naïvety of their
pictorial style, the illustrations offer a searching and in many ways critical analysis
of the masque. Blake seems to have discerned in his source two fundamental errors—
that of a sexual parable which casts Repressiveness in the role of virtuous heroine,
and that of a Neoplatonist and Christian vision of existence which fails adequately
to discriminate between the two—and to have attempted through his illustrations
to rectify these errors. Though the *Comus* plates are almost certainly the earliest of
his Milton sets they are in their own subtle way the most subversive of them all.

Blake was a tireless critic of the 'double standard' of sexual morality and of the
repression of 'natural desire'. It is therefore not surprising that he should have transformed Milton's 'sage/And serious doctrine of virginity' (ll. 785–6) into a sterile
and destructive dogma, and his virtuous Lady into a coy, deluded, and self-denying
miss whose maidenly refusal is to be seen as an error comparable with Comus's
aggressiveness, if not a necessary condition of it. Similarly, he represents Comus as
the embodiment not merely of Satanic evil but of the circumstantial errors to which
the rampant male is driven in a society governed by a repressive moral code. Comus
himself is of attractive appearance throughout, and his rout as it appears at its most
grotesque in the fifth and sixth illustrations of the series owes as much to the Lady's
sexual apprehensions as to the physical reality that was presented in the first—something that is confirmed in the sixth illustration when the rout vanishes in smoke
that emanates from the Lady's chair. Blake may have turned to the masque itself
for an assertion of the subjectivity of the Lady's fears:

> A thousand fantasies
> Begin to throng into my memory
> Of calling shapes, and beckoning shadows dire,

> And airy tongues, that syllable men's names
> On sands, and shores, and desert wildernesses[2]
>
> (ll. 204–8)

though the notion is entirely in keeping with his own belief in the subjective nature of perception.

The Book of Thel, with its timorous virgin-heroine, its pastoral setting and Neoplatonist overtones, and its evocation of the horrors of sexual experience in the lower world, owes much to *Comus*, though the darkened vision of the generative world which is offered in its concluding plate cannot necessarily be assumed to have been Blake's own, for it is entirely subjective: the voice which breathes out 'sorrow ... from the hollow pit' (K 130; pl. 6, 10)[3] is Thel's and it is not corroborated by any independent evidence.

More frankly and more fundamentally than the masque, the illustrations set out to investigate the state of adolescence—a state characterized for Blake by sexual obsession without release, the unfulfilled and unfulfilling condition of 'sex in the head'. Adolescence is presented as a time of great peril—a time in which the original innocence of the child is overtaken by emergent sexuality and in which the individual must exercise extreme vigilance if he or she is not simply to allow the establishment to repress and distort this new, potentially divine energy.

In the illustrations all three children are sexually conscious and Comus, though of 'full-grown age' (l. 59) according to the text, is also represented as an adolescent. Among them these four figures reveal all the typical 'errors' of adolescent sexuality— frigidity, aggressiveness, and (in the case of the Lady's brothers) homosexuality or self-regard. The skill and audacity of Blake's 'rewriting' of the masque is particularly evident here, both in his tilting at the forbidden subject of sexual deviation and in his transformation of the Brothers—vehicles in the masque of a philosophical discourse on the virtues of virginity and mere supernumerary figures in its plot—into key performers in the dance. By devising a central role for them Blake has transformed Milton's woman-centred allegory into a drama of male and female adolescence. He has also asserted the exigencies of the sex drive over those of the theorizing intellect, which was so fully exercised by the Brothers of the masque.

With the exception of the Lady's aged father, all the males in the illustrations

---

[2] To be sure she hastily adds (though with the haste that conceals uneasiness, Blake may have felt): These thoughts may startle well, but not astound/The virtuous mind' (ll. 209–10).

[3] Blake's description of Thel wandering beside her own 'grave plot' (cf. pl. 6, 6–9) is strikingly similar to the Elder Brother's account of the degraded souls that cannot bear even after death to forsake their bodies (*Comus*, ll. 469–74).

bear phallic emblems—torches, wands, swords, or crooks. This male sexuality is associated in every case with actual or potential aggression—an aggression which is laudable when channelled towards the defence of the weak or into healthy, normal sexual activity, but culpable when exercised tyrannically, in the service of the individual's own selfish desires. Repression of others begins for Blake with the repression by the individual of his own healthy, natural instincts. Part of the lesson of adolescence is to learn how to utilize the potentially spiritual and saving grace of sexuality without either repressing it or employing it to repress others.

Though youth may err in the *Comus* illustrations, it is attractive and—as the closing plates reveal—amenable to redemption. But behind the potentially redemptive state of adolescence stands the state of age, characterized by fixity of outlook and by uncompromising repressiveness, and represented in the series by the children's parents. They exhibit in unqualified form the 'error' to which the Lady, her Brothers, and Comus are all in some sense prone but to which they are all in one way or another also opposed.

Both Milton and Blake were at times seduced by the doctrines of Neoplatonism: Milton's *Comus* bears particularly strong marks of its influence, especially in its portrayal of the Attendant Spirit as a Neoplatonist daemon and in the many passages that suggest a divorce between the soul and the body, between the aerial mansions of the spirit and the wilderness of this world into which the soul descends. It is therefore not surprising that Blake's illustrations to the masque should show evidence of the same influence nor that Blake as well as Milton should have endowed the Lady with a secondary significance as the descended soul lost in the forests of the material world and fettered by the body (Comus). In this area Blake's revision of his source is far less radical than it is when he deals with the sexual parable, though he does take issue with Milton in the concluding plate, in which—instead of rendering the concordant Neoplatonist-Christian conclusion of the masque—he has the Attendant Spirit as a Christian soul headed for ultimate bliss in the heaven of heavens but leaves the Lady to the more questionable delights of a resting-station on the Neoplatonic cycle. The Neoplatonist interpretation can only be applied intermittently to the series, for unlike the sexual theme it renders the Brothers superfluous—though they were perhaps this in the masque—and is difficult to reconcile with certain aspects of the concluding plates.

Though Blake probably had both interpretations in mind when executing each version of the *Comus* illustrations, many details suggest a Neoplatonist emphasis in the Boston version and an emphasis on the sex drama in the Huntington plates. The most striking of these details are the position of the 'immanacled' Lady's hands—

in the Huntington version they are crossed over the breasts, suggesting sexual inhibition, whereas in the Boston plate they are simply resting on her knees—and the markings on the enchanted chair, which in the Huntington version take the form of serpent-entwined figures (a common emblem in Blake's works for the self-imprisoned personality) and in the Boston plate an ear of corn—a Christian and pre-Christian symbol of resurrection.

These different emphases find expression also in the different styles of the two sets—differences which are all the more striking because of the basic similarity between corresponding plates. The Boston series displays the impersonal solemnity and stylization appropriate to an incarnation ritual whereas the Huntington series, which is more delicately conceived and contains figures whose bodies and postures are supple and expressive, reveals the anguished involvement of participants in a personal drama—participants who are individually responsible for their actions and who must suffer or be rewarded for them.

In so far as sexual disharmony is a characteristic of the fallen condition, the two interpretations are wholly consistent: indeed, in his Prophetic books Blake often makes strife between the sexes a stage in the Fall itself. In other ways, however, the interpretations are mutually contradictory, especially as regards the extent of the characters' moral responsibility (and hence culpability) for their actions—an issue about which Blake was never wholly consistent. The tension is at its sharpest in the figure of Comus, who may be seen either as the misguided but redeemable apostle of sexuality, whose ends are admirable though the means he employs—perhaps of necessity—to bring them about, regrettable; or as the irreparably degraded Body of the Neoplatonists, an interpretation which accords with Milton's view of him as a principle of evil. Blake tends to suggest the former aspect by showing Comus as a comely—if rather priapic—youth, and to reveal the latter only through the monsters of his rout and the barrenness of his domain—the supposedly '*stately palace, set out with all manner of deliciousness*' (after l. 657). The dual significance of Comus is also in part the result of a divergence between the Lady's view of what he represents and a more sympathetic and (to Blake) impartial view of him—a view which Milton only entertains ironically in the flamboyant rhetoric with which he endows him. It may alternatively be taken as a reflection of the Lady's own ambivalent feelings: while she fears his importunings, she is doubtless also susceptible—though she would not have admitted it—to his attractions. In rather the same way, the terrifying beasts of prey which greet Lyca and her parents in Blake's lyrics 'The Little Girl Lost' and 'Found' turn out when seen with renewed vision to be gentle and compassionate spirits.

Like the Comus of the illustrations, Blake's Lady responds to two different interpretations. She may be regarded either as the wilful part-author of her own imprisonment, which thus becomes a kind of punishment for her 'error', or as the hapless
soul which is fated to descend but which, unlike the defiled soul described by the
Elder Brother at lines 462–74, rejects with philosophic dignity the depredations of
her bodily captor.

Whichever interpretation one applies, the Lady's release from captivity is assured,
although the illustrations unlike the masque qualify the feeling of joy that is associated with this release. Nevertheless, the prevailing mood of the illustrations is optimistic and the terrors which threaten the Lady are rendered as merely scarifying, or
even comic. Sexuality and generation are seen with the patient vision of maturity
and of eternity, and not as in the masque or in *The Book of Thel* through the tormented
eyes of an engaged being whose limited and partisan vision can only result in an
over-emotional rejection of experience.

COMUS I: COMUS WITH HIS ROUT (2, 3)

Comus and his rout are shown capering gaily down an incline that slopes steeply
downwards from right to left across the plate. Their chief appears as a comely youth,
naked and somewhat elvish in the Huntington version, and dressed in a sleeved,
leotard-like garment in the Boston. The rout is depicted as it is described in the
masque, with the bodies of men and the heads of beasts—a debasing of Blake's
'human form divine' as well as of Milton's 'human countenance' and 'Godlike
shape'. The Huntington plate shows the hog, the wolf, and the 'ounce' or lynx cited
in lines 70–1; the Boston picture has the hog and the wolf but adds an ox and a
parrot-like bird not mentioned in the text. In each case the foremost member of
the rout has the crossed legs which serve in many of Blake's illustrations to indicate
error. Magic rod, enchanted glass, and torches are all held aloft by the revellers.
In the Boston version, as in the masque, Comus holds both rod and glass; in the
Huntington plate the glass is held by the foremost reveller.

The energy and exuberance of the revellers contrast sharply with the Lady's seated
position, her anxious expression, and her gesture either of rejection (Boston plate)
or of helpless concern (Huntington). She is shown seated beneath the shoulder of
the incline, which in the Boston version forms a rough quadrant with the Lady towards the centre and the revellers on the rim. This arrangement may serve as an
ironic reminder of the Elder Brother's observation on the inner resources of the vir-

tuous: 'He that has light within his own clear breast/May sit i' the centre, and enjoy bright day' (ll. 380–1); or of Blake's association in his poetry of virtue with the 'centre' and the descended state with the 'circumference'.[4] According to this interpretation the Lady, here seated towards the centre of the circle, is to be 'drawn out' onto the rim under the influence of Comus and his rout. This influence is already apparent in the first illustration, in which she has been relegated to the lower right-hand corner of the plate and, in the Huntington version, considerably reduced in size relative to Comus and his rout. In both versions Comus is positioned just above her.

In the masque the Lady is not present when the revellers enter, and when she appears a few moments later, lost but in desperation following 'the sound/Of riot, and ill-managed merriment' (ll. 170–1), the rout has already concealed itself in the undergrowth and Comus himself has 'step(ped) aside'. In the illustration her isolated position on the flat surface of the plate and her bewilderment derive from the fact that she was not actually present when Comus entered; her anxious and alert expression, from the moment of her entry. Her seated posture suggests that in which she was left 'weary on a grassy turf' (l. 279) by her brothers while they went in search of sustenance but it also foreshadows that of her binding. By portraying her as he does in the first illustration of the series Blake is able to hint from the outset at the closeness of the relationship between her and Comus and the dominance of Comus over her, and to indicate that her bondage was not wholly the product of supernatural enchantment.

The Attendant Spirit, depicted in the Huntington version only, is shown hovering in the opposite corner of the plate, visually as well as symbolically cut off from the Lady by a chain formed from the interlaced arms and legs of the revellers. His absence from the Boston plate is justified by his decision, which he voices in the text, to make himself 'viewless' (l. 92) as the rout approaches. He is portrayed conventionally, as an effeminate-looking angel with shoulder-length hair, plump, cherubic features, and downward-pointing wings that elegantly frame his body. The conception may owe something to the Lady's invocation of the theological virtues:

> O welcome pure-eyed Faith, white-handed Hope,
> Thou hovering angel girt with golden wings,
> And thou unblemished form of Chastity,
> I see ye visibly

(ll. 212–15)

His expression and gesture betray his concern for the Lady's safety.

[4] Cf. e.g. *Milton*, K 498; pl. 17, 29–30: 'travellers from Eternity pass outward to Satan's seat,/But travellers to Eternity pass inward to Golgonooza.'

Comus's sexual rapacity, and a general association between aggressive sexuality and physical violence, are suggested by the uninhibited manner in which he brandishes his rod. The torches that are borne aloft by the other revellers also appear to have a phallic significance, and the enchanted glass—held by Comus himself in the Boston version but in the Huntington plate by the foremost monster—resembles the goblets that Blake elsewhere associates with such lustful figures as the Whore of Babylon and the Wife of Bath. It may here be pertinent, particularly in view of the other associations between *Comus* and *The Book of Thel*, to recall Thel's Motto: 'Can Wisdom be put in a silver rod?/Or Love in a golden bowl?' (K 127; pl. i). Neither love nor wisdom is offered by the tyrannous sexuality of Comus.

The illustration contains several features which do not appear in the masque but which are elsewhere associated by Blake with the fallen world: the rock upon which the Huntington Lady is seated, the tangle of exposed tree-roots that frame her head, the schematically-drawn stars—depicted in defiance of lines 194–9 of the text—and the vivid blue (cf. Blake's 'poisonous blue', *Jerusalem*, K 699; pl. 65, 9) that tints the enchanter's 'clustering locks' in this and subsequent illustrations from the Huntington series. Though the wood which appears in the background of the illustration and which is present throughout owes its origin to the text of the masque, Blake has made it his own by replacing 'the spreading favour of [Milton's] pines' (l. 183) with what appear to be oaks—the trees most frequently associated by him with the fallen world. In the masque the wood has similar associations, with moral confusion and the power of evil.[5]

The illustration strikes a whimsical, fairytale note which is particularly evident in the Huntington version with its exuberant monsters, its blue-green tonings—some of which have been carelessly applied—and its trees that appear in defiance of the laws of perspective to rise out of the incline itself.

COMUS II: COMUS ADDRESSING THE LADY (4, 5)

The second illustration shows the Lady—Virtue or Innocence, sexual frigidity or the human soul—allegorically placed between the opposing forces of sexual aggression or corporeality (Comus) and Divine Protection (the Attendant Spirit). Despite her symbolic significance, her fashionable, high-waisted *robe en chemise* is semi-transparent and clearly reveals the contours of her body. Comus, now disguised as a

---

[5] Cf. Blake's own 'forests of the night' ('The Tyger', K 214; 2).

'harmless villager' (l. 166), is approaching the Lady. In his left, or 'corporeal', hand he is carrying his magic rod,[6] wielding it as though it were a walking-stick and slyly concealing it behind him. We may be reminded of the eighty-first plate of Blake's Prophetic book *Jerusalem*, in which Gwendolen, one of the Daughters of Albion or guardians and tormentors of the mortal body, is depicted concealing a falsehood behind her back: 'she took a Falsehood & hid it in her left hand ... and utter'd her Falsehood,/Forgetting that Falsehood is prophetic: she hid her hand behind her' (K 725; pl. 82, 17 and 19–20).

In the Huntington version Comus is shown as an old man—one of Blake's favourite forms for the tyrant of this world but here a disguise presumably adopted in order to allay the Lady's fears for her virginity. His stoop contrasts both with the upright stance of the Lady and with the airborne grace of the Attendant Spirit, who is hovering nearby and glancing anxiously over his shoulder at the Lady.

The somewhat austere Boston version is characterized by strong vertical lines. In it all three figures, including the airborne Attendant Spirit, are placed side by side. The Spirit is hovering only a little way above the ground and his narrow and sharply-pointed wings are raised directly above his head. The trees have extremely tall, upright, and unblemished trunks that only bifurcate into branches high above the heads of the figures. They are similar to the classical pillars of the later banquet-scene and appear to be the product of art rather than of nature.

In the Huntington version Comus and the Lady are shown standing together between two more naturally-formed trees. The tree which is nearer the centre of the plate serves in its two-dimensional aspect to separate Comus and the Lady from the Attendant Spirit—an indication that the Lady's immediate fate lies not with her spiritual guardian but with her bodily seducer. Touches of 'poisonous blue' frame the Lady's head, neck, and arms as well as the head of Comus, thus further indicating that she is under his influence and in a state of error. The Attendant Spirit is hovering well above the ground, his wings again folded downwards so as to harmonize with the curve of his body. In his right, or 'spiritual', hand he is holding the golden flower of the divine haemony plant.

For Blake the wild flower in its minuteness, its beauty, its fragrance, and its obscurity recalls the 'infinite centre' of the Divine Vision:

> Thou percievest the Flowers put forth their precious Odours,
> And none can tell how from so small a center comes such sweets,

[6] For a discussion of the symbolism according to which a prominent right hand or foot indicates spirituality and a prominent left hand or foot corporeality, see Joseph Wicksteed, *Blake's Vision of the Book of Job*, 1924, pp. 18–22.

> Forgetting that within that Center Eternity expands
> Its ever during doors that Og & Anak fiercely guard.
> (*Milton*, K 520; pl. 31, 46–9)

In words which could serve as a gloss on the detail of *Comus* 2 Blake elsewhere aspires 'To see ... a Heaven in a Wild Flower,/Hold Infinity in the palm of your hand' ('Auguries of Innocence', K 431; 1–3). In the context of the *Comus* illustrations, the golden flower serves not merely as a charm against the enchanter's spells, like the haemony of the masque, but also as a symbol of the ideal love which opposes the tyranny of Comus's rod. As her position in *Comus* II suggests, the Lady must choose— or fail to choose—between them. The importance of the haemony flower to Blake is suggested by the fact that he includes it in this illustration even though it is not mentioned in the masque until much later (at lines 628–40), when it is not the flower but the root which the Attendant Spirit produces. We are told that the plant will only bloom 'in another country' (l. 631).

In both versions there is a marked correspondence between figures and background. Not only do the positions of the trees govern the grouping of the figures but the very attitudes of the figures seem to be mirrored in the shapes of the trees. Blake is not indicating, as he does in some of his protest poetry, the extent of the influence which the environment can have over the minds of men: he is merely emphasizing the connection (made in the masque) between the human and natural worlds, and hinting at the enchanted nature of the landscape. The forest foliage forms an impenetrable mass above the heads of the figures and, as in the masque, where it is described as a 'close dungeon of innumerable boughs' (l. 348), suggests the Neoplatonist prison of the material world.

COMUS III: THE BROTHERS PLUCKING GRAPES (6, 7)

In the masque this scene is presented as a flashback evoked by Comus in response to the Lady's anxious inquiry after her brothers. The illustration shows Comus watching them as they gather grapes from a 'mantling vine'. He is eyeing them not with the reverence that he asserts in the text but with sly malevolence. Blake indicates that the episode is a flashback by depicting the enchanter in his villager's disguise— which he did not don in the masque until he sensed the Lady's presence—and, by showing him as a furtive and unprepossessing figure, undermines the credential of 'good faith' which his speech to the Lady is intended to establish.

The Brothers, depicted at right foreground, are stretching upwards in order to reach the grapes. Their figures suggest the comeliness of youth; their actions an attractive, aspiring, and spontaneous sexuality. Their freedom of gesture and elegant balletic postures contrast strikingly with the stealthy aggression of Comus.

Yet despite their comeliness the Brothers as well as Comus and the Lady are deeply in error. In the masque it is they who expound the (to Blake) pernicious doctrine of virginity or sexual denial, but besides this the fact that the Lady falls into Comus's hands is at least partly the result of their desertion of her. This desertion appears to have been conceived by Milton purely as a plot convenience; but to Blake, for whom all events had a 'spiritual' cause, it was evidently a grave dereliction of duty. As much may be read into Comus's implied criticism of the Brothers' action and the weakness of the Lady's defence of it:

> *Comus.* What chance good lady hath bereft you thus?
> *Lady.* Dim darkness, and this leafy labyrinth.
> *Comus.* Could that divide you from near-ushering guides?
> *Lady.* They left me weary on a grassy turf.
> *Comus.* By falsehood, or discourtesy, or why?
> *Lady.* To seek i' the valley some cool friendly spring.
> *Comus.* And left your fair side all unguarded lady?
> *Lady.* They were but twain, and purposed quick return.
>
> (ll. 276–83)

Where the Brothers advocate sexual abstinence in the masque, they display in the illustration a potentially sexual intimacy. In both versions they are turned towards each other and are gazing adoringly into each other's eyes; in the Boston plate one is handing down a bunch of grapes to the other. (In 'The Ecchoing Green' from the *Songs of Innocence* Blake employs a similar design to suggest healthy, nascent sexuality but, significantly, it is there a girl who is the recipient of the youth's gift of the fruits of 'sweet delight'.)

In her plea to Comus the Lady casually associates the Brothers with Narcissus: 'Canst thou not tell me of a gentle pair/That likest thy Narcissus are?' (ll. 235–6), and it may be that Blake intended his Brothers to represent not a pair of lovers but a narcissistically self-regarding single being.

Although at the opposite pole to the other-directed aggressiveness of Comus, the 'sweet entrancing self-delusion' (*Jerusalem*, K 654; pl. 29, 39) which the Brothers display is equally far removed from ideal, procreative sexuality—as is indicated in the Huntington plate by the fact that the ominous blue shade originally associated with the enchanter here frames the heads of the Brothers and the grapes as well.

Blake is hinting that, while the aggressiveness of a Comus is inimical to love, a certain degree of masculine assertiveness or outward-directed energy is essential: the Brothers' pliancy is the corollary of their sterile self-regard. Their obsession with each other and the relationship between lack of sexual energy and general submissiveness are suggested in the Huntington version by the fact that their swords— traditional emblems of potency as well as of aggression—are shown lying idle together on the ground, with the strap of one of them suggestively entwined about them both.

Apart from the fact that in the Boston set one Brother is clothed in red and the other in green, and in the Huntington set one is barefoot and the other wearing sandals of varying designs and stages of completion, they are not distinguished at all from each other. Indeed there was no need for the artist to have individualized them or to have distinguished between them, for Milton draws between them only the rudimentary distinction of greater and lesser maturity and Blake's interpretation of their function necessitates no distinction at all. Their breeches and sleeved waistcoats, which are elegant if somewhat effete, resemble those found in many of Blake's Young and Gray illustrations and are based upon contemporary semi-formal dress.

'The 'small hill' along which Milton's vine is supposed to crawl has in both *Comus* III illustrations been transformed into a steep outcrop of rock—always in Blake's works associated with error. The vine is sturdy and flourishing in the Huntington plate, brittle and lifeless in the Boston version. A carefully-delineated ploughman depicted in profile and leading a 'laboured ox/In his loose traces' (ll. 290–1) (in the Boston plate there are two oxen) is appearing from behind the outcrop.

The Lady is to be seen in the distance, resting on her 'grassy turf' at the edge of the 'wild wood'—a diminutive and isolated figure yet one watched over by a hovering Attendant Spirit. The presence of the Lady and the Attendant Spirit indicates that Blake is working with thematic and temporal correspondences rather than with an exact transcription of the text, for although the outcrop largely shields the Brothers from the Lady's sight, she and they could scarcely at this point in the masque have been part of a single scene literally conceived.

The smallness and brilliance of the Attendant Spirit suggest the star to which he is compared by Milton:

> when any favoured of high Jove,
> Chances to pass through this advent'rous glade,
> Swift as the sparkle of a glancing star,
> I shoot from heaven to give him safe convoy.
>
> (ll. 78–81)

In the Boston version he is enshrined within a nimbus and his wings are placed together above his head. In the Huntington plate his wings are apart, thus indicating that he is still in the act of descending. His presence relates this picture to the Huntington version of *Comus* I, in which he was shown hovering near the Lady.

COMUS IV: THE BROTHERS WITH THE ATTENDANT SPIRIT (8, 9)

Both versions of the fourth illustration are similar to the second Boston plate. The Attendant Spirit, now disguised as a shepherd, is standing between the Brothers and displaying the magical haemony flower for their inspection. In the Boston version the figures appear as though recessed between tree-trunks, with one Brother turned towards the viewer and the other turned away though both of them are still facing each other—an arrangement that recalls the formal dance of the masque and suggests a row of statues set within niches. In the Huntington version all three figures are framed by trees and the Brothers are turned towards each other. In both plates the foliage and branches of the trees form a massy roof over the heads of the figures, again suggesting enclosure within the prison or cavern of the fallen world.

Crowded into the space above the trees is a chariot drawn by and formed from a pair of serpents, portions of whose bodies are coiled so as to suggest chariot wheels. They are slim and lithe in the Boston plate, plump, scaly, and extravagantly sinuous in the Huntington. Both pairs have beguiling, almost hypnotic eyes, and forked and flickering tongues. Despite their air of rapacity they appear, like the monsters of *Comus* I, to be the creations of whimsy rather than of revulsion or terror.

The chariot is being driven with some urgency by a spectral female figure, although in the instant captured by the picture it appears to be nestling snugly into the foliage. The woman's position reflects her role as guardian spirit of the woods, and in particular of the scene that is unfolded directly beneath her. A lunar crescent depicted alongside her head in the Boston version serves to identify her more precisely as the goddess of the moon. She is perhaps an ironic answer to the plea made by the Elder Brother at lines 330–3:

> thou fair moon
> That wont'st to love the traveller's benison,
> Stoop they pale visage through an amber cloud,
> And disinherit Chaos

—though had he seen her he would perhaps have invoked her less eagerly, for she appears more like the herald of chaos than its disinheritor.

Though she does not make an appearance in the masque, the virgin huntress Diana—who is one avatar of the moon-goddess—may be regarded as the ruling deity of the Brothers, with their sterile self-obsessions (Blake) or their eulogies in praise of chastity (Milton). She is associated by Milton's Elder Brother with the protective power of chastity (ll. 417–45). He also mentions her antique role as 'queen o' the woods' (l. 445).

Hecate, another aspect of the lunar goddess, was also the presiding deity of witch-craft and sorcery. Comus refers to her and invokes her riding companion, the sinister Thracian goddess Cotytto, before embarking upon his nocturnal rites. The parallel with the illustration is close, for Comus commands that the airborne chariot in which the goddesses are riding should be 'stayed', as that in the illustration is perforce:

> Hail goddess of nocturnal sport
> Dark-veiled Cotytto, to whom the secret flame
> Of midnight torches burns; mysterious dame
> That ne'er art called, but when the dragon womb
> Of Stygian darkness spits her thickest gloom,
> And makes one blot of all the air,
> Stay thy cloudy ebon chair,
> Wherein thou rid'st with Hecat'
>
> (ll. 128–35)

So by a compact and ironical device Blake has the same figure stand both for abstinence and for licence, for the values of the Lady and for those of Comus. This is of course appropriate to his own vision, in which adamant virginity and aggressive sexuality are simply opposing facets or corollaries of each other, but subversive of Milton's doctrine, in which they are principles implacably opposed.

Blake's source for the reptile chariot is an incident from Book VII of Ovid's *Metamorphoses*, in which Hecate sends a chariot drawn by dragons to the aid of her devotee Medea.[7] Milton alludes to this chariot in his Latin poem *In Obitum Praesulis Eliensis* (Carey & Fowler, p. 26, ll. 56–8), in *Il Penseroso* (ll. 59–60), and perhaps also in *Comus* itself when he speaks of 'the dragon womb/Of Stygian darkness' (ll. 131–2).

However, the creatures in *Comus* IV are not dragons but serpents (they have neither clawed feet nor wings) and for Blake the serpent has not only its traditional associations with sexuality and with the Judaeo-Christian Fall but also connections with the whole of the Neoplatonist material or 'vegetable' world: 'the vast form of Nature

[7] Circe, mother of Comus in Milton's genealogy, is according to myth Medea's aunt.

like a Serpent play'd before them' (*Vala*, K 294; 97); 'And thus with wrath he [Christ] did subdue/The Serpent Bulk of Nature's dross,/Till He had nail'd it to the Cross' (*The Everlasting Gospel*, K 749; 52–4). By placing the goddess of virginity and of licence in a serpent-drawn chariot and by placing this chariot directly above the wood of error and the cavernous space which encloses the Brothers and the Attendant Spirit, Blake is indicating an intimate and perhaps necessary connection between sexual strife and the fallen world.[8]

The Brothers, who are now beset on all sides by the signs and symbols of material evil, appear to have strayed still more deeply into error; yet the Attendant Spirit still stands between them, holding up the flower of saving grace for their inspection and separating or endeavouring to distract them from each other. The Brothers appear reluctant to abandon their accustomed mutual regard and are making negative gestures that indicate their eagerness to dismiss the flower from their minds— yet they are at least devoting some attention, however reluctant, to it. They have also taken up their swords, emblems of sexual potency as well as of combat, though they are wielding them with considerable diffidence. The shepherd's crook which the Attendant Spirit is holding (Boston version) or cradling under his arm (Huntington) suggests masculinity mellowed by an unselfish concern for others—a truly pastoral emblem.

COMUS V: COMUS'S BANQUET (10, 11)

Where Milton's banquet-scene revealed the sensuous attractions of Comus's philosophy, Blake's exposes its spiritual vacuity. Milton's 'stately palace, set out with all manner of deliciousness: soft music, tables spread with all dainties' (stage-direction after l. 657), has been transformed into a dim and dingy refectory—coloured a murky grey in the Boston version and an eerie greenish-yellow in the Huntington, illuminated only by three hanging oil-lamps and backed by austere, rounded arches and classical pillars. A few plates, goblets, and pitchers are scattered about on a long, cloth-covered table but none of Milton's 'dainties' are to be seen. The scene has a curious lack of recessive depth, which suggests its insubstantiality and prepares us for its eventual dissolution. The architectural style of the banqueting-hall is a tribute both to the many classical references in the masque and to Blake's association

---

[8] Blake's *Job* picture 'When the Morning Stars Sang Together' is similarly conceived. It shows the chariot of the moon, again drawn by serpents and this time in company with the sun, ruling over the benighted cavern of this world in which Job and his companions are trapped.

throughout his middle and later years of classicism with belligerency: 'The Classics! it is the Classics, & not Goths nor Monks, that Desolate Europe with Wars' (K 778).

The rabble is here shown as guests or waiters at table. Contrary to Milton's earlier stage-direction and to Blake's opening illustration, their bodies as well as their heads are now, if we allow for a slight anthropomorphizing of convenience, dehumanized—perhaps to suggest the nature of the Lady's fearful imaginings. All five of the monsters in the Huntington plate are depicted as birds—a beaky flock with blank, hooded eyes. The tufted head of the bird seated at far right seems to have degenerated still further, into a vegetable form. His companions at table suggest a cockerel and an eagle to the eye, though they clearly owe more to fancy than to ornithology. The two birds waiting at table are owl-like figures (representing what kind of desiccated wisdom?) with reptilian wings and bony fingers. Their heads resemble those of birds depicted in Stuart and Revett's *Antiquities of Athens*,[9] a work with which Blake had been associated when apprenticed to the engraver James Basire.

Seated at table in the Boston version are a long-billed bird, an elephant which is plunging its hoof into a plate, a lion with fierce, staring eyes, and a snouted animal —probably a dog or a wolf—which is avidly licking the 'shoulder' of the bird-figure beside it. Three of them suggest three of the seven deadly sins—the elephant, gluttony; the lion, wrath; and the snouted animal, lust. The tongue is often associated by Blake with sensuality: the viewer will of course recall the flickering tongues of the serpents of the previous illustration.

The Lady herself is depicted at left foreground of the picture, fixed in the enchanted chair—perhaps an ironical confirmation of the Elder Brother's encomium on chastity: 'She that has that, is clad in complete steel' (l. 420). In the Huntington version her hands are crossed over her breasts, a self-concealing gesture which serves as a reminder of the role of Chaste Woman which she plays in the masque. It also indicates that her 'binding' is in part the result of her own insistent virginity. Where to Milton her imprisonment contradicts and affronts the freedom and nobility of her mind and is wholly the result of Comus's evil designs and supernatural power, to Blake it is both the outcome of her state of mind and an accurate reflection of it.

Comus is shown standing over the Lady, his glass in one hand and his rod—which is poised just above her head and in a position suggesting phallic erection—in the other. He is perhaps giving the very wave of the wand that enchained his victim. In the Huntington version he appears to have been drawn to a larger scale than the Lady, something which suggests the axis of fear and aggression along which their

[9] James Stuart and Nicholas Revett, 1762–1816, iii, 19 and 29.

relationship moves as well as the tumescence of the would-be ravisher. His cloak, which is a brilliant sky-blue in the Boston plate, is reminiscent both of a magician's cape and of sheathed wings. In each case it indicates supernatural potency and corresponds to references in the masque to Comus as necromancer, juggler, magician, wizard, and brewer of enchantments.

In the Boston version a servant with an emaciated face reminiscent of a death's-head and with long, claw-like toes protruding from beneath his robe, is standing behind the Lady. He is holding a jar out of which emerges a serpent, framed by a cloud of smoke and flicking its tongue at Comus's rod. Its head is placed directly above the Lady's, thus suggesting that she is in its power. The Aladdin's-lamp nature of its emergence and its evident insubstantiality suggests both the impermanence of the error it represents and the illusory nature of that error. Its presence also accords with the masque's Christian frame of reference, which is particularly insistent in the banquet-scene, as well as with the Serpent's associations, both traditional and Blakean, with sin, sexuality, and the Fall. In this regard the death's-head countenance of the figure that bears the jar is also appropriate.

The Serpent is represented in the Huntington version as well, although there it is confined to a painting or low-relief carving that decorates the side of the Lady's chair. The decoration involves three figures, two standing one above the other along the spine and back leg of the chair, and the third within its front leg. At least two of the figures are women; all are enwrapped by serpentine forms and endowed with spiked wings or limbs that are reminiscent of the bat-wings of the waiters. Through this association Blake emphasizes that there is a direct thematic connection between the 'parable' depicted within the chair and the scene displayed without.

Just as Blake's Serpent symbolizes or is closely associated with the fallen world, so his serpent-entwined figures generally represent man—or as here, woman— trapped by the 'fallen' or self-regarding aspect of their own minds. The carved figures in the *Comus* design, two of whom are pathetically reaching out to one another along the base of the chair, demonstrate the constrictions of the mortal condition.[10] More specifically, they reveal the real nature of the Lady's plight: essentially she is imprisoned not by Comus but by her own state of mind.

The carving on the chair in the Boston version depicts not a serpent but an ear of corn, a traditional emblem for resurrection and one which in this context must be intended to reassure the viewer that the Lady will eventually be released from her trials.

So the illustration reveals Comus as the overlord of a drab and delusory regimen

[10] Cf. the domain of the earth-spirits in Blake's third illustration to *Il Penseroso*.

which affirms that 'lean and sallow Abstinence' that he professes to despise, and which exposes the joylessness and the sterility of a relationship based on tyranny and fear. The relations between Comus and the Lady are characteristic of those which to Blake obtain in the fallen world, in which the male pursues and the female withholds, or in which the soul is the hapless prisoner of the body.

COMUS VI: THE BROTHERS DRIVING OUT COMUS (12, 13)

The sixth illustration shows the Brothers routing Comus. In it Blake articulates a distinction that was not drawn by Milton: he shows the enchanter fleeing the scene unharmed, presumably to continue terrorizing lost maidens, but his rout and 'stately palace' dissolving into thin air. The distinction confirms that the monsters and the refectory depicted in the previous illustration were the creations of the Lady's mind; as further evidence of this their dissolving remnants are shown enveloped in a cloud of smoke that originates from behind her chair.[11] This dissolution indicates the Lady's liberation from hysterical imaginings, a necessary condition of her release from physical bondage. The fact that it occurs simultaneously with Comus's dismissal suggests that, though the error had its home in the Lady's mind, it was the natural result of the enchanter's threatening posture—one that he preserves, wand raised, even in retreat.

In *The Marriage of Heaven and Hell* Blake describes a similar triumph over subjective error which he himself had once sustained. An 'evil angel' has just evoked a vision of terror which, he assures Blake, is his 'eternal lot':

But [continues Blake] I arose and sought for the mill, & there I found my Angel, who, surprised, asked me how I escaped?

I answer'd: "All that we saw was owing to your metaphysics; for when you ran away, I found myself on a bank by moonlight hearing a harper.

(K 156; pls. 17–20)

As in the case of the Lady, the mental error that was generated by a third party disappears with the departure of that party.

The foreground of *Comus* VI is devoted to the disturbing diagonals that are generated by the figures of the Brothers as they rush the enchanter and by Comus's own figure as he performs his wide-stepping retreat. The 'weapons' of all three anta-

---

[11] The smoke probably derives from a reference made by the Attendant Spirit when instructing the Brothers on how to deal with Comus: 'seize his wand, though he and his cursed crew/Fierce sign of battle make, and menace high,/Or like the sons of Vulcan vomit smoke' (ll. 652–4).

gonists, which are raised aloft, create fresh lines of force and contribute to the general impression of upheaval. Behind the three figures sits the Lady, still immobile, and in the Huntington version still imprisoned in the enchanted chair. In the Boston version the chair has already vanished, leaving her seated on a grassy bank.

In both plates Comus is depicted as he was in the first illustration of the series—naked in the Huntington version, still wearing his 'leotard' in the Boston. His glass has been wrested out of his hand but, despite the Attendant Spirit's instruction to the Brothers above all to 'seize his wand' (l. 652), he retreats with this charm still firmly in his possession.

The Comus of the Huntington version is evidently disconcerted by the Brothers' assault, and his body, face, and hair are tinged with blue. His nakedness emphasizes the fact that he is being stripped of his magical powers. In the Boston plate he appears remarkably composed in the face of attack—something which suggests his secondary role as a philosophical principle rather than his primary one of individual and seducer. He is executing a kind of ballet step as he retreats—a last sign of his curious art. Flames and a blue mandorla-cloud, perhaps the remains of the cloak of *Comus* v, are to be seen behind him.

The rout in dissolution is depicted as a confused mass of heads and wings that cling as they disintegrate to Comus's wand, that sexuality which helped to give them birth. In the Huntington version an ass or horse, two horned and demonic faces, and a bird with a protruding tongue are shown; in the Boston version darkened and sinister, mask-like heads and reptilian wings. Severed heads, spiked wings, and imitations of the tragic mask are all frequently used by Blake to denote mental error.

In the Huntington plate the dissolving remnants of the palace are also represented—by a single, swaying lamp—and the Brothers are staring in horror not at Comus but at the dissolving heads—whose creation was partly the result of their own earlier, self-regarding neglect of the Lady. That they share the sight of them with the Lady indicates that they also to some extent share her 'error'.

By coming to the Lady's rescue with 'brandished blade' (l. 650) the Brothers at last succeed in directing their attention outwards instead of towards each other. At the same time, as is indicated by their raised swords, they experience a release of their own natural sexual energies: it is not only self-interested aggression that Blake associates with sexuality.

Comus's demesne is retreating to reveal, in the Boston plate, the burgeoning foliage of earlier illustrations. In the Huntington version two massive tree-trunks have appeared, each slanting away from the other so as to extend the diagonal stress established by the figures in the foreground, and with a single star—presumably

Venus, the star of the morning—visible between them. It is placed almost directly above the still 'immanacled' Lady—a sign of her imminent release from the bondage of sexual frigidity.

COMUS VII: SABRINA DISENCHANTING THE LADY (14, 15)

Here the river-goddess Sabrina is shown disenchanting the Lady by baptizing her with holy water. The Lady is now seated on a grassy bank in the Huntington version, on a rock in the Boston. She is gesturing freely and turning towards her Brothers, who are bending over her with prayerful gestures of thanksgiving. Behind the young people and to the far left of the picture stands the Attendant Spirit, who is gazing over his shoulder and pointing heavenwards with his right arm. His position and gesture, and their significance, are similar to those of Mercury in Botticelli's 'Primavera'.

The text for the Attendant Spirit's attitude is the couplet, 'Come let us haste, the stars grow high,/But night sits monarch yet in the mid sky' (ll. 955–6). The stars of Blake's illustration have indeed risen in the sky, leaving the hills beneath in darkness, but the solemnity of the Attendant Spirit's countenance and the deliberateness of his gesture suggest an urge to recall his companions to the true source of their aid rather than a pedestrian observation on the lateness of the hour.

Sabrina, whose 'maiden gentleness' (l. 842) is stressed by the Attendant Spirit, is shown as a young and attractive figure. In the Boston version she is attended only by two smaller nymphs, and—as in the text of the masque—is sprinkling water on the Lady's breast (ll. 910–12). She has the free-flowing hair mentioned in line 862 of the masque. In the Huntington version she is wearing a coronet of pearls in her hair, which is now short and stylish, and a pearled bracelet on each wrist—again after Milton, who at line 833 mentions the 'pearled wrists' of the nymphs who originally welcomed Sabrina to the river. She is accompanied by four attendants and is sprinkling water on the Lady's forehead (or lip—see ll. 914) rather than on her breast—a gesture which supports the hints of baptism that are associated with the episode in the masque. The nymphs of both plates have gracefully curved and attenuated bodies that appear to glide over the ground without actually making contact with it, as though they were all still within their watery element.

In the Huntington plate one of the attendants is carrying a whelk-shell and another, a shell-like jar. The Sabrina of the Boston version is bearing a leaf-shaped shell from which she takes the water that she is sprinkling on the Lady, and the smaller nymphs in both versions are holding conch-shells. Apart from a reference to 'scaly Triton's winding shell' (l. 872), which the Attendant Spirit swears by when summoning Sabrina, these shells are entirely of Blake's invention.

As Irene Tayler observes in an article on the *Comus* designs, 'The shell in Blake is usually an emblem of the mortal body—the circumference of the spirit ... —and sea shells are especially clearly so, since water itself is an emblem of the material world'.[12] In Blake's writings Sabrina and Gwendolen—Sabrina's 'stepdame' in the masque—are the names of two of Blake's Daughters of Albion or guardian-tormentors of the body.

The Sabrina of *Comus* VII with her shell-bearing nymphs is also associated with the body, but particularly with the loveliness of emancipated female sexuality which the Lady, already released from her own negative imaginings, must apprehend before attaining to full maturity. (Here too the radical nature of Blake's 'rewriting' is striking, for the Sabrina of the masque represents not matronly maturity but 'maiden gentleness'—l. 842.) It is perhaps worth noting that in Blake's conceptual drama it is the lady who must bring about the final liberation of the Lady, just as it was the Brothers who had to banish male aggression.

The nymphs have influence over the Lady's physical but not over her spiritual destiny. They can show her the way to the freedom of the body, the freedom to live a spontaneous sexual life, and through their own bodies can reveal the beauties of the liberated state; but they cannot initiate her into the deeper wisdom which the Attendant Spirit commands. The sky-pointing gesture of the Attendant Spirit, made with his right or 'spiritual' arm, is intended to remind the 'children' of the real source of man's aid—a higher, spiritual power of which the nymphs are perhaps agents—and maybe also that the divergent interests of male and female will only finally be reconciled in heaven. For the moment his gesture goes unheeded.

In the Boston plate a small rainbow hovers over Sabrina and her attendants. No rainbow is cited at this point in the text, although one is mentioned several times in the masque—in the Attendant Spirit's description of his celestial robes (at ll. 82–3), in Comus's evocation of the Brothers gathering grapes (at ll. 297–300), and in the Attendant Spirit's description of the Elysian Fields (at ll. 991–4). In devising his arrangement Blake may have been drawing upon a passage from Milton's *Nativity*

---

[12] 'Say First! What Mov'd Blake? Blake's *Comus* Designs and *Milton*' in *Blake's Sublime Allegory*, ed. Stuart Curran and Joseph Anthony Wittreich, Jr., 1973, p. 247. For Blake on shells, cf. *Vala*, K 301; 135, in which fallen man is described as a 'cold sleeper of weeds & shells'; and the designs for *America*, pl. 13, and *Jerusalem*, pl. 28.

Ode, which describes a similar grouping of figures in a parallel context—the descent to man of the divine principle of mercy:

> Yea Truth, and Justice then
> Will down return to men,
>   Orbed in a rainbow; and like glories wearing
> Mercy will sit between,
> Throned in celestial sheen
>
> (ll. 141–5)

For Blake himself the rainbow often suggests that of the covenant—a sign of the mercy which God shows to man. It can also imply transience, as it does for instance at the beginning of *The Book of Thel*. In the context of *Comus* VII it serves to link Sabrina's limited, 'corporeal' significance with the infinite riches of divine grace. As a physical phenomenon it is of course a manifestation of the coincidence of (rising) sun and (baptismal) water—both emblems of regeneration.

Just as the Lady of *Comus* VII is turning with an air of wonderment to her Brothers, they are bending over her with gestures of devotion, evidently recognizing the new spirit of emancipation within her.

The release of the Brothers as well as the Lady from sexual 'errors' and inhibitions is attested to by the complete absence of phallic emblems from the picture: self-assured and fulfilled masculinity does not need ostentatiously to assert itself. It is significant that the Brothers have discarded their swords, though without succumbing to their earlier 'error' of self-absorption, at precisely the moment at which the Lady sheds her crippling fears. Finally it is the woman's release from bondage that enables men to become the bearers of a sexuality that combines outer sweetness with inner strength. Even the crook of the Attendant Spirit—energy spiritualized or devoted, Christlike, to the redemption of others—has vanished.

The sun's rays are now feeling their way up the sky and lightening the upper part of the plate. In both versions the forest has retreated a little though in the Huntington picture it still dominates the upper half of the plate, giving the scene a slightly oppressive character. As in the previous Huntington illustration the Lady is seated directly beneath the trunks of two trees—though, significantly, the space between them has widened.

COMUS VIII: THE LADY RESTORED TO HER PARENTS (16, 17)

Milton's *Comus* concludes with the safe delivery of the Lady and her Brothers to their parents, and with the ascension of the Attendant Spirit. The 'ceremony' of the children's return takes place to the accompaniment of songs and country dancing, and against the background of 'Ludlow Town and the President's Castle' (stage-direction after l. 956). The 'wild wood' and the evil it contained have vanished, to be replaced by the reassuring verities of specificity, lineage, and celebration. The mood of rejoicing is heightened by a general consciousness that the children have triumphed in their battle against 'sensual folly, and intemperance' (l. 974).

Milton's Attendant Spirit, who has the only speaking part in the scene, presents the children to their parents, 'epiloguizes' at some length, then departs—apparently unnoticed by the rest of the company—for 'the broad fields of the sky' (l. 978). These appear to encompass both the 'lesser' heaven of Venus and Adonis and the 'greater' heaven of the celestial Cupid and of Psyche. The ultimate rewards of a virtue like the Lady's, marriage and eventual translation to heaven, are thus both suggested in the 'aspiring flight' of the Attendant Spirit.

In his version of the masque's closing scene Blake makes several significant changes. First, he exorcizes all of the 'occasional' and ceremonial elements incorporated by Milton—mere puffs for a potential patron, after all. The President of Wales's castle is reduced at his hands to a dwelling-house which is simple, even crude, and neither Ludlow Town nor Milton's 'Country Dancers' are to be seen. In this allegory of the human journey there is no place for such local and in a sense prosaic elements. On the other hand the dark wood of earlier illustrations—excluded from Milton's stage-direction—is still present, even though it has been distanced a little from the centre of events, and the sun, also not mentioned by Milton but a traditional image for the deity, is shown appearing above a nearby hillside.

Secondly, although Milton emphasizes that all three children are presented to their parents ('Three fair branches of your own'—l. 968) by the Attendant Spirit, Blake arranges the figures in two distinct groups of three, with the parents receiving the Lady on the right and the Brothers, having turned away from this group, farewelling the already airborne Attendant Spirit on the left. The two dissociated but artistically balanced sets of figures, and their respective preoccupations with parting and with reunion, counterpoint each other with masque-like formality.

Thirdly, the mood of festal rejoicing that characterizes the scene in the masque has been replaced in the illustration by one of solemnity, even of severity. Neither the perturbation of Blake's Brothers over the Attendant Spirit's departure nor the gravity with which the Parents receive the Lady are touched upon in the masque, where the Brothers remain apparently unaware of the Attendant Spirit's departure and the Parents' reaction to the Lady's return is not recorded.

The Attendant Spirit is shown ascending to heaven with due magnificence. In the Boston version his body, arms, and wings are all curving towards the sun and his hands are outstretched towards it as though he were willing it to rise. His posture asserts the urgency of his desire to attain the heavenly fields. In the Huntington version the Brothers have momentarily captured his attention: he is regarding them with anxiety, his body curving away from the sun and his left hand hovering, as if in blessing, over the Elder Brother's head. In both versions he is watched keenly by the Brothers, whose earlier insipidity and shallow self-regard have given way to an intense, outward-looking, and entirely unselfconscious preoccupation with the agent and hence with the values of eternity. Blake emphasizes the Brothers' apparent determination to take up the Attendant Spirit's concluding challenge—'Mortals that would follow me,/Love Virtue, she alone is free' etc. (ll. 1017–18)—but in no way suggests the traditional closing device of breaking the masque's dramatic spell, which was part of the purpose of the Miltonic lines.

In the spiritual sun which is the goal of the Attendant Spirit's flight and in the straitened hovel to which the Lady returns, Blake has preserved Milton's notion of the gradation of the states of bliss but he has preserved it with irony, for whereas the 'lower heaven' of the Attendant Spirit's closing soliloquy is a brave imitation of the 'greater', the Lady's resting-place appears more like an antithesis to the blessed state than its antechamber. It should not be overlooked that here, as well as in his treatment of the Brothers, Blake has given dramatic relevance to an element that was not a central preoccupation of the Miltonic narrative. The tension between the two states is emphasized in the illustration by the Brothers' distress over the departure of the Attendant Spirit.

The Lady—self-assured in the Boston version, more cautious in the Huntington— may be regarded either as the soul which has found a temporary haven yet which is fated perpetually to descend into the fallen or material state and to rise again, or as the young woman who, freed from her own sexual inhibitions, turns to her parents to provide her with models for a renewed sexuality.

The first interpretation, suggested more strongly in the Boston version, necessarily involves a contrast between the cyclical, classical theory of the soul's journey and the linear, Christian theory, in which the virtuous soul—which would here be represented by the Attendant Spirit—ascends to final, eternal glory. The classical garb of the Lady's parents and their air of prophetic strangeness suggest a pagan connection and hence the Platonist conception of historical recurrence, but the magnificence of the departing figure of the Attendant Spirit asserts Blake's sympathy with the Christian resolution. Classical and Christian references are interwoven throughout the masque. At the conclusion to *Jerusalem* Blake again pays tribute to both systems by making the mysterious cycle of life continue even after the Apocalypse:

All Human Forms identified, even Tree, Metal, Earth & Stone: all
Human Forms identified, living, going forth & returning wearied
Into the Planetary lives of Years, Months, Days & Hours; reposing,
And then Awaking into his Bosom in the Life of Immortality.

(K 747; pl. 99, 1–4)

Alternatively the Lady, having come through her own personal trial, may be regarded as about to confront her own former attitudes in the figures of her parents. Her position would then be that of any individual attempting to achieve freedom in a repressive world. Freedom may here be understood narrowly as sexual freedom, or in more general terms as the liberation of the individual from the restraints of the establishment. The portrayal of the Lady's parents as aged and careworn figures who greet her with stern and proprietorial expressions—the father with white hair and flowing beard, the mother veiled and in the Huntington version clutching at her daughter's wrist and waist—and the austerity of their dwelling-house, suggest this interpretation. In 'A Little Girl Lost', a lyric from the *Songs of Experience*, Blake concludes the tale of another maiden's discovery of the delights of love with a scene in which another father with 'hoary hair' (l. 34) confronts her with the terrors of the moral code masquerading as love and religion:

To her father white
Came the maiden bright;
But his loving look,
Like the holy book,
All her tender limbs with terror shook.

"Ona! pale and weak!
"To thy father speak:
"O, the trembling fear!
"O, the dismal care!
"That shakes the blossoms of my hoary hair."

(K 219; 25–34)

The words written by Blake on the back of a sketch for plate 43 of the Prophetic book *Milton*—'Father & Mother, I return from flames of fire tried & pure & white' (K 535)—have also been associated with *Comus* VIII.

As his poetry reveals, Blake believed that man in his unfallen condition was androgynous, that the female was formed from his body, and that her creation as an independent entity was itself a stage in the Fall. He also envisaged an apocalypse in which the sexes are finally and completely, physically as well as emotionally, reconciled.

Though she has been emancipated from her fears of the body, the Lady of *Comus* VIII still has no notion of the possibility of such a reconciliation. One is however suggested in the sexually ambivalent figure of the Attendant Spirit—ambivalent even by Blake's standards—who while on earth assumes the garb of a male but when in the air is depicted in his own form, as a conspicuously effeminate figure with flowing hair and a loose robe. He appears to represent for Blake not merely the spirit which descends to assist man (or woman) but the spirit which reconciles in its own form the sexual antagonisms of the 'night of error' by returning to the androgynous nature of original, unfallen man. The Brothers' present tragedy is that, though they have come to understand something of the mystery which the Attendant Spirit embodies, they are for the moment at least unable to follow him.

Thus in *Comus* VIII Blake has substituted for the prematurely triumphal certitudes of Milton's final scene a masterfully ironical and deliberately inconclusive ending which suggests that, although the Lady and her Brothers have learnt much from their *rite de passage* into maturity, their earthly travails are by no means ended.

III PARADISE LOST

Blake executed his first set of *Paradise Lost* illustrations in 1807, his second the following year. The original purchaser of the first set is not known for certain although Leslie Parris suggests that it may again have been the Rev. Joseph Thomas of Epsom;[1] the second was bought by Thomas Butts. The illustrations now have the same ownership as the *Comus* sets: the earlier is in the Huntington Library, the later in the Museum of Fine Arts, Boston, Massachusetts.

Both *Paradise Lost* sets are similar in arrangement and detail although they differ considerably in size and in style. The Huntington plates are drawn in a delicate and free-flowing manner. The Boston plates are considerably larger than those of the earlier set, and rather more ornate. Their ink outlines are also more distinct. Most of the figures in the Huntington series are represented as delicate and quasi-disembodied beings; those of the Boston series are Michelangelesque nudes with a commanding physical presence.

There are now thirteen plates (including two of 'Satan, Sin and Death') in the Huntington Library and only nine in the Boston Museum of Fine Arts. However, in an article published in 1950[2] Morse Peckham argues persuasively that both sets originally contained twelve drawings. The missing plates from the Boston series are, he believes, the larger of the two 'Satan, Sin and Death' plates in the Huntington Library, a drawing of 'Satan Rousing his Legions' in the Victoria and Albert Museum, London, and a plate which he was unable to trace but which had been described by William Rossetti in his catalogue as 'So judged He man'. It is in fact a version of 'The Judgement of Adam and Eve' and is now in the possession of the Houghton Library, Harvard University, Cambridge, Massachusetts. The dimensions of the three 'missing' plates correspond quite closely to those of the nine already in the Boston Museum. If Peckham is right, as he surely is, then eleven of the twelve subjects chosen for illustration in each series are the same.

[1] See 'William Blake's Mr. Thomas', op. cit., and my general Introduction.

[2] 'Blake, Milton, and Edward Burney', *Princeton University Chronicle*, XI, iii (Spring 1950), 115–16. Peckham's conclusions are echoed by Martin Butlin in 'A "Minute Particular" Particularized: Blake's Second Set of Illustrations to *Paradise Lost*', *Blake Newsletter*, VI, ii (Fall 1972), 44–6.

A third set of *Paradise Lost* illustrations, commissioned from Blake by the painter John Linnell, was begun in 1822. Only three drawings for this series were completed—'Satan Spying on Adam and Eve', 'The Creation of Eve', and 'Michael Foretelling the Crucifixion'—and these were bought from the artist by Linnell in 1825. They are very similar in style, size, and general design to their equivalents in the Boston series. The first two are now in the National Gallery of Victoria, Melbourne, Australia; the third is in the Fitzwilliam Museum, Cambridge, England.

Of the twelve plates which Blake appears to have executed for each of his two completed *Paradise Lost* sets, one plate, with one or two exceptions, served each Book of the poem.[3] The adoption of this 'one plate, one Book' formula probably owes something to the artist's sensitivity to epic design—a sensitivity which was later to be reflected in the grandiose but numerically 'perfect' proportions of his own epic poem, *Jerusalem*. It may also be attributed partly to convention, for almost all of the illustrated editions of *Paradise Lost* produced in the century preceding Blake's pictures were designed according to this formula,[4] appropriate as it was to the display considerations and financial exigencies of book illustration. There is no record of Blake's ever having sought or having been offered a commission to illustrate *Paradise Lost*—or indeed any of Milton's poems.

In approximately one half of his *Paradise Lost* plates Blake focuses upon a single episode; in the rest he makes pictorial reference to a couple of separate incidents or figure-groups which are or which could have been taken from the same Book. The single-episode plates enable him to give undivided attention to the poem's crucial dramatic moments: Satan rousing his fellow devils from the floor of hell and confronting Sin and Death at the gates of hell, the expulsion of the rebel angels from heaven and of man from Paradise, the birth of Eve, and the fall of man. In the dual-reference plates he attempts visually to intimate the poem's elaborate pattern of cross-references, as well as to convey something of its episodic variety. The relationship between the two scenes so depicted is generally symbolic: in 'Satan Spying on Adam and Eve' for instance the Devil is shown hovering just above Adam and Eve's bower, his outstretched finger penetrating its sanctity, and in 'The Descent

[3] The exceptions are that both sets contain two illustrations to Book XII and none to Book XI, and the Boston series has two illustrations to Book IV and none to Book V. Only in the case of *Paradise Lost* V (1) and *Paradise Lost* XI, therefore, do the numbers of the plates in their series differ from the numbers of the books from which the texts of the plates were drawn: the subject of *Paradise Lost* V (1) is taken from Book IV, that of *Paradise Lost* XI from Book XII.

[4] Whereas the great majority of those produced in the nineteenth century ignore it, partly because the Romantics and post-Romantics tended to place more emphasis on the episodic and scenic appeal of *Paradise Lost* than on its structure.

of Raphael' the figure of the descending angel separates the intruder from Adam and Eve. In the seventh illustration, 'Raphael Warning Adam', one of the 'scenes' derives from directly enacted narrative and the other from reportage—a distinction crucial to the nature and organization of the epic itself.

Similar figure-studies that appear in two separate plates provide a visual association between plates—a pictorial equivalent to narrative sequentiality and to Milton's own complex pattern of cross-references. The Satan who hovers beneath God's throne in *Paradise Lost* III, for instance, foreshadows the serpent-entwined Satan depicted above the bower of Adam and Eve in *Paradise Lost* IV; and the prone figure of Eve in 'Michael Foretelling the Crucifixion' recalls that of Adam in the Creation scene—a connection made by Milton himself: 'let Eve .../Here sleep below while thou to foresight wakest,/As once thou slep'st, while she to life was formed' (xi, 367–9).

Where he wishes to convey either physical distance or spiritual antipathy between characters represented in separate scenes but within the same frame Blake does not differentiate between them in scale but simply separates the scenes with a pictorial boundary—usually a simplified version of the stylized cloud-bands common in medieval manuscript illumination. By drawing all his figures according to the same scale and his separate scenes in mostly symbolic relation to each other he manages to retain the holy and heroic proportions of the 'human form divine' and to suggest the equal perceptual (though not moral or spiritual) validity of different experiences. This distinguishes his method from that of John Baptist Medina,[5] the only other major *Paradise Lost* illustrator to incorporate several episodes from the poem within a single frame but who employed Baroque perspective in combination with a kind of cartoon technique according to which a major episode or figure-group in the foreground was spatially related to other, subsidiary, small-scale scenes—which in the narrative generally followed the major scene, were causally dependent on it, or represented events whose reportage was the subject of the major scene.

Blake's illustrations to *Paradise Lost* provide ample evidence of the artist's sympathy for Milton's vision. Like Milton, he offers an optimistic view of the Fall by presenting Christ's final victory as assured and evil as proleptically vanquished. He selects subjects which are directly relevant to the central Creation–Fall–Redemption story instead of, for example, the brief allusions chosen (among other topics) by Fuseli for his Milton Gallery, and he does not, as other illustrators have done, adhere slavishly to biblical illustrative tradition. He also incorporates in his pictures many unobtrusive textual details that escape other less observant or less sympathetic illustrators.

[5] Who executed designs for all except one of the engravings in the first illustrated edition of *Paradise Lost*, published by Jacob Tonson in 1688.

Yet in certain significant respects Blake differs sharply from his poetic text. Though he accepts the Protestant emphasis placed by Milton on the psychological rather than on the literal aspects of evil, he takes this notion a stage further (and thus transforms it) by suggesting that evil is without metaphysical reality: his hell serves in part as a metaphor for the fallen world, his Satan as the negative aspect of Adam.

Blake attempts assiduously to mellow what he saw as the harsher aspects of Milton's vision—his repressive attitude towards sex, his respect for a withdrawn and tyrannical deity, and his lengthy account of the violence and lust of the post-lapsarian world—by indicating that for him sex, one of the blessings of Paradise, should be openly enjoyed, by portraying the Godhead in the guise of the repressive Urizen (though as an anonymous rather than as an actively malignant figure), and by ignoring all the scenes that are set in the harsh historical world. Only at the moment of Eve's fall do the grotesque passions and cruel forms of this world reveal themselves.

Besides his occasional 'rewritings', Blake had also modified the significance of the major characters of Milton's epic and the nature of the relationships between them, so that they more nearly reflect his own vision—both more compact and more complex than that of Milton—of the nature and history of man.

According to the *Paradise Lost* of Blake's illustrations Adam, Eve, and Satan are all aspects of an original, androgynous personality that has become divided against itself in a falling and a fallen world. The nature of this original personality is adumbrated in the Christ of the Crucifixion scene. The Adam of the *Paradise Lost* illustrations plays the role assigned in the Prophetic books to Albion—that of man fallen yet potentially redeemable. Eve stands for his Emanation, the female portion of originally androgynous man, whose assertion of her separate identity was itself a step in the prolonged process of the Fall. (Her materialization out of her 'contrary' has a parallel in the creation of the Eve of the text from the supernumerary rib of Adam.) For the most part Satan represents Adam's 'Spectre' or 'Selfhood', his negative characteristics of self-will, sterile ratiocination, and hypocritical puritanism, although in the first two plates of the series he is perhaps better seen simply as a representation of fallen man. The Spectres of the Prophetic books are frequently referred to as Satan.

Blake's Serpent, which is first shown entwined about Satan himself and later about the Tree of Knowledge, about Eve, and about the Cross (supposed in legend to have been made from the wood of the Tree), represents a further objectification and 'hardening' of the negative qualities that are manifested by the Spectre. Through it Blake emphasizes the bestiality and degradation associated with those qualities, and the way in which they fetter or restrict the freedom of their possessor. Though in origin a mere attribute of the Spectre, the Serpent appears to assume a will of its own, for its differences of attitude from Satan are at times evident. The degradation which results from Satan's continuance in evil, conveyed in the poem through bestial imagery and transformations, is indicated in the illustrative series by the fact that he does not appear in human form after the Book IV and Book V illustrations but is represented only through the Serpent.

The Spectre and Serpent of Blake's writings are frequently associated with an orthodox and self-righteous morality: 'Cloth'd in the Serpent's folds, in selfish holiness demanding purity,/... he (Satan) drove/Me from his inmost Brain' (*Milton*, K 493; pl. 12, 46–8).[6] The Satan-Spectre of the *Paradise Lost* illustrations is himself the first victim of this attitude, for the Serpent that is wound about him is carefully covering his genitals and thus 'bruising [his] minute articulations'[7]—a representation of Reason crushing the sexual and artistic impulses as well as of the tyrannous and self-destructive effects of strict sexual morality. With Freudian insight Blake associates this repressive puritanism with a corrupting and rapacious sexuality—as in the *Paradise Lost* 'Fall' illustration, in which the Serpent is coiled about Eve's body and she receiving the fruit from its jaws. (The association of corrupt sexuality with the Fall is traditional, and is also to be found in Milton's account and in many other pictorial representations.)

The pursuit of the Emanation by the Spectre—himself 'A male without a female counterpart' (*Vala*, K 347; 253)—and their coital embrace are described many times in the Prophetic books. The following passage, in which the Spectre of Urthona tempts the shadow of Enitharmon,[8] is particularly closely related to Blake's 'Fall' illustration:

> Intoxicated with
> The fruit of this delightful tree, I cannot flee away
> From they embrace, else be assur'd so horrible a form
> Should never in my arms repose;
> (*Vala*, K 326; 233–6)

In other works Blake also asserts a close connection between Satan and Adam. He associates them with the two 'limits' of the fallen world: 'The Divine hand found

---

[6] Leutha, Blake's Sin-figure, describing her birth out of the head of Satan.

[7] Cf. Los, Blake's Zoa of the redemptive Imagination, speaking of the depredations of Satan, which threaten him in the fallen world: 'Reasonings like vast Serpents/Infold around my limbs, bruising my minute articulations' (*Jerusalem*, K 635; pl. 15, 12–13).

[8] The Spectre or degraded aspect of the female: the process of decline and division, once begun, seems potentially limitless—and might indeed have become so without the intervention of Christ.

the Two Limits, first of Opacity, then of Contraction./Opacity was named Satan, Contraction was named Adam' (*Milton*, K 494; pl. 13, 20–1); he lists Satan as the fifteenth and Adam as the nineteenth 'son' of Los and Enitharmon (who are here, as often in Blake's writings, Adam and Eve figures and hence progenitors of the human race); and in his engraving of 'The Laocoön' he describes them as the two sons of 'Jah' (Jehovah).

The close metaphysical relationship between Satan and Adam is indicated in the *Paradise Lost* illustrations by their physical similarity. Both are portrayed as handsome, curly-haired nudes and (apart from the large wings which he displays in the illustrations to Books III, IV, and V, and which have their equivalent in the 'sail-broad vans' of the text) Satan is not represented with any of the paraphernalia of the traditional Gothic devil—horns, hooves, tail, pointed ears, spiked wings. These omissions are consistent with Milton's emphasis upon the psychological aspects of evil and its initial heroic appeal, and with his own rejection of the Gothic stereotype in his portrayal of Satan; and also with the representation of Satan in the paintings and writings of Blake's contemporaries as an attractive and courageous Romantic rebel, a martyr to the tyranny of the establishment.

In his controversial prose-poem *The Marriage of Heaven and Hell* Blake appears to endorse this portrait by associating what the world and the Church call Evil—and in particular, the devils of *Paradise Lost*—with reformist or revolutionary energy, with an urgent desire to establish those social and political liberties whose attainment might be thought to herald the millennium. Responding as many readers have done to the appeal of the Satan of Milton's Books I and II, and again employing Freudian insight, Blake associates the author of the poem with his anti-hero—and hence links Satan with the ultimate in artistic and redemptive genius:

> Note: The reason Milton wrote in fetters when he wrote of Angels & God, and at liberty when of Devils & Hell, is because he was a true Poet and of the Devil's party without knowing it.
>
> (K 150, pls. 5–6)

Yet these assertions must be placed in context, where they can be seen to be part of a sustained attack upon the moral and religious orthodoxies of the establishment—orthodoxies whose real aim according to Blake was the suppression of political, sexual, and artistic freedom: what the establishment sees as a threat to its existence, it smears as evil and attempts to eradicate. So with a gesture of mock deference the poet himself adopts the terminology of the establishment and calls upon his readers to follow Evil towards the light.

The unorthodox attitude which he adopts in *The Marriage* towards Milton's Satan, and which has become celebrated on account of its controversial nature, is by no means Blake's only or even his usual attitude towards him. Indeed, in an annotation to Swedenborg's *Heaven and Hell* that was penned at about the same time as *The Marriage*, he reveals considerable antipathy to Satan's attitudes and asserts his creator's independence from him: 'Thus Fools quote Shakespeare; the above is Theseus' opinion Not Shakespeare's. You might as well quote Satan's blasphemies from Milton & give them as Milton's Opinions' (K 939).

Many of Blake's Spectres are bat- or dragon-winged figures, and the enormous, spiked wings that frame the body of Satan like a kind of infernal mandorla in the illustrations to Books III, IV, and V therefore suggest his role as Spectre. They do not, however, appear in the illustrations to Books I and II, and their late addition may also be attributed to an attempt on Blake's part to suggest the moral and physical deterioration of Satan,[9] to a desire to evoke his epic journey through space, which is described in Book III, and to a wish to distinguish him from the Adam from whose form he was derived and who is represented with him in the fourth and fifth illustrations of the series. The omission of the wings in the first and second illustrations, in which Adam is not featured, facilitate the identification of the Satan of those plates with fallen man.

In the end man's Spectre and Serpent-Selfhood are to be overcome, his Emanation laid to rest, and his 'divine humanity' reasserted—the equivalent of Milton's 'paradise regained'.[10] These apocalyptic events are envisaged in the Crucifixion illustration, which shows the Serpent nailed to the Cross and Eve sleeping at its foot. Adam is standing to one side, gazing devoutly up at the crucified Christ. His hands are placed together in a gesture of prayer. This posture suggests the intimacy of the metaphysical relation between sinful man and the Divine Humanity—image and essence—as well as the compelling emotional bond that connects them. It also suggests the capacity of man to approach beatitude through contemplation and example. An even more moving and more explicit rendering of these notions is given in plate 76 of *Jerusalem*, which shows Christ crucified on the Tree of Knowledge and an adoring Albion gazing up at him, his arms outstretched in imitation of the crucifixion posture but his side-pointing left foot unobtrusively asserting his own identity.

[9] As Edward J. Rose observes, 'Winged forms, angelic or otherwise, are not a step up from the Human, but a step down.' ('Blake's Illustrations for *Paradise Lost, L'Allegro*, and *Il Penseroso*: A Thematic Reading', *Hartford Studies in Literature*, II, i, (1970), 53.)

[10] Cf. *Paradise Lost* xii, 461–5.

In *Milton and English Art* Marcia Pointon has listed the most frequently illustrated subjects from each Book of *Paradise Lost*:

The first two books ... were undoubtedly the most popular, 'Satan summoning his Legions' and 'Satan, Sin and Death' being the most favoured scenes respectively in these books ... 'Uriel and Satan' was the preferred subject in Book III followed by 'Satan Watching Adam and Eve' in Book IV. For the subsequent eight books the most favoured scenes were as follows: 'Raphael Arriving in Eden', 'The War in Heaven', 'Raphael Discoursing', 'Adam Sees Eve Approaching', 'Eve Tempted' with 'Adam Tempted' as a close second, 'Adam and Eve in Sad Discourse', 'Michael in Eden' and finally 'The Expulsion'.[11]

Despite the originality of most of his designs Blake chooses the traditional favourite subject for seven out of his twelve illustrations. The remaining five—those for Books III, VI, VIII, X, and XI—all depict Christ in one of his roles as Saviour (twice), Warrior, Creator, and Judge. In each case he appears as a dignified and gentle figure. It seems that when Blake differs from tradition in his choice of subject he does so at least partly in order to emphasize the beneficence and central importance of Christ. The protectiveness of the Saviour of Blake's Judgement scene and his mildness when expelling the rebel angels far exceed those of his Miltonic counterpart.

Blake pays tribute to Milton's nobility of conception and to the epic or 'classical' features of *Paradise Lost* by depicting his figures as statues with long limbs and deep chests, small heads and noble gestures, that 'bring hints to us of Greek models'.[12] Other allusions to classical sculpture include the raised platforms and plinths, the blank eyes of some of the figures, God's throne in the Book III illustration, and the light, clinging garments—perhaps partly derived also from the *robes en chemise* worn by fashion-conscious women of Blake's time—which render the bodies within them 'both more mysterious and more comprehensible'.[13] The toning of the figures is also reminiscent of marble.

Though sometimes hostile to classical culture, Blake often associates the permanence and beauty of sculptured marble with ideal forms and on occasion even speaks of his characters as though they were exquisitely sculptured figures. In *A Descriptive Catalogue 1809* for instance, he describes some of his favourite Greek statues as 'representations of spiritual existences, of Gods immortal ... embodied and organized in solid marble' (K 576), and in *Jerusalem* (K 638; pl. 16, 61) he envisages the ideal Platonic forms in Los's halls of memory as 'bright Sculptures'. In a climactic passage from *Milton* (K 502; pl. 20, 7–9) he compares the redeemer-poet moulding

[11] 1970, p. xxxix.
[12] Elisabeth Luther Cary, *The Art of William Blake*, 1907, p. 19.
[13] Kenneth Clark, *The Nude*, 1956, p. 68.

a humanized Urizen out of clay, to a sculptor, and in *Jerusalem* (K 709; pl. 70, 21–4) he even portrays the evil seductress Rahab as a marble form:

> On her white marble & even Neck, her Heart,
> Inorb'd and bonified, with locks of shadowing modesty, shining
> Over her beautiful Female features soft flourishing in beauty,
> Beams mild, all love and all perfection

PARADISE LOST I and separate plates: SATAN ROUSING HIS LEGIONS (18–20)

Blake executed two water-colour and two tempera versions of this subject. One of the water-colours is the first plate of the Huntington series and the other, which is in the Victoria and Albert Museum, is almost certainly a missing plate from the Boston series. The Victoria and Albert water-colour is a slightly revised version of the central portion of the Huntington plate. One of the tempera versions was painted for the Countess of Egremont and remains today at Petworth House, Sussex; the other, which is a study for it, is in the Victoria and Albert Museum. The water-colour plates are delicately tinted in pink and grey, and apart from their overhanging curtains of cloud convey little off the sublimity and obscurity of Milton's Infernal landscape. The tempera plates do convey these qualities, though quite divorced from the heroism with which Milton endows his devils. They are executed in rich, deep reds and browns with flecks of gold that highlight the figures and the flames: the 'experiment Picture' in particular is so dark that the shapes within it are barely discernible. Blake expresses his own dissatisfaction with it in his *Descriptive Catalogue 1809* (K 582):

This picture was ... painted at intervals, for experiment on colours without any oily vehicle; it may be worthy of attention, not only on account of its composition, but of the great labour which has been bestowed on it, that is, three or four times as much as would have finished a more perfect Picture; the labour has destroyed the lineaments; it was with difficulty brought back again to a certain effect, which it had at first, when all the lineaments were perfect.

All four versions of 'Satan Rousing his Legions' show the devils as nude male figures, stripped of their traditional demonic attributes and placed within a sombre and cavernous landscape. Satan is perched on a ledge above the lesser devils, his shield and spear propped up against the rock face behind him and his arms raised in a gesture of encouragement to his fellows to 'Awake, arise, or be for ever fallen' (i, 330). Behind him (below, in the tempera version) is the reclining figure of

Beelzebub, his back turned to the viewer and his head sunk on his hand. The mournful resignation of his posture reflects that part of his opening speech in which he suggests that God may be working out his purpose through the devils (i, 143–52)—something Satan is not yet prepared to acknowledge.

In the Huntington version several of the lesser devils are shown groping their way up through the 'dusky air' in response to their general's call:

> They heard, and were abashed, and up they sprung
> Upon the wing, as when men wont to watch
> On duty, sleeping found by whom they dread,
> Rouse and bestir themselves ere well awake.
>
> (i, 331–4)

Those who are rising in the tempera version are being driven upwards not by their own exertions but by two enormous, steel-grey tongues of flame—'darkness visible'[14] against a lighter, fiery background. Several of their companions are still floating or falling downwards.

The inhibited actions and postures of the rising devils hint at the fact that their apparent freedom to rise from the floor of hell is merely the result of a tactical concession on the part of God. The impression of defeat and doom is reinforced by the oppressive rock faces in the background and (in the water-colour versions) by the overhanging clouds. These, though they part around the figure of Satan, remain above his head to hem him in. Some of the devils—in the V & A water-colour all of them except Satan and Beelzebub—remain chained to the fiery lake or floor of hell. However, their cramped postures convey still more clearly than their chains the restraints to which they are subject.

In the Huntington version there are close parallels in expression and position of the head or body between Satan and the two devils to either side of him on the one hand, and the devils directly beneath them on the other—an attempt by Blake to suggest progressive movement within a single frame.

The rising devils are reminiscent of some of the figures in Michelangelo's 'Last Judgement' fresco. One of these forms the subject of a study in oils that had been executed by Blake some thirty years before he embarked on the *Paradise Lost* illustrations. Other similarities between the fresco and 'Satan Rousing his Legions' reside in their vertical structuring, their use of cloud- or rock-masses, and their emphasis

---

[14] Cf. *Paradise Lost* i, 62–4: 'from those flames/No light, but rather darkness visible/Served only to discover sights of woe'. These lines are echoed by Blake in *The Book of Urizen*, K 225; pl. 5, 17–18: 'But no light from the fires: all was darkness/In the flames of Eternal fury.'

on a single key figure, depicted with arms raised and positioned above centre—Christ in the case of Michelangelo, Satan (ironically, perhaps) in the case of Blake.

The attitudes taken up by most of the other devils in 'Satan Rousing his Legions' are clichés in Blake's rhetoric of the visionless state—knees or heads clasped, arms outstretched with body supine or floating in the air, kneeling or crouching positions. A kneeling and head-clasping figure with staring eyes and open mouth, who is represented in the lower right-hand corner of the tempera versions, closely resembles the Los of the furnaces depicted in the seventh plate of *The Book of Urizen*; and the pinkish stream of molten lava that runs down the rock face in the Huntington plate, is reminiscent of the 'thousands of rivers in veins/Of blood [which] pour down the mountains to cool/The eternal fires' in the same work (K 225–6; pl. 5, 30–2).

The figure of Death, depicted in all the versions of 'Satan Rousing his Legions', also makes his presence felt in the hell of *The Book of Urizen:*

> He [Los] dug mountains & hills in vast strength,
> He piled them in incessant labour,
> In howlings & pangs & fierce madness,
> Long periods in burning fires labouring
> Till hoary, and age-broke, and aged,
> In despair and the shadows of death.
>
> (K 225; pl. 5, 22–7)

In the water-colour *Paradise Lost* plates he is lying prostrate on the floor of hell— a living embodiment of death—and in the tempera, sitting over another figure, whom he appears to have strangled. He is portrayed with white hair and beard, and with blank, sightless eyes. In the Huntington plate his arms are hidden but in the V & A water-colour they are outstretched—the position in which he is shown, vanquished, in the eleventh illustration of the series. The fact that he is here (as in *Paradise Lost* XI) given a solid body and not merely an outline, as in *Paradise Lost* II, suggests that his nature has already become realized—in other words, that the scene is an allegorical representation of life in the fallen world.

In all versions of the picture one devil is represented in the foetal posture in which Urizen, overlord of the fallen world, is frequently depicted—perhaps because it is Urizen who in Blake's cosmogony was responsible for the birth of the flesh.

In the Huntington version Beelzebub is reclining, with his buttocks and leaning arm on opposite sides of the stream of hell—a position which suggests that of the classical river-god. In his catalogue of devils turned pagan deities Milton lists Thammuz-Adonis and refers to the myth of how the River Adonis was supposed annually to have been discoloured by his blood:

> Thammuz came next behind,
> Whose annual wound in Lebanon allured
> The Syrian damsels to lament his fate
> In amorous ditties all a summer's day,
> While smooth Adonis from his native rock
> Ran purple to the sea, supposed with blood
> Of Thammuz yearly wounded
>
> (i, 446–52).

There is no evidence that any of the risen devils in the Huntington water-colour have had to struggle to free themselves from their fetters, though most of their fellows below them are still chained to the floor of hell. This apparent anomaly has its equivalent in *Paradise Lost*, where the devils are also imprisoned in 'adamantine chains' (i, 48) but where the chains are conveniently forgotten when the devils come to rise from the lake. In Blake's case at least the anomaly is unlikely to have been an oversight, and may well reflect his belief in 'mind-forg'd manacles'—abstract fetters which have been created by the mind and which must therefore be broken through mental rather than through physical exertion. The only chains that are visible in the tempera versions are those that bind the foetus-figure.

Satan, who dominates the scene, is depicted as a full-frontal nude with Michelangelesque torso and legs. His proud displaying of his beauty corresponds to the vaunting rhetoric of his public speeches in the epic, particularly his facile boast that 'Here at least/We shall be free' (i, 258–9). He reflects something of the charisma of the devils of *The Marriage*—that of brave rebels against tyranny—yet the artistic and sexual freedom which his nudity implies is compromised by the lightly-sketched codpiece of scales which he is wearing.

Satan's alarmed gaze, which appears to have been arrested by some new threat that has arisen beyond the confines of the plate, reflects his inner uncertainty and the strains of his recent experiences. Milton too emphasizes his careworn expression—one of the first signs of his fall from grace—and the searching attitude which he strikes: 'round he throws his baleful eyes/That witnessed huge affliction and dismay/Mixed with obdurate pride and steadfast hate' (i, 56–8).

Blake has introduced into the landscape of 'Satan Rousing his Legions' several elements which do not feature in the text but which are frequently associated by him with the unlovely aspects of the fallen or material world—the rock faces, the dark and billowing clouds, and a tiny cave in the lower left-hand corner of the plate. The symbolic nature of this cave is emphasized in the water-colour versions by the fact that its prisoner is able to gaze up through its rock wall at the risen Satan.

In the tempera plates its cramped spaces are inhabited by two devils who appear unaware of each other's existence: extreme self-centredness and lack of fellowship are part of the diabolic character.

For Blake hell is synonymous with the mental condition of fallen man. In his *Annotations to Lavater* he exclaims in a moment of exasperation with the writer: 'To hell till he behaves better! mark that I do not believe there is such a thing litterally, but hell is the being shut up in the possession of corporeal desires which shortly weary the man' (K 74); and in *Jerusalem* he laments: 'What are the Pains of Hell but Ignorance, Bodily Lust, Idleness & devastation of the things of the Spirit?' (K 717; pl. 77).

'Satan Rousing his Legions' may therefore be seen as a proleptic representation of man in the fallen world—an interpretation facilitated by Blake's portrayal of the devils without their traditional demonic attributes, though the gnarled and lined faces of the figures in the V & A water-colour and the mannikin-Satan of the tempera versions do indicate the depths to which they have descended. Some verses in his *MS Note-book 1808–11* confirm that Blake regarded the tempera versions as an analogue at least of his own fallen condition:

> But now the Caves of Hell I view:
> Who shall I dare to shew them to?
> What mighty Soul in Beauty's form
> Shall dauntless View the Infernal Storm?
> Egremont's Countess can controll
> The flames of Hell that round me roll.
>
> (K 558; 3–8)

Blake's allegorical interpretation of hell is consistent with the close connection established by Milton himself—particularly in the first Books of the poem—between the devils and fallen man, and with his representation of the Infernal landscape in general and abstract terms that suggest a psychological or spiritual condition rather than a particular location: 'bottomless perdition' (i, 47); 'The dismal situation waste and wild' (i, 60); 'The seat of desolation' (i, 181); 'this mournful gloom' (i, 244); 'the oblivious pool' (i, 266).

SATAN RISING (21, 22)

To a Notebook sketch for plate 5 of his emblem-book *The Gates of Paradise* Blake appended the lines from *Paradise Lost* which describe Satan rising from the lake of hell: 'Forthwith upright he rears from off the pool/His mighty stature' (, 221–2). (The first two words have been scored out.) These suggest that the completed engraving, ostensibly a personified representation of the element fire and the last of a group depicting the four elements, has another referent in the Satan of *Paradise Lost*.

The emblem-book exists in two versions—the earlier, of 1793, 'For Children' and the later, of 1818, 'For the Sexes'. Both versions of plate 5 show the fire-spirit or Satan-figure as a naked warrior holding his shield and spear aloft and springing upwards in a burst of flame. He is drawn as though elevated above the viewer's level of vision. In the first edition he is represented as vigorous and even noble, his energy and naked beauty recalling those of the Devil of *The Marriage of Heaven and Hell*; for the later version the portrait has been altered and darkened so as to conform to the added 'Keys of the Gates' and to comply with the new dedication to humanity in a fallen world. The figure is now blinded ('Blind in Fire with shield & spear', K 770; 10), its hair has been restyled so as to suggest a pair of horns ('Two Horn'd Reasoning, Cloven Fiction', K 770; 11), scale-like markings are visible on its body and in the flames that surround it, and an added caption associates it with 'endless Strife'. Youthful idealist has been transformed into visionless assassin—'The selfhood in a flame of fire' (K 421).

PARADISE LOST II: SATAN, SIN, AND DEATH AT THE GATES OF HELL (23, 24)

For his second illustration of the *Paradise Lost* series Blake 'freezes' the moment in which Sin intervenes to prevent a clash of arms between Satan and Death:

> So frowned the mighty combatants, that hell
> Grew darker at their frown, so matched they stood;
> 　　　　　. . . and now great deeds
> Had been achieved, whereof all hell had rung,
> Had not the snaky sorceress that sat
> Fast by hell gate, and kept the fatal key,
> Risen, and with hideous outcry rushed between.
> 　　　　　　　　　　(ii, 719–20, 722–6)

The antagonists have raised their weapons for the strike and Satan is brandishing his shield above Sin's head. Sin herself, who is placed between the would-be duellists—father and son, her father and her son—is trying to thrust them apart, her gesture serving visually to link the assailants as well as to separate them:

> O Father, what intends thy hand, she cried,
> Against thy only son? What fury, O Son,
> Possesses thee to bed that mortal dart
> Against thy father's head?
>
> (ii, 727–30)

Sin is presented as a promiscuous young woman, though with serpentine tails for her lower parts; Death as a pellucid outline. Satan retains the naked human form which he enjoyed in the preceding illustration.

The subject was a popular one with Blake's artist friends and contemporaries. William Hogarth executed an oil-painting and an engraving of it in 1764, and between 1775 and 1799 it was illustrated by Barry, Burney, Corbould, Fuseli, Gillray, Mortimer, and Stothard. Anthony Blunt attributes part of its popularity to the fact that Edmund Burke selected it—or, to be precise, the 'portrait of the king of terrors'—as 'the purest example of the sublime in literature'.[15] However, a passing attack on Burke's *Enquiry into . . . the Sublime and Beautiful* in the *Annotations to Reynolds* ('Obscurity is Neither the Source of the Sublime nor of any Thing Else', (K 473)) suggests that in Blake's case at least the motive is more likely to have been a determination to take issue with the Burkean conception of the sublime than a desire to pay tribute to it. Certainly he transfers to his illustration none of the terrible obscurity of Milton's 'execrable shape' (ii, 681) and 'gloom of Tartarus profound' (ii, 858). The 'Sin intervening' arrangement of *Paradise Lost* II is similar to that employed by Hogarth and by several of Blake's contemporaries. One or more of these designs, perhaps those of his friend Fuseli, may have served him as a model.

Despite its chaotic subject, Blake's picture shows a high degree of artistic organization. His Satan and Death are depicted in virtual mirror-positions of each other, and the two coiled serpent-tails with which he endows his Sin stretch neatly from her lower parts to the margins of the plate. His background, which is left obscure and undefined in the works of most of his contemporaries, is dominated on the left by the soaring flames of hell and elsewhere by oppressive, square-cut forms—the latticed portcullis on the right, the two massive stone arches 'impaled with circling fire,/Yet unconsumed' (ii, 647–8) on the left, and, as a foundation for the encounter of the giants, a stone slab with flames licking at its edges.

Blake emphasizes the sensuality of his Sin, portraying her with provocatively displayed arms and torso and with abundant, free-flowing curls. The hell-hounds which

---

[15] *The Art of William Blake*, 1959, p. 20. Burke's actual words were, 'In this description all is dark, uncertain, confused, terrible, and sublime to the last degree.'

Milton grouped 'about her middle' (ii, 653) are placed by him in front of her sexual parts, and her tails appear to have their origin there as well:

> The one seemed woman to the waist, and fair,
> But ended foul in many a scaly fold
> Voluminous and vast, a serpent armed
> With mortal sting: about her middle round
> A cry of hell hounds never ceasing barked
>
> (ii, 650–4)

Where with Blake's artist-contemporaries Sin's gesture was the simple, stiff-armed one of separating the antagonists, here she is intimate and even caressing as she touches Satan and Death—a reflection of the sexual favours that she has already enjoyed with them both. In the larger plate she is shown with wildly upstanding hair—perhaps a reference to the Medusa myth, which was alluded to by Milton when he described her as 'the snaky sorceress' (ii, 724). In his cartoon engraving James Gillray made the reference explicit by depicting his Sin with snakes writhing in her hair.

Milton's Sin also appears in Blake's poetry, thinly disguised as the 'immortal, heart-piercing' (*Milton*, K 492; pl. 11, 32) Leutha. As in *Paradise Lost* her 'parent-power' is Satan; a 'Dragon-Form' (pl. 12, 2) issues from her loins; and she is the bearer of Death. Her emergence from the head of Satan is interpreted by Blake as the Selfhood's rash expulsion of its Emanation:

> Cloth'd in the Serpent's folds, in selfish holiness demanding purity,
> Being most impure, self-condemn'd to eternal tears, he drove
> Me from his inmost Brain ...
>
> (*Milton*, K 493; pl. 12, 46–8)

In the larger version of *Paradise Lost* II Sin's coiled tails terminate in serpents' heads.[16] These look menacing and fiendish, and are evidently acquainted with the very roots of evil. One head is nudging impatiently at hell's gate and the other is belching its poison back into the furnace. They prefigure the Serpent of the Fall, and their appearance here serves to indicate the closeness of the association between Sin and the Serpent. The owe their origin to a hint dropped by Milton in his description of Sin (quoted above), a hint which Blake has characteristically picked up and articulated.

The Janus-position of the serpent-heads—one is looking forward towards the

---

[16] Morse Peckham (op. cit., p. 122) suggests that Blake may have borrowed this idea from Edward Burney's illustration of the scene, but if this is the case then he has transformed the original conception, for Burney's insignificant and fanciful heads bear little resemblance to Blake's.

future, the other back towards the fiery lake—suggest the crucial nature of Satan's encounter with Sin and Death. The coils of Sin's tails appear ready to imprison the Devil, just as one has already encircled some of the hell-hounds. The scales which in the larger version can be seen covering his genitals hint at his connections with the Serpent. They also suggest a distortion of his sexual energies: as with Comus, repressed sexuality is associated with aggression.

Though not mentioned again in the poem the hell-hounds reappear, together with Sin and Death, in 'The Judgement of Adam and Eve' and in 'Michael Foretelling the Crucifixion'. Their mood varies according to the fortunes of the Satanic Trinity. In *Paradise Lost* ii, just before Satan escapes from hell, they are baying eagerly and with an air of expectation; at the moment of judgement, when the power of Death over the world is confirmed, they appear rapaciously triumphant; and at the Crucifixion, the event which symbolizes the defeat of the unholy Trinity, they are sunk in slumber. The fact that there are three of them in all cases except one—the larger version of *Paradise Lost* ii—suggests that they may be compared with Cerberus, as they are at *Paradise Lost* ii, 655.

Blake's Death is represented as a pellucid figure in human form—shadowy and phantasmal indeed (cf. ii, 669 and 743) though without the grisly indeterminateness of his counterpart in the epic. The intention is clearly to convey not the horrors of death but its relevance to the human condition and the fact that at the time of the encounter with Satan it was still unrealized, and inconceivable to man. The description of its origins which Blake gives in *Milton* emphasizes its illusory nature: 'In dreams she [Leutha] bore the shadowy Spectre of Sleep & nam'd him Death' (K 494; pl. 13, 40); and in the quartering of the original man which is described in *Jerusalem* Death is the shadow of the Spectre Satan—yet another cleavage in the primal unity and in part a reference to his issue from the single line of Satan: 'I see the Four-fold Man, The Humanity in deadly sleep/And its fallen Emanation, The Spectre & its cruel Shadow' (K 635; pl. 15, 6–7).

In the smaller version of *Paradise Lost* ii Death retains the beard which he possessed in the first illustration; in the larger he is unfledged but his face has assumed the mask-like character frequently found in Blake's figures of evil. In both versions he is shaking his 'dreadful dart' (ii, 672), which, like the comet to which Satan is compared at ii, 708, streams with fire. He is also wearing a spiked crown—frequently an attribute of Blake's Urizenic tyrant but here according with Milton's description: 'what seemed his head/The likeness of a kingly crown had on' (ii, 672–3).

Suspended from the ceiling above Sin's head is a large chain. Its function, like that of a similar chain in Hogarth's painting, must be to raise the portcullis; but whereas the earlier chain is attached to the portcullis and appears to be purely functional, Blake's is dangling just above the characters' heads and serves as a concise figurative reminder that the chains from which Satan and his crew have just escaped still hang threateningly over them.

The two arches in *Paradise Lost* ii through which Satan has already passed, together with the portcullis gate which still lies ahead of him, may be compared to the 'three-fold gates' of the text: 'And thrice threefold the gates; three folds were brass,/Three iron, three of adamantine rock,/Impenetrable, impaled with circling fire' (ii, 645–7). These gates are incorporated by Blake into his own system, where they stand in the first instance for the perilous delights of female beauty:

> ... every one [of Los's daughters] in their bright loins
> Have a beautiful golden gate, which opens into the vegetative world;
> And every one a gate of rubies & all sorts of precious stones
> In their translucent hearts, which opens into the vegetative world;
> And every one a gate of iron dreadful and wonderful
> In their translucent heads, which opens into the vegetative world;
> ... [the gates] are incircled with flaming fires.
>
> (*Jerusalem*, K 635; pl. 14, 19–24 and 28)

The forcing of these gates is associated by Blake both with sexual intercourse and with birth. His gates, like Milton's, are guarded by a female figure; they cannot be closed again once opened; and penetration of them is associated with the Fall, and hence with death:

> She burst the Gates of Enitharmon's heart with direful Crash,
> Nor could they ever be clos'd again; the golden hinges were broken,
> And the gates broke in sunder & their ornaments defac'd
> Beneath the tree of Mystery
>
> (*Vala*, K 328, 323–6)

Their possible presence in *Paradise Lost* ii suggests an intimate association between sexuality and descent, and between generation and Satan's irruption into the wider world. It also hints at the incestuous origins of Sin and Death, though without drawing attention in any way to their allegorical aspect. Having passed through two arches and now confronting the third, Satan is portrayed in the midst of an action which stands both for copulation and for generation.

In contemporary literary and artistic circles the 'Satan, Sin, and Death' episode lay at the heart of a debate on the propriety of including allegory in a dramatic epic. Blake's picture stands above the debate for it is no narrowly allegorical episode but a powerful rendition of the clash of evil with evil, the disintegration of the disordered personality, and the familiar disputes—'War and deadly contention Between/Father and Son' (*Jerusalem*, K 640; pl. 18, 20–1)—which characterize the fallen world.

PARADISE LOST III: CHRIST OFFERING TO REDEEM MANKIND (25, 26)

Here Christ is shown offering himself as a sacrifice for mankind. He is hovering in mid-air before the Father, with his back to the viewer and his arms outstretched. The Father is seated on a simple throne, with his hands prominent but his face and body hidden from sight. The pair are framed by the figures of four downward-gliding angels who are offering up their crowns in adoration of Christ. Beneath the group glides a darkened and disconsolate Satan.

In the Huntington version Christ is represented as a slight and insignificant youth but in the Boston plate his identity as the future Prince of mankind is already revealed in his gravity and dignified self-assurance. In this version his head is turned to one side, thus displaying his 'conspicuous countenance' (iii, 385) in profile—a significant aspect to an amateur physiognomer like Blake.[17] His outstretched arms and upright, attenuated body prefigure the Crucifixion-posture and so suggest the offer of atonement which he made to God:

> Behold me then, me for him, life for life
> I offer, on me let thine anger fall;
> Account me man; I for his sake will leave
> Thy bosom, and this glory next to thee
> Freely put off
>
> (iii, 236–40)

The posture hints at his filial devotion as well as at his love of man.

The Father, 'High throned above all highth' (iii, 58), is frontally portrayed though his face, which is buried in Christ's right shoulder, is not visible. His large and magnificently expressive hands are lightly touching the Son's sides but not supporting him, so that he appears both to be arrested in mid-air and to be on the verge of slipping downwards out of the Father's grasp—a position which admirably conveys the momentousness and emotional tension associated with his offer. It also suggests God's

---

[17] Cf. *The Everlasting Gospel*, K 748; pl. a, 1–4: 'The Vision of Christ that thou dost see/Is my Vision's Greatest Enemy:/Thine has a great hook nose like thine,/Mine has a snub nose like to mine'; and my discussion of *Nativity Ode* IV.

own responsibility for the sacrifice. In *The Marriage of Heaven and Hell* Blake asserts that 'in Milton, the Father is Destiny' '(K 150; pls. 5–6)'[18]: he might have added that he is also as good as the murderer of his son. Martin Butlin[19] points out that Blake has 'contrasted the ecstatic, open-gestured figure of Christ with the closed, slumped form of God the Father'.

The Father's bowed head and caressing hands convey tender feelings towards Christ, sorrow at the projected sacrifice, and possible reluctance to permit the Son to descend, but to those familiar with Blake's visual symbolism his hidden face and his prominent, Urizenic knees are ominous signs indicating the hypocrisy of his sorrow, the despotism of his rule, and the impersonality of his nature. He may also have been shown with hidden face in deference to Milton's description of him 'invisible/Amidst the glorious brightness where [he sits]/Throned inaccessible' (iii, 375–7). Blake himself mocks the unapproachable godhead of *Paradise Lost* and the Old Testament in some early satirical verses:

> Why art thou silent & invisible,
> Father of Jealousy?
> Why dost thou hide thyself in clouds
> From every searching Eye?
>> (*Poems from the Note-book*
>> *1793*, K 171, no. 21)

In *Paradise Lost* iii only a feeble burst of light emanates from behind the head of him who is Milton's 'Fountain of light' (iii, 375), and his throne is so plain as to suggest that it was ironically conceived. The portrait is similar to that in Fuseli's 'Das Schweigen' (an illustration for *Il Penseroso*), which may have served Blake as a model.

Although it is often difficult to ascertain whether Blake's symbolism of 'right' and 'left' has been applied to any particular figure, it is clearly relevant in this illustration, in which God, who remains in heaven, shows only his right foot and Christ, who is about to descend to earth, displays only his left.

On each side of the Father and Son two downward-gliding angels offer up their golden crowns in homage to Christ. Apart from their heads, which are represented severally, each pair of angels is shown with a single body—a living demonstration of the harmony of the blessed state. Their postures combine humility with exultation and—like Christ's—suggest the paradox of arrested motion. They add a note of grace

---

[18] A charge that in *Paradise Lost* is made by the Devil—appropriately, in view of Blake's sympathies in *The Marriage*.

[19] *William Blake*, 1978, p. 113.

and lyricism to the somewhat severe lines of the central arrangement and they also accentuate the downward impulse of the figure of Christ. Their robes, particularly those in the Boston version, are executed according to a principle proclaimed by Blake in his *Annotations to Reynolds*: 'Drapery is formed alone by the Shape of the Naked' (K 462), and frequently practised by him.

The bands of the crowns in the Boston version are surmounted by designs shaped like vine leaves so as to suggest the Passion. Springs of greenery are interwoven around them—the 'Immortal amarant' (iii, 353) of the poem. The same connotations of immortality, or triumph, and death are to be found in the Huntington version in the two stately crowns that are held aloft by the angels nearest the viewer and in the two plain, spiked crowns similar to that worn earlier by Death, that are held at a slightly lower level by the other angels. So as well as the Incarnation and Passion, the Triumph that resulted from them is alluded to in the illustration, as it is in the third Book of the poem. The fact that there are four angels and four crowns hints at the fourfold nature of the redeemed man (cf. *Jerusalem*, pl. 98).

'Coasting the wall of heaven on this side night' (iii, 71) is Satan, excluded from the celestial region by a belt of cloud.[20] His presence brings to mind that other world of Milton's Book III—the world of immense and terrifying spaces, of physical and spiritual isolation, of Chaos and Night, and of the Limbo of Vanity. His isolation, his sulky or anxious expression, the body-length bat-wings with which he is now endowed, and the dark blue shading that surrounds his figure, provide a sharp contrast with the figures in the upper region of the picture. Unlike Christ and the angels, he is turned away from the Father—perhaps because Blake had learnt from his reading of Swedenborg's *Heaven and Hell* that:

all the angels constantly turn their faces towards [the Lord] ... whereas the infernal spirits turn themselves to that blackness and darkness which are opposite thereto, having their backs towards the Lord, forasmuch as all that are in hell are in the love of self and of the world, and as such in opposition to his Divine Majesty.[21]

Despite weaknesses in draughtsmanship the illustration is highly successful. It is remarkable for its flowing beauty, its balanced design, its rendering of arrested motion, and its capacity to convey incident directly and affectingly in terms of symbolic gesture. Its dramatic impact and its fidelity to the text far exceed those of most illustrations of the subject, which generally show an inert and enfeebled Christ seated

---

[20] Cf. the 'rolling Cloud which separates the Wicked from the Seats of Bliss' (*A Vision of the Last Judgment*, K 614).

[21] Emanuel Swedenborg, *A Treatise Concerning Heaven and Hell*, trans. from the Latin, 1778, p. 74 (para. 123).

in heaven at the right hand of God and supporting a Passion cross not mentioned in the text.

PARADISE LOST IV and separate plates: SATAN SPYING ON ADAM AND EVE (27–30)

In *Paradise Lost* IV Adam and Eve are watched by Satan as they recline upon a 'soft downy bank damasked with flowers' (IV, 334):

> our general mother ... with eyes
> Of conjugal attraction unreproved,
> And meek surrender, half embracing leaned
> On our first father, half her swelling breast
> Naked met his under the flowing gold
> Of her loose tresses hid: he ...
> ... pressed her matron lip
> With kisses pure: aside the devil turned
> For envy, yet with jealous leer malign
> Eyed them askance
>
> (IV, 492–7 and 501–4)

Almost every detail of this description has been faithfully rendered or suggested—with the exception of Eve's hair, which flows down her back instead of covering her breasts, a pointed repudiation of Milton's puritanism and an affirmation of Blake's belief that 'Art can never exist without Naked Beauty displayed' (*The Laocoön*, K 776).

Adam and Eve are shown embracing—attractive in their nudity though displaying all the awkwardness of two statues in a clinch. The legs of the Huntington Adam are particularly poorly drawn and were revised for the Boston version.

Adam is wearing a coronet of roses in both plates—a proleptic allusion to the crown of thorns which in a later, less happy time is to be worn by Christ, his descendant and more perfect self. Earlier in Book IV Milton reminds us that the paradisal rose was 'without thorn' (IV, 256).

In the Boston version Adam and Eve, who are caressing each other with one hand, are both shown plucking a flower with the other. The traditional sexual significance of this action is relevant and is underlined by a reference in the poem to the ravishing of Persephone, whom Milton associates both with flower-plucking and with descent into the nether world:

> Not that fair field
> Of Enna, where Proserpine gathering flowers
> Her self a fairer flower by gloomy Dis
> Was gathered, which cost Ceres all that pain
> To seek her through the world ...
> ... might with this Paradise
> Of Eden strive
>
> (iv, 268–72 and 274–5)

Later Eve, separated from her spouse and watched by the Serpent, is herself imaged as 'fairest unsupported flower' (ix, 432), and her fall is described by Adam in his first anguished apprehension of it as a deflowering (ix, 901).

In *Paradise Lost* iv Adam is shown about to pluck a lily, Eve a rose. Blake frequently juxtaposes these flowers, using the lily to represent the incorruptible beauty of the soul and the rose, the transient mortal beauty which is forced to defend itself against the ravages of the world. It is appropriate that Adam, the original member of what was to Blake as well as to Milton the more 'godlike' sex, should be grasping the stem of a lily and Eve, who is the first to fall, a rose.

Two curved palm-fronds decorated with roses spring from either corner of the illustration, the rose-sprays meeting above the heads of Adam and Eve. The sanctuary thus formed is reminiscent of the 'blissful bower' (iv, 690) in which Milton's Adam and Eve take their conjugal pleasures. The illustration appears to be a collation of this episode with the earlier scene in which Satan was shown spying upon Adam and Eve.

The varied plant-life of Milton's bower reflects the plenty of God's world; Blake's design, which is restricted to palms and roses, is more severely emblematic. The palm traditionally stands for Christ's sacrifice and triumph, and the rose, as has already been noted, for fragile beauty. The frame of the bower in Fuseli's 'Adam entschlossen, das Los Evas zu teilen' (Milton Gallery no. 20) is very similar to that of *Paradise Lost* iv, and may have influenced Blake in his design.

Adam and Eve's couch is also composed largely of roses. Their size and abundance, and the rotundity of their forms, serve admirably to suggest the fecundity of paradisal nature, and the beauty and fragility of love before the Fall. Though their apparent solidity in the illustration sorts oddly with their natural frailty, their identity as roses is confirmed by the fact that their leaves, shown beneath the couch in the Huntington version and peeping out from between the heads of the flowers in the Boston plate, are identical to those depicted on the stems of the roses that overhang the bower— and, in the case of the Boston illustration, on that of the rose by Eve's right hand. In colour they are a delicate pink.

That curiously unyielding quality which enables the roses to support Adam and Eve some distance above the ground may derive from Blake's memory of a detail in the *Iliad*—a work which he had occasion to know well, for he had already engraved several of Flaxman's second set of plates for it. The detail occurs in a description of Hera and Zeus's freshly formed connubial bed:

> into his kind embrace
> He took his wife. Beneath them both fair Tellus strewed the place
> With fresh-sprung herbs, so soft and thick that up aloft it bore
> Their heavenly bodies, with his leaves did dewy lotus store
> Th'Elysian mountain; saffron flow'rs and hyacinths helped make
> The sacred bed. And there they slept.[22]

A connection between the two scenes had already been made by Milton, who chose for his 'blissful bower' the flowers 'of the Atlantic Isles, [combined] with those that sprang up beneath Zeus and Hera to raise them from the soil of Mt Ida'.[23] Hera's deceptiveness, so pronounced in the episode from which this extract is taken, parallels that of Eve at the climax of *Paradise Lost*.

Blake's delicate and carefully delineated flowers and the ornate, fully or partially formed leaf-mats upon which Adam and Eve are reclining, are reminiscent of the conscious craftsmanship which Milton himself associates with the bank and the bower of Book IV:

> they sat recline
> On the soft downy bank damasked with flowers
> (iv, 333–4);

> it was a place
> Chosen by the sovereign planter, when he framed
> All things to man's delightful use; ...
> ... each beauteous flower,
> Iris all hues, roses, and jessamine
> Reared high their flourished heads between, and wrought
> Mosaic; underfoot the violet,
> Crocus, and hyacinth with rich inlay
> Broidered the ground, more coloured than with stone
> Of costliest emblem
> (iv, 690–2 and 697–703).

Above the bower hovers the Devil, with the Serpent entwined about his limbs and torso. The Serpent's power over Satan is indicated not only by the way in which

[22] *Homer's Iliad*, trans. George Chapman, 1887, pp. 222–3 (Book XIV).
[23] Alastair Fowler, note on iv, 697–701.

it has him imprisoned within its toils but also by the deferential expression with which Satan is regarding it as he points inquiringly down at Adam, his hand penetrating the protective shell of the bower near its topmost (and therefore weakest) spot. It is the Serpent and not Satan which is to instigate the Temptation: Satan appears dismayed, even woeful, as he learns of the plot.

Considered as a single entity, Blake's Satan and Serpent (the Serpent imprisoning Satan in its coils and Satan gazing mournfully but deferentially down at the Serpent) form a strikingly appropriate analogue to Satan's psychological state in the opening lines of Book iv—that of a tormented and self-divided being in whom despair battles with resolution, and fleeting remorse with bitter hatred; and one who is imprisoned within the compulsions of his own nature.

That Satan and the Serpent are not wholly of one mind is indicated by the divergence in their expressions—apparent mournfulness in the case of the first, implacable malevolence in the other. The difference arises from the fact that Adam, upon whose downfall the Serpent is intent, is Satan's own fundamental self: if not remorse then self-interest at least has a last pang of regret for the victim, blissfully happy yet doomed to fall.

If we discount the emblematic serpent-heads of the second illustration in the series *Paradise Lost* iv marks the first pictorial appearance of the Serpent. Milton's Serpent, too, is mentioned for the first time in Book iv:

> close the serpent sly
> Insinuating, wove with Gordian twine
> His braided train, and of his fatal guile
> Gave proof unheeded
>
> (iv, 347–50)

The false morality and jealous isolation which Blake frequently associates with his Spectres are both manifested in this picture, in which Satan is contemplating an Adam and Eve whose gestures suggest the act of love-making. The Adam of *Paradise Lost* observes to Eve that conjugal love is perhaps the human bliss which most excites Satan's envy (ix, 263–4)—something which is borne out by the Devil's own lament as he catches sight of the embracing couple:

> Sight hateful, sight tormenting! Thus these two
> Imparadised in one another's arms
> The happier Eden, shall enjoy their fill
> Of bliss on bliss, while I to hell am thrust
>
> (iv, 505–8)

One or two stars appear to be trapped in Satan's reptilian wings—a curious but arresting detail which indicates his connection with the Newtonian world of scientific materialism while at the same time stressing the illusory nature of that world:

> Then [Los] sent forth the Spectre: all his pyramids were grains
> Of sand, & his pillars dust on the fly's wing
>
> (*Jerusalem*, K 739; pl. 91, 48–9)

The rounded shell of Adam and Eve's bower suggests the 'outside bare/Of this round world' (x, 317–18) upon which Satan landed shortly before he began to spy on the human pair. To one side of it the sun is shown setting into the sea while on the other side a crescent moon and the evening star are rising. Milton indicates that it was evening at this point in *Paradise Lost*, and he also describes the sun sinking into the sea—though in a patently cosmic context and without in any way implying that the sun is contained within the immediate environment of the bower.[24] To Blake the sea ('Time's Ocean' or the 'Sea of Time and Space') is an emblem for the contingent material world and its presence in this illustration therefore serves as a portent of man's fall. He often uses a setting sun as an emblem of evil or of imminent disaster.

Besides the Huntington and Boston versions of 'Satan Spying on Adam and Eve', other illustrations of the subject are to be found in the National Gallery of Victoria, Melbourne, and in the Fogg Art Museum, Cambridge, Massachusetts. The Melbourne picture is a near replica of the Boston illustration and was one of the three late drawings bought from Blake by John Linnell. The Fogg picture, which is dated 1806, is the earliest of the four versions and is incomplete. It is similar to the other designs, although its Serpent is not entwined around Satan's body but is coiled lavishly along the ground at the bottom of the plate. Adam is shown resting the ball of his foot on one of its coils.

The Satan of the early picture is depicted within a burst of flame, which is itself surrounded by cloud. He is clutching his head and gazing down at the lovers in a paroxysm of jealousy. He is not winged. Whereas he and Adam had resembled each other in the Huntington and Boston versions, here they are quite dissimilar: Satan's face is old and careworn and his hair upstanding, whereas Adam's face is youthful and his hair is arranged in well-tended curls. The conception of Satan as Adam's Spectre and the Serpent as a projection of the Spectre's evil has not yet emerged.

The lower part of the illustration has a rococo delicacy not to be found in the other plates. Eve is presented as a fashionable lady with curls piled daintily on top

[24] Cf. *Paradise Lost* iv, 352–4 and 539–41.

of her head, ankles delicately crossed, and toes pointed. That part of her hair which is visible behind Adam's right hand is reminiscent of the leaf-formations of the other versions. Adam has no coronet, and the lovers are reclining not on a bed of flowers but on a bank of leaves. Neither the sun nor the moon is represented.

PARADISE LOST V (1): SATAN AS A TOAD AT THE EAR OF EVE (31)

The Boston series contains a second drawing for Book IV. This shows the angels Ithuriel and Zephon catching sight of Satan 'Squat like a toad, close at the ear of Eve' (IV, 800). Marcia Pointon observes that Blake, by choosing to represent this scene instead of the more popular one that immediately follows it, of Satan surprised by Ithuriel and leaping up in his own shape, 'intentionally and calculatedly lays the emphasis of *Paradise Lost* where Milton intended it, on the human pair'.[25]

The 'human pair' are represented sleeping side by side on their couch of roses. A leaf-mat is shown beneath Eve's legs and feet. The toad is squatting on another leaf just below her hand and she, 'With tresses discomposed, and glowing cheek,/ As through unquiet rest' (V, 10–11), is bending her head towards it. Her long, sensitive fingers appear to be stroking the roses of the couch and she seems entranced by her Satanic dream. Adam's right hand, which had evidently been embracing the woman before he fell asleep, now hangs limply down below him and affords her no protection.

Directly above the pair hover their guardian angels Ithuriel and Zephon, their closeness to Adam and Eve and the size of their figures lending an overcrowded quality to the picture. The slanting line of their figures suggests a compositional unease which corresponds to that of the picture's subject. It also gives the illustration a diagonal stress which, together with the pointing finger of the more distant angel, serves to rivet our attention on the tiny, though dramatically significant, figure of the toad in the lower left-hand corner.

Because the bower has been violated it is no longer represented as a protective enclosure but merely by a few palm-fronds, upright or crossed. These may suggest Christ's sacrifice, as before; but the palm, especially when its branches are touching, twined about each other, or crossed, is also a traditional emblem for chastity and concord in marriage:

> ... we may imitate the loving palms,
> Best emblem of a peaceful marriage,
> That ne'er bore fruit, divided.[26]

[25] Op. cit., pp. 148 and 151.   [26] John Webster, *The Duchess of Malfi*. I, i. 485–7.

In this context, therefore, its presence must be ironic. Beneath the crossed palm-fronds in the upper right-hand corner of the illustration are the crescent moon and evening star depicted in the previous illustration. The sun, like that in the text, has set.

Beyond the bower a couple of small grape-vines,[27] one entwined about a stake, a tiny mosaic of leaves, and a thin band of cloud are shown. As in 'Satan Spying on Adam and Eve' the band at the foot of the illustration is devoted to dainty and decorative plants. The couch is fringed with rose-leaves.

PARADISE LOST V (2): RAPHAEL DESCENDING TO PARADISE (32)

Book V is illustrated only in the Huntington series, and there by a plate remarkable for its economy and directness of statement. It shows a youthful Raphael descending from heaven in an arrow-head of cloud. The base of the arrow-head is formed from the figure of God—a pale and bodiless deity with arms, wings, and beard that extend to the margins of the plate. To either side of the descending Raphael are two contrasting figure-studies set within emblematized landscapes of Innocence and Experience that both reflect and reveal their occupants' states of mind.

Marcia Pointon has observed that 'Blake makes Raphael, descending in cloud, the arrow-head or the executor of the divine will represented by the all-embracing gesture of the Almighty ... Raphael's position—separating Satan and the human pair—symbolizes his function.'[28] The shape of the cloud also suggests the speed of his descent ('the angelic choirs/On each hand parting, to his speed gave way'—V, 251–2) and his sureness of purpose. In addition, it adumbrates the bow and arrows wielded by Christ in the next illustration.

Raphael, who is compared to 'Maia's son' as he lands on the eastern cliff of Paradise (V, 285), is here portrayed, like the Hermes of classical art, as a handsome and youthful figure. Though he is naked his hands and wingtips cover his sexual parts ('the middle pair (of wings) .../Skirted his loins and thighs'—V, 280, 282)—a hint of the modesty he later shows when he blushes in response to Adam's inquiry about how the angels make love. Blake shows him fully clothed when he appears before the human pair in the seventh illustration of the series. In *Paradise Lost* V (2) he is represented gazing back up at him who had decreed his journey.

---

[27] The supported vine is a traditional emblem for the female partner in a marriage.
[28] Op. cit., p. 147.

Although his form fills only the wide but shallow space at the top of the picture God's image broods over the whole scene. His outstretched wings and the abstraction which his figure suggests identify him as another tyrant of the fallen world, but one far less human than the sorrowing, anthropomorphic deity of *Paradise Lost* III.[29]

Simlar figures with the same outstretched arms or wings and vestigial bodies occur frequently in Blake's works. The figure in *Paradise Lost* v (2) is despite its inhumanity much less ferocious than the majority of its counterparts and thus conforms to the comparatively tranquil tone of the *Paradise Lost* series. The source of the image has been traced[30] to an engraving of Jupiter Pluvius depicted on Marcus Aurelius' column in Rome.[31] A sketch by Fuseli based on this engraving was elaborated and engraved by Blake for Erasmus Darwin's *Botanic Garden*.[32]

To the left of Raphael stands Satan, enwrapped by his Serpent-selfhood and with his legs crossed—a sign of the ungainliness and contorted nature of error. The Serpent's head is positioned directly above Satan's and so indicates its continuing mastery over him. The Devil again seems distressed as he gazes across at his future victims but the Serpent is now gloating openly. The bare, gaunt branches of the trees and the darkness behind them suggest the wretched state of Experience and hence draw attention to Satan's role as fallen man.

The human pair, 'erect and tall,/Godlike erect, with native honour clad/In naked majesty' (iv, 288–90), are strolling hand in hand through the landscape of Innocence on the right of the illustration.[33] They have turned their backs to the viewer and are gazing into each other's eyes. Though they are themselves as yet unaware of the Devil's presence their positions are a reversal of his face-forward stance.

Unlike the world of Experience, that of Innocence is not terminated by its own darkness. In the background it shows tree-trunks enwrapped by vines and backed by foliage—an ambiguous symbol suggesting the plenty of Paradise and the still-prevailing marital harmony of Adam and Eve but also the twining of the Serpent about the Tree of Knowledge, or indeed about the body of Satan: the two scenes, like the states of Innocence and Experience in the *Songs*, are not as totally opposed

---

[29] The portrait may owe something to Milton's descriptions of the Holy Spirit at *Paradise Lost* i, 20–1, and vii, 234–5. Cf. also Blake's assertion in *The Marriage of Heaven & Hell* that 'in Milton ... the Holy-ghost [is] Vacuum' (K 150; pls. 5–6).

[30] By Anthony Blunt in *The Art of William Blake*, p. 41.

[31] Depicted in Montfaucon's *Antiquité expliquée*, 1719, I, i, pl. xiii (facing p. 44).

[32] 1791, i, facing p. 127. The engraving is entitled the 'Fertilization of Egypt'.

[33] In *Paradise Lost* the joining of hands by Adam and Eve becomes a subtle indication of the state of their relationship: cf. Fowler's note to xii, 648. Blake has a rudimentary touch-symbolism of his own for he generally depicts Adam and Eve in physical contact before the Fall yet not during or after it.

as might at first have been expected. The vine-wrapped trees are also a reminder of the light work in which Adam and Eve were engaged when God caught sight of them and, pitying, determined to send Raphael down to warn them of the danger posed by Satan.

PARADISE LOST VI: THE EXPULSION OF THE REBEL ANGELS (frontispiece, 33)

For his illustration of this scene Blake rejects both the vast spaces conceived by Martin and Turner and the gigantic masses favoured by Barry, Flaxman, Fuseli, Romney, and Gustave Doré. Instead he offers a simple, almost diagrammatic representation of Christ the archer kneeling within an enormous, rose-tinted circle that is surrounded by angels, and tautening the string of his great bow in order to release the arrows of his wrath upon the falling devils—ideal Man expelling the Spectre of Albion (cf. *Jerusalem*, pl. 98). The devils, having dropped their 'idle weapons' (vi, 839), are descending 'drained,/Exhausted, spiritless, afflicted, fallen' (vi, 851–2), into hell.

Along with several others of Blake's pictures, *Paradise Lost* vi appears to have been influenced in its conception by Renaissance diagrams demonstrating the proportions of the human body. Like the figures in some of these diagrams, the Christ of *Paradise Lost* vi fills the circle within which he is represented. He is shown kneeling inside its lower arc with his arms—one bent at the elbow and the other, which holds the bow, extended downwards—forming its vertical diameter. Its shape is underlined by the great bow which frames the lower part of its circumference and stretches across almost the whole width of the picture. This bow points straight down towards the abyss and serves on the flat surface of the plate to cut Christ off from the falling devils. By omitting all reference to the cosmic chariot, the most splendid element in Milton's Expulsion-scene, Blake places particular emphasis upon the Son's 'human form divine'.

The rose-tinted circle itself serves as a reminder of the 'spacious gap' (vi, 861) in the wall of heaven through which the rebel angels fell, but it has a more substantive significance as that other Sun, the celestial sphere. Circle and Christ in conjunction form but one example of the 'figured sun' which recurs throughout Blake's poetry and paintings as an index of spiritual vision.[34] Exceptionally, the sun-god himself will, as here, step down from or reach out of his globe in order to imbue the world

[34] Cf. also the third and sixth illustrations of the *L'Allegro* series.

beneath with his strength as well as his radiance. Another such occasion is depicted in *Milton*, pl. 43, which shows Los, Blake's Zoa or divine principle of the Imagination, stepping out of his sphere in order to infuse his disciple, the poet Blake, with his vigour:

> And Los behind me stood, a terrible flaming Sun, just close
> Behind my back ...
> And I became One Man with him arising in my strength.
> 'Twas too late now to recede. Los had enter'd into my soul:
> His terrors now posses'd me whole! I arose in fury & strength.
>
> (K 505; pl. 22, 6–7 and 12–14)

Blake sometimes identifies the god within the sun as Los, and he sometimes presents Los as an avatar of Christ—an artist-redeemer who keeps the fires of the Imagination burning in the cellars of the fallen world. At the climactic conclusion to *Jerusalem* these two figures merge into one: 'Then Jesus appeared standing by Albion as the Good Shepherd .../And the Divine Appearance was the likeness & similitude of Los' (*Jerusalem*, K 743; pl. 96, 3 and 7). The conception of the Christ of *Paradise Lost* VI must also owe something to the classical sun-god Apollo—archer, prophet, and creative artist.

The apocalypse at the end of Blake's *Jerusalem* is envisaged in terms of images drawn from the sixth Book of *Paradise Lost* and therefore it is perhaps not surprising that it should offer an appropriate gloss on the illustration. In *Jerusalem* it is the redeemed man, Albion, who is the victorious warrior:

> ... Then Albion stretch'd his hand into Infinitude
> And took his Bow. ...
> And the Bow is a Male & Female, & the Quiver of the Arrows of Love
> Are the Children of this Bow, a Bow of Mercy & Loving-kindness laying
> Open the hidden Heart in Wars of mutual Benevolence, Wars of Love:
> And the Hand of Man grasps firm between the Male & Female Loves.
>
> . . .
>
> Then each an Arrow flaming from his Quiver fitted carefully;
> They drew fourfold the unreprovable String, bending thro' the wide Heavens
> The horned Bow Fourfold; loud sounding flew the flaming Arrow fourfold.
> Murmuring the Bowstring breathes with ardor. Clouds roll round the horns
> Of the wide Bow; ...
> The Druid Spectre was Annihilate, loud thund'ring, rejoicing terrific, vanishing,
> Fourfold Annihilation; & at the clangor of the Arrows of Intellect
> The innumerable Chariots of the Almighty appear'd in Heaven,
> And Bacon & Newton & Locke, & Milton & Shakspear & Chaucer,

> A Sun of blood red wrath surrounding heaven, on all sides around,
> Glorious, incompreh(en)sible by Mortal Man
>
>   (K 744–5; pl. 97, 6–7 and 12–15, and pl. 98, 1–11)

The spiritual or intellectual character of the battle fought by the 'divine warrior' is emphasized many times in Blake's poetry—for instance, in the balad-like poem 'The Grey Monk':

> But vain the Sword & vain the Bow,
> They never can work War's overthrow.
> The Hermit's Prayer & the Widow's tear
> Alone can free the World from fear.
>
> For a Tear is an Intellectual Thing,
> And a Sigh is the Sword of an Angel King,
> And the bitter groan of the Martyr's woe
> Is an Arrow from the Almightie's Bow.
>
>   (K 430, 25–32)

and on plate 38 of *Jerusalem*:

> ... Albion! Our wars are wars of life, & wounds of love
> With intellectual spears, & long winged arrows of thought.
>
>   (K 664; 14–15)

The multiple nature of Christ's bow—it is duplicated six times in the Huntington version of *Paradise Lost* VI and four times in the Boston plate—and the fact that in the Boston version it is represented without a shaft suggests that it too is metaphorical and therefore that the violence which is expelling the devils is that of the mind or spirit. Many Milton critics also incline towards a metaphorical rather than a literal interpretation of the celestial battle in Book VI of the epic.

The groups of three arrows refracted on either side of the central weapon in the Huntington plate may owe their origin to the 'three-bolted' thunder(s)' (vi, 764) of the poem; the four refracted arrows of the Boston plate to the 'fourfold-visaged four' (vi, 845) who draw the celestial chariot and whose quaternity—or that of the four living creatures of Ezekiel, from whom they were derived—is found also in Blake's own vision.

The figures of six of the 'ten thousand thousand saints' (vi, 767)—i.e. angels—who attended upon Christ, are depicted on either side of the rose-tinted circle. 'Eye witnesses of his almighty acts' (vi, 883), they convey through their facial expressions and raised hands their genteel indignation at the rebellion of Satan's divisions. To Blake the six figures, together with Christ himself, represent the seven Eyes of God which in his own 'system' were successively appointed to descend into the world in order to atone for man. All of them except the seventh, who was Christ, selfishly refused:

> Then they [the Family Divine] Elected Seven, called the Seven
> Eyes of God & the Seven Lamps of the Almighty.
> The Seven are one within the other; the Seventh is named Jesus,
> The Lamb of God, blessed for ever, & he follow'd the Man
>
> (*Vala*, K 279; 553–6)

This refusal is suggested in *Paradise Lost* vi by the inactivity of the six angels—something which accords conveniently with Milton's representation of Christ as 'Sole victor' (vi, 880) in the celestial battle. Several of Blake's other Bible-related pictures employ a similar arrangement—that of a central deity surrounded by six attendant spirits.

The grace, radiance, and harmony of the celestial group—evident despite the angels' refusal—is counterbalanced by the falling devils' darkened and contorted figures. Nudity here serves not to indicate beatitude but to reveal degradation. The celestial forms above show how much the devils have 'changed in outward lustre' (i, 97). Their figures are inverted and contained within flames—a reminder of Milton's 'headlong flaming' (i, 45) epithet. The picture may be interpreted Neoplatonically, as a representation of the one ideate essence residing within the perfect sphere or circle and confronting the disordered multiplicity of its parts, alternatively to be regarded as the wanton individualism of the fallen mind.

Some of the devils are clutching their heads, the seat of the perverted rational intellect; others have their hands over their eyes, ears, or mouths so as to indicate the lack of sensory experience which pertains in the fallen state. The genitals of the centre figure are covered in scales, and the familiar face of Blake's bearded tyrant is just visible in the lower left-hand corner of the Huntington illustration. In the same version one of the devils is wearing both a crown and what appears to be a monk's cowl—a reference to the Satanic alliance of Church and State.

The Boston devils have the mask-like features and knotted foreheads that they revealed in the first illustration of the series, but on the whole they appear far more grotesque here than in *Paradise Lost* i—even though the earlier plate is a chronologically later representation of them. This apparent discrepancy may perhaps be explained by Blake's belief that appearances are dictated by the eye of the perceiver: here the demonic 'opposition' is being viewed by the 'Eye' or figure that above all others is opposed to it. In *The Marriage of Heaven and Hell* Blake treats ironically of the same phenomenon: 'It indeed appear'd to Reason as if Desire was cast out;

but the Devil's account is, that the Messiah fell, & formed a heaven of what he stole from the Abyss' (K 150; pls. 5–6).

Though the necessity for representing the final annihilation of man's 'Druid Spectre' (*Jerusalem*, K 745; pl. 98, 6) in the middle of the illustrative series was dictated by the narrative scheme of *Paradise Lost*, it was by no means alien to the structure of Blake's own longer poems, with their disregard of chronological sequence and their emphasis upon the irruption of extra-temporal redemptive agencies into the arena of the descended world.

PARADISE LOST VII: RAPHAEL WARNING ADAM (34, 35)

Adam and Eve are here shown entertaining Raphael within their 'silvan lodge ... that like Pomona's arbour smiled/With flowerets decked and fragrant smells' (v, 377–9). The illustrative lodge, more elaborate than the 'natural' abode of the poem, offers chairs and tables in the Gothic style and a palm-framed window with an extensive view of Paradise. Its floor is covered with a mosaic of grasses and tiny, flowering plants. The landscape outside is crowned by an enormous Tree of Knowledge laden with fruits and with the Serpent coiled about its trunk in a prefiguring of the position which it adopts in most illustrations of the Fall (though not in Blake's). The trunk of the Tree is covered in thorns.

A stern Raphael is seated to one side of the window-frame. He is pointing with one hand to the Serpent and with the other to the wall of the lodge, thus indicating the threat that the Serpent poses to man's present happiness and security. As God had earlier warned Adam,

> The day thou eat'st thereof, my sole command
> Transgressed, inevitably thou shalt die;
> From that day mortal, and this happy state
> Shalt loose, expelled from hence into a world
> Of woe and sorrow.
>
> (viii, 329–33)

By his gesturing Raphael is also hinting at the travail that the Fall will engender for Christ. Adam, seated opposite, appears in the Huntington version only mildly startled by the warning, but in the Boston plate perturbed and perhaps indignant. Eve, who does not appear to have heard it, is in the Boston plate seated submissively beside her mate; in the Boston version she is standing between Adam and the angel and beneath the Tree of Knowledge, a position which emphasizes the centrality of her role in the Fall and the way in which she is to turn Adam away from God's will—represented here by the divine messenger, Raphael.

The rounded window-frame of the lodge rises on either side of the figures to form an archway far above their heads. It dictates the basic design of the illustration and provides much of its symbolism. Like the nuptial bower of the fourth illustration of the series, it is formed from curved palm-fronds and decorated with flowers—lilies and roses in the Huntington version, lilies only in the Boston. Bunches of luscious-looking grapes also hang from the Boston frame. Despite their similarities the bower of *Paradise Lost* IV and the lodge of this illustration are functionally opposed, for the shell of the bower attempts to isolate man from evil, the window-frame of the lodge to draw it to his attention.

The palm, as has already been mentioned, is a traditional emblem both for Christ's sacrifice and for his triumph. To Blake the 'gadding vine' is another emblem of Christ the Saviour: 'All Things are comprehended in their Eternal Forms in the divine body of the Saviour, the True Vine of Eternity' (*A Vision of the Last Judgement*, K 605–6), but here the enormous 'grapes that burst in summer's vast Excess' (*Vala*, K 325; 190) suggest as well the ecstasies of carnal love—another traditional signification of the grape and something that was also mentioned by Milton's Raphael in the warning that he gave to Adam.

The lilies that fringe the upper section of the window-frame serve both as an emblem of paradisal purity and as an attribute of the incarnate Christ. They are used in both these senses by the German mystic Behmen, with whose writings Blake was familiar:

the Noble Lily Twig or Branch *grows* in *Patience and Meekness*, and *takes* its essence, power and smell out of the soil of God, as also out of Christ's Incarnation; for Christ's Spirit is its Essence; God's Substance is its Body. Not out of any *strange* or heterogeneous property, but out of its own included and shut-up in Death, and in Christ's sprouting Essence grows the virgin-like *Lily* Twig or *Branch*: It seeks not *nor desires* the fairness or excellence of this world, but of the Angelical world. For it also grows, not in this world in the Third Principle, but in the Second Principle in the *Paradisical* World.[35]

Lilies are depicted in the lower left-hand corners of both plates, and roses in the lower right—an arrangement used in several of the Milton designs and one which suggests a contrast between absolute purity and fragile beauty. The heads of the lilies, and of the roses in the Huntington version, are drooping, though with a certain studied elegance. This, and the visible roots of the palm plant in the Boston picture, may be intended to sound a note of warning to the viewer.

[35] Jacob Behmen, 'The Treatise of the Incarnation'; in *The Works of Jacob Behmen*, 1764–81, ii, 80.

The lilies of the window-frame in the Huntington version resemble the stylized fleurs-de-lis on plate 6 of Blake's designs for Thomas Gray's *Ode for Music*, which are identified in the text: 'Great Edward, with the lilies on his brow/From haughty Gallia torn...' (IV, 5–6). The more ornate lilies of the Boston version are reminiscent of the lily of Calvary and of the white lily. A picture of the latter was contained in *The Temple of Flora* (1799), a lavishly illustrated book of flowers compiled by Dr. Robert Thornton, one of Blake's patrons.

A bowl of 'savoury fruits' (v, 304) is shown in both versions. In the Huntington plate it rests on the ledge between Raphael and the human pair, in the Boston between Adam and Eve. In this version another vessel containing only a single fruit is placed between Eve and Raphael. A jagged line appears above its curving rim, and most though not all of the area between this line and the rim has been coloured orange so as to suggest flame. It seems likely, however, that it was originally intended to represent a leaf-mat and that the orange colour was applied in error.

Eve is holding a bunch of grapes in her right hand and a gourd in her left, while several fruits, one apparently half-eaten, are lying on the ledge beside her. The gourd has a long, twisting stem that echoes the twining of the Serpent about the Tree of Knowledge and the tendrils around the window-frame of the lodge, as well as the kinks in Eve's own flourishing locks. It suggests female sexuality but is also reminiscent of the 'vessels of seed' with their 'bends of self interest & selfish natural virtue' (*Jerusalem*, K 723; pl. 80, 74–5) that were woven by Gwendolen, one of Blake's Daughters of Albion or guardians of the body.

The Raphael of *Paradise Lost* VII is a magnificent creation. Two of his wings are raised above his head to form a soaring, flame-like peak while two more wings sweep down to his feet and others—tiny ones this time, like tongues of fire—are dusted about on his long white robe:

> six wings he wore, to shade
> His lineaments divine; the pair that clad
> Each shoulder broad, came mantling o'er his breast
> With regal ornament; the middle pair
> Girt like a starry zone his waist, and round
> Skirted his loins and thighs with downy gold
> And colours dipped in heaven; the third his feet
> Shadowed from either heel with feathered mail
> Sky-tinctured grain.
>
> (v, 277–85)

His magnificence singles him out as an agent of the Divine Vision and recalls Los's description of the resurrected Jerusalem:

I see the River of Life & Tree of Life,
I see the New Jerusalem descending out of Heaven,
Between thy Wings of gold & silver, feather'd, immortal,
Clear as the rainbow, as the cloud of the Sun's tabernacle.

Thy Reins, cover'd with Wings translucent, sometimes covering
And sometimes spread abroad, reveal the flames of holiness
Which like a robe covers & like a Veil of Seraphim
In flaming fire unceasing burns from Eternity to Eternity.
(*Jerusalem*, K 731; pl. 86, 18–25)[36]

The shape formed by his upraised wings[37] and the delicate plate-tracery that supports the table and chairs are in the Gothic style, which for Blake was always associated with the spiritual life: 'Grecian is Mathematic Form: Gothic is Living Form, Mathematic Form is Eternal in the Reasoning Memory: Living Form is Eternal Existence' (*On Homer's Poetry and On Virgil*, K 778). He often indicates the spirituality of the child of Innocence or of the man of Imagination by the Gothic of natural growth—the tracery of *Paradise Lost* VII or the Arbour in plate 17 of *Pilgrim's Progress* for instance—and suggests the spirituality that is the apanage of the Eternals by the joined and raised wingtips of celestial beings, as in *Nativity Ode* II and VI or plate 28 of the *Pilgrim's Progress* series, as well as in *Paradise Lost* VII.

Raphael is unquestionably the most splendid figure in the *Paradise Lost* series. We may ask why the insignia of the Divine Vision have been heaped so lavishly upon him. Is it perhaps because he is the only heavenly being who is concerned not with judging but with assisting mankind, or because he is an adherent (though a tentative one) of two theories that Blake appears elsewhere to support—the doctrine of descent from unity[38] and the notion that the earth is but the shadow of eternity?[39]

Besides serving as the frame for an enormous window that looks out over the landscape of Paradise, the floral arch of *Paradise Lost* VII is an image for the expansive vision of unfallen man—a vision that is soon to be narrowed by the experience of the Fall. Windows blocked or screened are a common Blakean image for the dulled perceptions of fallen man.

[36] The association both of the Jerusalem of this quotation and the Raphael of *Paradise Lost* VII with fire, is supported by Raphael's nature as a seraph (v, 277). 'Seraph' is derived from the Hebrew verb meaning 'to burn': cf. v, 875, in which Milton refers to Abdiel as 'The flaming seraph fearless'.

[37] Curiously, the space enclosed by these wings is in the Boston version coloured an opaque blue and so reveals nothing of the paradisal landscape behind.

[38] Cf. *Paradise Lost* v, 469–500: 'O Adam, one almighty is, from whom/All things proceed, and up to him return', etc.

[39] Cf. *Paradise Lost* v, 574–6: 'what if earth/Be but the shadow of heaven, and things therein/Each to other like, more than on earth is thought?'

Far from looking out on the traditional paradisal landscape, however, the window gives onto a scene which is itself an elaborate ironic emblem for the fallen world. Several of its topographical features—mountains, the expanse and fall of water,[40] and the creeper-entwined trees—suggest that the Fall has already taken place, and the bed of flowers from the bower of love, which reappears in the Boston version, is now placed *outside* Adam and Eve's dwelling-place—in order presumably to suggest the debasement of love into lust and self-interest. Almost all of the animals depicted in the paradisal landscape are used by Blake himself at some point in his writings as emblems for meekness and rage, reason and energy, creativity and destructiveness—the complementary qualities of the mind which become dissociated only at the time of the Fall.

While the view afforded by the window suggests the true character of Experience, the decorativeness of the window-frame indicates the deceptively attractive appearance of that life to the as yet unfallen soul:

> For many a window ornamented with sweet ornaments
> Look'd out into the World of Tharmas, where In ceaseless torrents
> His billows roll, where monsters wander in the foamy paths.
>
> (*Vala*, K 286; 255–7)

Interestingly, George Mills Harper links these lines with the Raphael of *Paradise Lost* though apparently without having the illustration in mind:

The deliberate contrast of the terrible ocean with the ornamented window is Blake's symbolic device for reminding us that although the appeal of the life of the senses is very great we must not be deluded about the nature of the world 'where monsters wander in the foamy paths.'... Like Milton's Raphael he is warning us not to be deceived by a 'fair outside.'[41]

PARADISE LOST VIII and separate plate: THE CREATION OF EVE (36–8)

Considered in itself the Creation of Woman was to Blake an overwhelming tragedy, a crucial stage in the catastrophe of the Fall:

> At length in tears & cries imbodied,
> A female form, trembling and pale,
> Waves before his deathy face.

[40] The fall of water is clearly represented in the Huntington version but its equivalent in the Boston version has been coloured in brown so that it resembles a gate rather than a waterfall.

[41] *The Neoplatonism of William Blake*, 1961, pp. 166–7.

> All Eternity shudder'd at sight
> Of the first female now separate,
> Pale as a cloud of snow
> Waving before the face of Los.
>   (*The Book of Urizen*, K 231; pl. 18, 6–12)

For his own *Illustrated Genesis* he summarizes the contents of Genesis 3 as, 'the Sexual Nature & its Fall into Generation and Death' (K 942). He therefore tends when contemplating the event in isolation to emphasize its darker side. His 'Creation of Eve' which figures on plate 35 of *Jerusalem*, for instance, shows a coarse-featured woman emerging from man's abdomen and man wide-eyed with terror, turning towards the earth. The two figures, and the Christ who is shown floating above them, are bathed in flames. The rendering is remarkable for its uncompromising natural-ism and for its atmosphere of potential violence.

On the other hand the Creation of Woman was also for Blake an essential part of the Creation–Redemption or Generation–Regeneration cycle, and an example of Christ's saving grace:

> But when Man sleeps in Beulah, the Saviour in Mercy takes
> Contraction's Limit, and of the Limit he forms Woman, That
> Himself may in process of time be born Man to redeem.
>   (*Jerusalem*, K 670; pl. 42, 32–4)

In *Paradise Lost* VIII the artist conveys the ambivalence of his attitude towards the Fall by presenting a scene which contains portents of adverse significance but which is of an exquisite surface beauty.[42] He catches Eve in the first moments of her separate existence, hovering just above the rib-cage of Adam and beneath the controlling and life-giving hand of Christ. Her eyes are raised heavenwards and her hands coming together in a tentative gesture of prayer. She is as 'Pale as a cloud of snow' (*The Book of Urizen*, K 231; pl. 18, 11) and as delicate and graceful as Botticelli's Venus Anadyomene.

Above the trees in the background stretches an immense, light-filled sky that deepens into an opaque, blackish blue at the top of the plate. A moon—appropriately new—glows in the sky above Eve's head and suffuses the scene with a soft and radiant light, which glows the more intensely about the head and body of Christ. The artistic relationship between the two upright figures and the supine Adam is balanced but not rigidly symmetrical. The spaces which surround the group, with their connota-tions of tranquillity and primordial emptiness, have become a part of the beauty

---

[42] Milton's version of the Creation combines spirituality with a physicality not suggested at all in Blake's *Paradise Lost* illustration: see viii, 465–73.

and the artistic design of the picture. The balanced arrangement of figures, the delicate colouring, the representation of arrested motion, and the absence of physical contact between any of the figures, also evoke a mood of harmony and innocence, and suggest a spiritual interpretation of the birth.

Both the atmosphere and the subject of the painting liken it to Blake's Beulah, the lower, lunar heaven that stands between the solar intensities of Eden and the formless darkness of Ulro:

> There is from Great Eternity a mild & pleasant rest
> Nam'd Beulah, a soft Moony Universe, feminine, lovely,
> Pure, mild & Gentle, given in Mercy to those who sleep,
> Eternally created by the Lamb of God around,
> On all sides, within & without the Universal Man.
>
> (*Vala*, K 266; 94–8)

In *Paradise Lost* VIII Christ is represented in profile and as a small-headed, pot-bellied, Grecian–Gothic figure. He is standing on a low platform or plateau at Eve's left hand and is clad in a fine white robe through which the contours of his body are clearly visible. As befits one who is initiating a significant stage in the descent of man, he reveals only his left foot.

Beneath Eve and Christ lies an entranced Adam, his eyes closed but his head inclining attentively towards his companions.[43] His hands too suggest mental alertness. His body is placed along the lower edge of the picture and appears to be resting on the side of a slope—an attitude that enables a frontal portrait to be made of him despite the fact that he is lying on his back, and which because it sets him slightly apart from his context appears to acknowledge the fact that in *Paradise Lost* it was he who reported the episode of Eve's creation. Adam's attitude also suggests the precariousness of his present position, the ease with which he might fall from the heaven of Eden into the abyss of Ulro, Blake's region of darkness and despair.

A huge and highly ornate leaf is shown beneath Adam's body, and part of a similar growth covers the 'plateau' on which Christ is standing. Adam's serves him as a mandorla, its topmost 'fronds' framing his head like a sunburst halo and its lower portion fitted neatly to the contours of his body; Christ's forms a luxurious carpet.

Throughout the series this leaf provides a foundation for those figures who are at the time of depiction most closely involved in the formation of the mortal or 'Vegetable' world. It first made its appearance in the illustrations to Book IV—beneath Eve's legs and buttocks in 'Satan Spying' and beneath her legs and the figure

---

[43] Cf. *Paradise Lost* viii, 460–1: 'Mine eyes he closed, but open left the cell/Of fancy my internal sight'.

of the toad in 'Satan as a Toad'. There it was partially formed; here and in the 'Judgement' illustration, where it reappears, it is displayed in full splendour. It is also suggested, though as a travesty of its former magnificence, in the barren space which frames the sleeping Eve of the 'Crucifixion' illustration.

The leaf itself indicates the presence or imminent formation of the 'Vegetable world', in particular its seductive but deceiving beauty. The repeated manifestations of the leaf, its development throughout the pictorial narrative, and its lack of justification in the text, are all measures of its significance to Blake.

Low in the background of *Paradise Lost* VIII stands a row of squat, closely-planted trees—the 'Infernal Grove' that Blake associates with 'Female Love' and with the material world in general:

> Till I turn from Female Love,
> And root up the Infernal Grove,
> I shall never worthy be
> To Step into Eternity.
> *(Poems from the Note-book 1800–3;* K 417)

The trees appear to be oaks, and the oak is closely associated by Blake with the degraded material world. Their straight trunks and ordered foliage are characteristic of this type of tree when closely planted, and the tiny leaves that form a mosaic between the trunks in the Boston version are very similar to those of the English oak. (The shapes of the leaves actually on the trees are not clearly delineated in either version.) In the Huntington plate these trees are shadowy and indistinct; in the Boston they are clearly visible but a sense of mystery has been retained, for the spaces between their trunks have been blocked out by the leaf-mosaic. An almost identical row of trees appears in the background to *Paradise Lost* x, and groves are represented in 'Raphael Warning Adam' and in 'The Fall'.

A near replica of the Boston version of 'The Creation' was bought from Blake by John Linnell. It is now in the National Gallery of Victoria in Melbourne, Australia.

PARADISE LOST IX: THE FALL OF EVE (39, 40)

The typical illustration of the Fall displays the Tree of Knowledge at centre, the Serpent wound about its trunk, and Adam and Eve to either side. Eve is generally eating the fruit or accepting it from the Serpent, and Adam either accepting the fruit from Eve or plucking his own. While still drawing on this arrangement Blake

modifies it considerably by altering the positions of the man and the woman so that
Eve is portrayed frontally and Adam with his back to the viewer, and Eve in
front of the Tree with Adam behind it and to one side, and by having the Serpent
wound not about the Tree but about the body of Eve. Eve is tasting the fruit, which
is held between the jaws of the Serpent.

These modifications serve to disturb the symmetry of the traditional arrangement
and thus to renew the drama of the moment so starkly rendered by Milton: 'So
saying, her rash hand in evil hour/Forth reaching to the fruit, she plucked, she ate'
(ix, 780–1). They also accord with Blake's interpretation of the Fall as the appropria-
tion of individuality by the separated male and female entities:

> Los said: 'When the Individual appropriates Universality
> 'He divides into Male & Female, & when the Male & Female
> 'Appropriate Individuality they become an Eternal Death.
> (*Jerusalem*, K 737; pl. 90, 52–4)

and as the violation of man's Emanation by his unnatural and mateless Serpent-
Spectre. Blake's conception suggests as well Milton's portrayal in the text of an Eve
completely self-absorbed as she plucks the fruit.

The ravishing of Enion by the Spectre of her principal, Tharmas, is described
in terms that may remind us of the Eve-and-Serpent group of *Paradise Lost* ix:

> Mingling his brightness with her tender limbs, then high she soar'd
> Above the ocean; a bright wonder, Nature,
> Half Woman & half Spectre; all his lovely changing colours mix
> With her fair crystal clearness; in her lips & cheeks his poisons rose
> In blushes like the morning ...
> (*Vala*, K 269; 182–6)

Even the colouring in this passage accords with that of the illustration, which shows
the Serpent with 'turret crest' of red and 'sleek enamelled neck' (ix, 525) of red,
blue, and yellow, and the cheeks of the figures with heightened colour.

Blake's portrayal is faithful to other, more significant elements in Milton's Book
ix episode—in particular, its association of carnality with the Fall. The coiled embrace of Blake's Serpent, Eve's caressing of its 'chin' and body as she bends forward
to receive the fruit from its jaws, and the actual oral transference of the fruit—the
mouth in *Paradise Lost*, whether eating or speaking, is frequently a channel for sin—
all emphasize this carnality, though true to its puritanical nature the Serpent hides
Eve's private parts—which had been innocently revealed up to now—even as it
ravishes her. As John Broadbent observes,

Most paintings of the temptation [also] emphasize its erotic qualities. Raphael's snake bears

Eve's head . . . and the tree it twists round is phallic. In Michelangelo's painting, Eve's head as she takes the apple lies between Adam's thighs; Titian's Adam touches Eve's breast at the same moment; Tintoretto's Eve, as she offers the apple to Adam, gazes on his genitals.[44]

Blake's representation of an Adam present within the illustrative frame but with his back turned against the drama of Eve's fall, and with transfixed gaze, upheld hands, and tautly curved body, admirably conveys the plight of Milton's Adam, who although absent from the scene at the time had a premonition of disaster: 'Yet oft his heart, divine of something ill,/Misgave him; he the faltering measure felt' (ix, 845–6).

In *Paradise Lost* ix he is shown trailing tiny strands of greenery from his hands— the remnants of the garland which he had woven while awaiting Eve's return but which he numbly lets fall on hearing of her 'fatal trespass' (ix, 889). The representation is probably indebted to the tradition of portraying classical Floras and Graces holding flowers or scraps of greenery.

So *Paradise Lost* ix records both the moment of Eve's fall and that in which the news of it was communicated to Adam. In the forks of lightning that rend the sky it also portends the fall of Adam himself, though without resorting to the stereotyped and textually inaccurate 'double' Fall scene rendered by many Milton illustrators:

> Earth trembled from her entrails, as again
> In pangs, and nature gave a second groan,
> Sky loured and muttering thunder, some sad drops
> Wept at completing of the mortal sin
> Original
>
> > (ix, 1000–4)

The branches of Blake's Tree of Knowledge are, like Milton's, 'Loaden with fruit of fairest colours mixed,/Ruddy and gold' (ix, 577–8), and, its roots form a prominent, fan-shaped arrangement in the lower foreground. Their unnatural presence above ground emphasizes that the fallen condition is at hand.

In the Boston version the trunk and roots of the Tree of Knowledge are covered in huge thorns. These suggest the menace of the Tree, recall Milton's description of paradisal 'Flowers of all hue, and without thorn the rose' (iv, 256), and anticipate the terms of the Judgement: 'Cursed is the ground for thy sake . . ./Thorns also and thistles it shall bring thee forth' (x, 201 and 203). They are displayed on a thin cluster of stems which covers the surface of the Tree's trunk and leads at its lower extremity directly into the roots.

[44] *Paradise Lost: Introduction*, Cambridge, 1972, p. 22.

The thickly foliated trees in the background to the picture suggest those of the Creation illustration but they are also justified by the text of *Paradise Lost* IX: Satan 'after Eve seduced, unminded slunk/Into the wood fast by' (x, 332–3). Mountains are shown behind them.

The luxuriant and pacific natural world of the Book IV illustrations has been reduced to the broken garland and (in the Boston version) a tiny cluster of pinkish roses beside Adam's left foot, all that remains of the couch of marital bliss; a mound covered with a mosaic of leaves; and grasses scattered between the Tree's roots. The ground about the Tree in the Huntington version is coloured green but is bereft of natural detail.

The world of *Paradise Lost* IX is a tense and sombre one, depicted in dark and threatening tones and with a preponderance of harsh, jagged lines. Expressionist forms heighten the drama of the scene and are particularly pronounced in the Boston version with its spikey tree-stems and roots, and enormous thunderbolts. The land-scape contrasts sharply with the delicate beauty of that in the previous illustration and with the restrained grief portrayed in the next, and is itself a foretaste of Experience.

THE TEMPTATION OF EVE (41)

Blake's tempera painting of the Temptation of Eve, which was completed about 1796 and which is now in the Victoria and Albert Museum, differs sharply in design, colouring, and mood from the Huntington and Boston 'Falls'. Blake has abrogated any suggestion of the traditional, quasi-symmetrical arrangement by placing the Tree to the far left-hand side of the picture; his colouring is rich and luminous; and the mood of the picture is not one of abandoned lust but of enchantment and sacramental evil.

Eve and the Serpent occupy the centre of the plate. The woman is again frontally portrayed. She is standing poised, with her right arm raised in a kind of salute but also presumably in order to accept the fruit, and her left arm pushed out behind her. The porcelain-doll rigidity of her joints contrasts strikingly with the sinuosity of the Serpent's coils and suggests an absence of conscious volition. She is gazing fixedly before her as though in a trance.

The Serpent is a magnificent beast—huge, brilliantly coloured, and towering aloft—an image of sinister beauty derived directly from the text of *Paradise Lost*:

> on his rear,
> Circular base of rising folds, that towered
> Fold above fold a surging maze, his head
> Crested aloft, and carbuncle his eyes;
> With burnished neck of verdant gold, erect
> Amidst his circling spires, that on the grass
> Floated redundant: pleasing was his shape,
> And lovely, nor since of serpent kind
> Lovelier
>
> (ix, 497–505).

Its coils spiral downwards beside Eve's body and spin a magic circle about her feet. They are then wound in a grimly decorative manner about the head of Adam, who is lying behind and to the left of his mate. The Serpent's crested head is placed directly above Eve's, thus indicating its power over her. It is holding the fatal fruit between its jaws.

The rich, almost iridescent tones of the painting give it an atmosphere of diabolical enchantment. The sky (a night sky, although in *Paradise Lost* the Fall took place in daytime) is a lustrous peacock blue; Eve's tresses and the Serpent's body are tinged with gold, a gold that intensifies where Eve's body meets the Serpent's; and flecks of turquoise and silvery white are scattered throughout the scene. These flecks are particularly concentrated on the body of Adam (and, to a lesser extent, on that of Eve), giving it a deathly glow. The 'deadly fading Moon' (*Milton*, K 491; pl. 10, 18) in the upper right-hand corner of the plate adds a final touch of eeriness to the landscape.

A spade shown lying on the ground beside Adam suggests that *Paradise Lost* rather than Genesis is the subject of the illustration, for in the poem Adam was absent and tending to his garden when the Serpent tempted Eve. The spade also suggests the toil with which God punished Adam for his part in the Fall. The state of sleep is to Blake a metaphor for earthly existence, and his primordial man Albion is, like the Adam of this illustration, overcome by sleep at the time of the Fall: 'Satan first the victory won,/Where Albion slept beneath the Fatal Tree' (*Jerusalem*, K 650; pl. 27, 28–9).

The massive, double-stemmed trunk of the Tree reflects the 'duality of the tree of the knowledge of good and evil'.[45] Its coils also suggest those of the Serpent, and its overhanging bough is reminiscent of the rounded-arch motif which often controls the upper limit of a Blake design, and which almost invariably indicates the rule

---

[45] Kathleen Raine, *Blake and Tradition*, 1969, i, 135. (Miss Raine is speaking of a similar tree, depicted on plate 3 of 'The Little Girl Found'.)

of the tyrant of this world. Other evidence of his rule resides in the background presence of rivers, two falls of water, and the pallid moon.

PARADISE LOST X: THE JUDGEMENT OF ADAM AND EVE
(42, 43)

A frontally portrayed Christ commands the centre of the 'Judgement' picture. He is clad in a full-length white robe and invested with a large disc-halo. To either side of him stand Adam and Eve—Gothic–Grecian figures with small heads and long, slightly distended bellies. They are now wearing fig-leaves. Adam's hands are held in the position of prayer and in the Huntington version his head is bowed. Eve, whose head is also bowed, covers her face with her hands. As befits those who are about to descend into the fallen world, they are both standing with their left or 'material' feet in advance of their right or 'spiritual' ones.

Above this simple frontal-profile arrangement of figures, and separated from it by a cloud-belt, are Sin and Death. Sin is placed above Eve, Death above Adam: the she-devil has influence over the woman, the male devil over the man. At the centre of the plate their bodies meet or even merge: 'For Death from Sin no power can separate' (x, 251). They are engaged in unleashing their weapons—darts in the case of Death, vials of disease in the case of Sin[46]—down the margin of the page and into the world beneath. Sin's dogs, sensing the turn of events, are gloating in jubilation.

Blake's Christ, like Milton's, is 'mild judge and intercessor both' (x, 96), for while delivering his judgement upon mankind he also acts as the supporting pillar for an Adam and Eve beset on all sides by the figures and symbols of evil. His arms—disproportionately large in the Houghton version—are raised and his palms turned upwards.

The Serpent, which has already received its punishment ('Upon thy belly grovelling thou shalt go'—x, 177), glides sinuously along the ground behind the three figures. Its expression betrays the exultation of evil accomplished. It appears unaware that the raised heel of Adam's right foot is poised beside its head—a reference to its eventual overthrow by Christ and incidentally an indication of the intimacy of the relationship between Adam and Christ, progenitor and seed, type and antitype. Christ's prophecy of the Serpent's doom is contained in his judgement of it:

[46] The detail may derive from the tradition of endowing the fickle goddess of fortune with a pair of urns; see Howard R. Patch, *The Goddess Fortuna in Mediaeval Literature*, 1967, pp. 52–3.

> Between thee and the woman I will put
> Enmity, and between thine and her seed;
> Her seed shall bruise thy head, thou bruise his heel.
>
> (x, 179–81)

·The wood of the fallen world forms the background to the illustration, as it did in *Paradise Lost* VIII, and all three figures are standing on a replica of the decorative leaves that were figured there. The repetition of these details indicates a close association between the two subjects.

The mood of this monumental illustration is one of dignity and solemnity. Order and self-restraint have for the moment triumphed over emotionalism and violence. Any suggestion of the strife between Adam and Eve that Milton records in Book x has been omitted, and neither is the rapacious malevolence of Sin and Death evoked. The stillness of the scene is disturbed only by the subdued weeping of Eve, and Sin and Death are calm and graceful—in the Huntington version, even attractive. Their roles are suggested only by their weapons, their true character only by the elation of the hell-hounds. In the Houghton version (the larger) the hounds are fancifully depicted, with spiked hackles and the gnarled countenance of the Spectre.

With the Fall Death becomes able to realize his powers. Accordingly he is here depicted not as a pellucid outline (as in *Paradise Lost* II) but as a solid figure.[47] The Infernal causeway 'Over the foaming deep high arched' (x, 301), which Sin and Death were constructing while the Judgement was being delivered, is suggested in the archway which their bodies form above the Judgement scene—another example of Blake's genius for employing symbolic posture and for relating separate but thematically or chronologically associated scenes.

THE HOUSE OF DEATH (44–6)

Three impressions of the colour-print 'The House of Death'[48] are known. Their basic design is of course identical but as each was finished separately with water-colour and ink Blake was able to render slight but intriguing differences in detail between them. All were executed around 1795. They show the fate of the intemperate as it was revealed to Adam through Michael in Book XI of *Paradise Lost*.

The ghastly image of Death, a desembodied tyrant with outstretched arms, blank eyes, and an enormous, fan-shaped beard,[49] presides over the scene. A thick, miasmic

---

[47] Similarly, Adam's prelapsarian inability to conceive of death may be contrasted with his long and anguished discourse on the subject at x, 769–824.

[48] Also known as 'The Lazar House'.

[49] It is reminiscent of that of Urizen, as described in *America*, K 204; (cancelled) pl. b, 16: 'His snowy beard ... streams like lambent flames down his wide breast'.

bow of cloud frames his image and a winding-sheet or scroll that terminates in a phallus-like shape or in arrested darts that he 'delayed to strike, though oft invoked/ With vows' (xi, 492–3), is spread out just beneath his arms. The allegorical figure of Despair—'busiest from couch to couch' in *Paradise Lost* (xi, 490)—is standing at far right, a brooding and listless figure portrayed in profile and with bald, bowed head and bestial features. Like the Despair of Spenser's *Faerie Queene* (i, ix, verse 51) he is wielding the dagger of self-slaughter. A near replica of the figure is shown in similar position and context in *Jerusalem*, plate 51.

The 'many shapes/Of death' (xi, 467–8), the tyrant's victims, are shown in agonized postures on the ground beneath him. Three of them are lying prostrate on a woven pallet—the 'Sick Couch [that] bears the dark shades of Eternal Death' (*Milton*, K 493; pl. 13, 1). The nearest has turned his face towards the ground in an apparent effort to escape from pain; the next—the most fortunate perhaps— seems to have died already, for he appears to have been overcome by rigor mortis; the third, the most degraded of the victims, has drawn his knees up to his chest and is groaning or gritting his teeth in agony.

All three figures differ slightly in colouring, and each has adopted a different position and is facing in a different direction. John E. Grant suggests that they may represent the Strong Man, the Beautiful Man, and the Ugly Man[50]—Blake's types of the 'three general classes of men' (*A Descriptive Catalogue 1809*, K 577). If correct this would indicate that Blake's intention, like Milton's, was to stress the universality of Death's dominion in the post-lapsarian world.

Another victim is kneeling with his head touching the ground and his hands placed on either side of it so that only the top of his head, part of his back, and the sides of his hands are visible. A fifth, a gruesome life-in-death figure with bald head and gaping mouth, has raised himself onto his elbows and is staring up in horror or in fruitless supplication at the presiding deity.

The picture is Blake's vision not so much of death as of life in the fallen world— a life of pain, degradation, inertia, and sensory deprivation whose summation or truest image is its logical opposite, death. The naked bodies of the figures here reveal not the lineaments of the 'human form divine' but the distorted outlines of the Spectre:

> Their maker's image ...
> Forsook them, when themselves they vilified
> To serve ungoverned appetite
>
> (xi, 515–17)

[50] 'You Can't Write About Blake's Pictures Like That', *Blake Studies*, i, ii (Spring 1969), 196.

Even Death is deathly, a figure whose triumph is as hollow as it is absolute, although his rule shows as yet no sign of ending.

The starkness of the illustration contrasts dramatically with the lyrical and generally optimistic mood of the Milton sets. It was probably composed under the influence of Fuseli, whose sketch for no. 24 of the Milton Gallery, 'Die Vision des Elendsspitals' (1793), is still extant. It shows a Jupiter-Pluvius figure of Death, naked and massive, presiding over a group of anguished victims. These include a figure on the far right with bent head and depicted in profile, who is reminiscent of Blake's Despair.

An earlier Blake illustration of 'The House of Death', finished in pen and wash and now owned by the Tate Gallery, London, is even more strongly marked by the influence of Fuseli. Here Despair is an agile, waistcoated youth with a short, dark beard. He is lunging forward and gesturing agitatedly towards Death, and has turned his suicidal dagger towards himself. He is still shown in profile but is now on the left-hand side of the plate. Death bears no relationship to his counterpart in the colour-prints. He is shown in three-quarter profile, sweeping down from the upper right-hand corner of the plate with raised and vengeful dart. The dramatic gestures of the Death and Despair of the washed drawing suggest a motion and an urgency quite alien to the colour-prints.

Four of Death's victims correspond to the figures on the pallet in the later pictures, though a fifth—apparently a female, with arms raised to her face—has been added to the group. She may be an early version of the kneeling figure with bowed head in the colour-prints. Behind Despair the faces of two recumbent figures are visible. They are clearly indebted in style to the drawings of the Royal Monuments in Westminster Abbey made by Blake during his apprenticeship to James Basire, and are similar to the 'portraits' on the frontispiece to the *Songs of Experience* and to those in 'The Counsellor, King, Warrior, Mother & Child in The Tomb' from the designs to Blair's *Grave*.

PARADISE LOST XI and separate plate: MICHAEL FORETELLING THE CRUCIFIXION (47–9)

While most of the poem's illustrators ignore the Crucifixion scene and concentrate instead upon incidents drawn from the strife-torn history of mankind, Blake disregards the passing show of history altogether, and also breaks with his scheme of illustrating one incident from each Book of the poem, in order to depict the supreme subject of the Crucifixion.

The simple wooden Cross of *Paradise Lost* xi is placed on the brow of a hill, with Michael and Adam standing on either side of it and Eve sleeping at its foot. The head of the Serpent is nailed to the Cross and the bodies of Sin and Death lie prostrate beneath it. The hill recalls both the biblical Golgotha and the Miltonic 'top/Of speculation' (xii, 588–9) on which Michael reveals to Adam the history of the world. The sky behind the Cross is grey in the Huntington version, blackish-blue in the Boston version. Both skies deepen towards the base of the Cross.

As the Raphael of *Paradise Lost* vii revealed the magnificence of the Divine Vision, so Michael and Christ respectively display its tenderness and its supreme mercy. In the Huntington version Christ is a gaunt Gothic figure; in the Boston version a peaceful sleeper; and in the third version, executed for John Linnell and now in the possession of the Fitzwilliam Museum, a radiant Saviour with beams of light streaming from his body.

In the poem Michael approaches Adam

> Not in his shape celestial, but as man
> Clad to meet man; over his lucid arms
> A military vest of purple flowed
>
> . . .
>
> His starry helm unbuckled showed him prime
> In manhood where youth ended; by his side
> As in a glistering zodiac hung the sword,
> Satan's dire dread, and in his hand the spear.
>   (xi, 239–41 and 245–8)

Blake is not completely faithful to the Miltonic portrait: he shows Michael clad in decorative military garments—a diaphanous tunic and a plumed helmet—and with a spear in his hand, but without belted sword and with body-length wings that are draped behind him and frame his figure handsomely. However, the angel does appear, as in the poem, reassuring and 'Without remorse' (xi, 105).

Adam is gazing up at Christ, 'lost in contemplation of faith/And wonder at the Divine Mercy' (*Jerusalem*, K 743; pl. 96, 31–2). Christ's head has sunk downwards and is turned towards his. Here we have man as the image of Christ, contemplating his whole and redemptive self which has in prophecy 'put off the dark Satanic body' (*Vala*, K 346; 196) and thereby vanquished the whole of the fallen, material world as well:

> And thus with wrath he did subdue
> The Serpent Bulk of Nature's dross,
> Till He had nail'd it to the Cross.
>   (*The Everlasting Gospel*, K 749; 52–4)

The Serpent of *Paradise Lost* XI is entwined about the lower part of the Cross. Its head is transfixed by the nail that pierces Christ's feet. At the foot of the Cross lie the prostrate bodies of Sin and Death. This section of the illustration shows the fulfilment of Michael's prophecy to Adam:

> to the cross he nails thy enemies,
> The law that is against thee, and the sins
> Of all mankind
>
> (xii, 415–17);

> this act
> Shall bruise the head of Satan, crush his strength
> Defeating Sin and Death, his two main arms,
> And fix far deeper in his head their stings
> Than temporal death shall bruise the victor's heel,
> Or theirs whom he redeems
>
> (xii, 429–34).

Death's body is partly covered in winding-sheets; Sin's is scaly in the Huntington version but composed simply of blank coils in the Boston and Fitzwilliam plates. The eyes of both figures are closed and their arms (poorly drawn even for Blake), flung out sideways in a parody of the Crucifixion posture. This attitude may owe something to line 431 of Book X (quoted above); but as we have seen it is also an attitude in which Blake frequently depicts his tyrant-figures. (Death himself was earlier shown in this position in the water-colour versions of 'Satan Rousing his Legions'.) The dogs' heads are resting on Sin's breasts—a reminder of the carnality of the Fall.

Before the Cross lies Eve, apparently in a trance-like slumber. Her posture resembles that of Adam in the Creation illustration, and the patch of earth upon—or within—which she is lying is similar in shape to the giant leaf upon which Adam's body was placed. The association is also made in *Paradise Lost* when Michael says to Adam:

> let Eve (for I have drenched her eyes)
> Here sleep below while thou to foresight wakest,
> As once thou slep'st, while she to life was formed.
>
> (xi, 367–9)

Just as Adam's leafy carpet represented the 'Vegetable world' in the freshness of its first creation, so the bare earth on which Eve is lying represents that world in its decay—another indication that it is to be annihilated through the sacrificial gesture of Christ.

The woman's recumbent position at the base of the Cross is a literal rendering of Michael's lines, 'let Eve (for I have drenched her eyes)/Here sleep below while thou to foresight wakest' (xi, 367–8), but it is also an allusion to her secondary role as earth-mother and mother of mankind, and to her typological identity as 'second Eve'—associations which are all made in the poem. In so far as her position corresponds to that which she actually adopted during Michael's visionary revelation to Adam, she must be regarded as part of the 'actual' or directly enacted scene containing Michael and Adam; in so far as it is symbolic, she must be regarded as part of the 'vision' revealed by Michael to Adam. Thus her figure helps to integrate the 'literal' and 'visionary' levels of the picture.

Eve's rest has a further significance as the sleep of oblivion in which the errant Emanation returns at last to her rightful place within the male, an event concomitant to Blake with the resurrection of mankind:

> Los answer'd swift as the shuttle of gold: 'Sexes must vanish & cease
> 'To be when Albion arises from his dread repose, O lovely Enitharmon
> (*Jerusalem*, K 739; pl. 92, 13–14)

PARADISE LOST XII: THE EXPULSION (50, 51)

Many eighteenth-century illustrators of *Paradise Lost* used the 'Expulsion' of John Baptist Medina as a model for their own Expulsion scenes. As Medina's design was merely a slavish imitation of the Vatican fresco by Raphael—itself based on Masaccio's version of the incident, which of course owed its inspiration to the Bible—the details of the biblical incident became standard items in the Miltonic illustrative tradition.

Blake's 'Expulsion' however is quite closely related to the *Paradise Lost* version of the incident. It shows a firm yet sorrowful Michael clasping Adam and Eve by the hand. They too, 'though sorrowing, [are] yet in peace' (xi, 117). Behind and above them are four awesome guards mounted on horseback, and an enormous coil of flame. In the Huntington version Adam and Eve are gazing back up towards Paradise, and Adam is waving farewell to it:

> In either hand the hastening angel caught
> Our lingering parents, and to the eastern gate
> Led them direct, and down the cliff as fast
> To the subjected plain; then disappeared.

> They looking back, all the eastern side beheld
> Of Paradise, so late their happy seat,
> Waved over by that flaming brand, the gate
> With dreadful faces thronged and fiery arms
> (xii, 637–44)

The Serpent, which is not mentioned in Milton's account of the Expulsion, is shown slithering out of Paradise with Adam and Eve, and leering up at Adam as it does so. Michael is stepping over it and treading close to its head, a detail that draws attention to his traditional role as a type of Christ. In the Boston version Adam and Eve are gazing down at the Serpent and Adam's right hand is raised as if to strike it: the detail marks him too out as a type of Christ. It is of course entirely appropriate to Blake's vision of the Expulsion that the Serpent-Selfhood should be accompanying man into the fallen world: 'I do not consider either the Just or the Wicked to be in a Supreme State, but to be every one of them States of the Sleep which the Soul may fall into in its deadly dreams of Good & Evil *when it leaves Paradise following the Serpent*' (K 614, italics mine).

The composition is frontal and vertically organized. Thunderbolts rend the spaces between Adam, Michael, and Eve, thus precluding the rendering of recessive depth. Thistles, brambles, and grasses are depicted in the foreground—all that remains of the luxuriant vegetation of Paradise. They are so placed as to suggest the harshness of the world of Experience:

> And their sun does never shine,
> And their fields are bleak & bare,
> And their ways are fill'd with thorns:
> It is eternal winter there.
> ('Holy Thursday', K 212; 9–12)

One possible model for Blake's Expulsion scene is a rendering by Rubens of Lot's escape from the doomed city of Sodom, which was engraved by Blake himself for the *Protestant's Family Bible*.[51] (See pl. 52.) It shows a bearded Lot leading his daughters away from the burning city of Sodom while his wife casts her fatal backward glance. The stoical resignation and the hand-clasping of Lot and his daughters are closer to Milton's vision of the Expulsion than are the Bible-based illustrations of the Expulsion, with their despairing and humiliated figures.[52] The arrangement of the three figures is frontal in Blake's picture and almost frontal in Rubens's, and

---

[51] 1780; opp. Genesis 19: 26.

[52] Several of the details of *Paradise Lost* that are acknowledged by Blake in his illustration are echoes of the Lot story; cf. xii, 637–8 and 641 with Genesis 19: 16, 26.

in Blake's Huntington version Adam and Eve are looking behind them—as is Lot's wife in the Rubens picture.

Clusters of thistles, brambles, and grasses appear at the foot of the Rubens design as well as in the Blake picture, although in the Rubens they serve merely as background detail. Two streaks of forked lightning which are shown in the sky above the city in the engraving also have an equivalent in *Paradise Lost* xii: the four tremendous thunderbolts which rend the spaces between the three figures, endowing the scene with an atmosphere of catastrophic violence and bringing to mind the Day of Judgement as well as the weather-torn world of Experience.

The blazing city of the engraving corresponds in Blake's picture to an enormous coil of fire depicted directly above Michael's head. This represents the 'flaming sword' that the guardian cherubim are waving 'In signal of remove' (xii, 592–3). Its dwindling tail suggests the image referred to at lines 633–4: 'The brandished sword of God before them blazed/Fierce as a comet'.

In his writings Blake suggests that the fallen world will endure only as long as the angelic sword remains at the entrance to Eden:

The ancient tradition that the world will be consumed in fire at the end of six thousand years is true ... For the cherub with his flaming sword is hereby commanded to leave his guard at the tree of life; and when he does, the whole creation will be consumed and appear infinite and holy, whereas it now appears finite & corrupt.

(The Marriage of Heaven and Hell, K 154; pl. 14)

and in another context he identifies the sword with the 'Wheel of fire' that represents the false religion of the fallen world:

> I stood among my valleys of the south
> And saw a flame of fire, even as a Wheel
> Of fire surrounding all the heavens: it went
> From west to east, against the current of
> Creation, and devour'd all things in its loud
> Fury & thundering course round heaven & earth.
> By it the Sun was roll'd into an orb,
> By it the Moon faded into a globe
> Travelling thro' the night; for, from its dire
> And restless fury, Man himself shrunk up
> Into a little root a fathom long.
> And I asked a Watcher & a Holy-One
> Its Name; he answered: 'It is the Wheel of Religion.'
> I wept & said: 'Is this the law of Jesus,
> 'This terrible devouring sword turning every way?'

He answer'd: 'Jesus died because he strove
'Against the current of this Wheel; its Name
'Is Caiaphas, the dark Preacher of Death,
'Of sin, of sorrow & of punishment:
'Opposing Nature! It is Natural Religion;
'But Jesus is the bright Preacher of Life
'Creating Nature from this fiery Law
'By self-denial & forgiveness of Sin.
(Jerusalem, K 717-18; 1-23)

The sword of *Paradise Lost* XII is also reminiscent of Blake's Vortex, a symbol for those areas of a man's life which, having been experienced, become in retrospect ordered and significant:

The nature of infinity is this: That every thing has its
Own Vortex, and when once a traveller thro' Eternity
Has pass'd that Vortex, he percieves it roll backward behind
His path, into a globe itself infolding like a sun

. . .

the eye of man views both the east & west encompassing
Its vortex, and the north & south with all their starry host

. . .

Thus is the heaven a vortex pass'd already, and the earth
A vortex not yet pass'd by the traveller thro' Eternity.
(Milton, K 497; pl. 15, 21-4, 28-9, and 34-5)

So the 'Vortex' or sword of *Paradise Lost* XII marks the conclusion of man's sojourn in Eden—a sojourn which takes on a new significance after the Expulsion—and the beginning of his trials on earth.

The row of daemonic horsemen depicted behind and above Michael, Adam, and Eve are the 'flaming warriors' (xi, 101) that '[thronged] the gate/With dreadful faces' (xii, 643-4). In his poetry Blake associated them with the sacred western gate of his holy city of Golgonooza: 'The Western Gate fourfold is clos'd, having four Cherubim/Its guards' (*Jerusalem*, K 633; pl. 13, 6-7). They are placed two on each side of the great coil of fire, and a smaller, twisting pyre of flame is shown between each pair. They all have long beards, wild, staring eyes,[53] and upstanding hair. Their appearance suggests that alien justice which is soon to operate in the fallen

---

[53] Cf. Milton's description of the 'eyes' in Christ's chariot:

One spirit in them ruled, and every eye
Glared lightning, and shot forth pernicious fire
Among the accursed, that withered all their strength
(vi, 848-50).

world. Similar faces are depicted on plate 6 of *The Book of Urizen* behind three descending, serpent-entwined Eternals, and in Blake's illustration of the Transfiguration. However, the ears of the mounts in the Boston version are touching, and thus form a whimsical imitation of the sacred Gothic arch.

The fourfold nature of the horsemen owes its origin largely to Milton's description of the cherubim: 'four faces each/Had, like a double Janus' (xi, 128–9), which is in turn derived from the fourfold creatures of Ezekiel's Vision, though the four horsemen of Revelation may also be relevant.

In Blake's system the four mounted guards have their counterpart in the primordial fourfold man who is eventually to be resurrected from the scattered fragments of the Divine Image—the disunited Zoas—at the time of the Apocalypse:

> And every Man stood Fourfold; each Four Faces had: One to the West,
> One toward the East, One to the South, One to the North, the Horses Fourfold.
> (Jerusalem, K 745; pl. 98, 12–13)

Endowed with such a significance, the figures of *Paradise Lost* xii become not only the guardians of the Edenic gate but a pledge of man's eventual renewal, and their stern gaze becomes the gaze of prophecy.

IV *NATIVITY ODE*

Blake's two sets of *Nativity Ode*[1] drawings both comprise six illustrations. The same six subjects recur in each, and the corresponding plates from each series are of similar design although—as with the *Comus* and *Paradise Lost* sets—they differ somewhat in detail.

The larger of the two sets was executed in 1809 and is now in the Whitworth Art Gallery, Manchester. The identity of its first owner is not known for certain although it may be assumed to have been the Rev. Joseph Thomas again.[2] The other set, which is undated, was bought from the artist by Thomas Butts and is now with Joseph Thomas's *Comus* and *Paradise Lost* drawings in the Huntington Library, San Marino, California.

The Whitworth paintings are really pen-and-ink drawings to which washes of colour have been applied; the Huntington pictures are in comparison highly coloured, and their ink outlines are not prominent. The Whitworth series is the more detailed of the two, and it includes more points drawn from Blake's 'system' and more traditional pictorial motifs than the Huntington set. It is therefore likely to have been the later of the two.

Unlike many of their successors, which were influenced by the conventions of the Victorian Christmas-card industry and by those of Romantic landscape-painting as well as by a tradition in Nativity illustration that dates back to the fourth century, Blake's *Nativity Ode* sets faithfully reflect the concerns of the poem. Its illustrations draw their subjects from those which are of fundamental importance to the text, they display a wealth of detail mentioned in it, and they base on its structure their own over-all construction. They also reflect the emphasis it places on the paradoxical nature of the Nativity.

The closeness of sympathy between poem and paintings is not surprising, for the Platonically influenced conception of the Nativity that we find in Milton's Ode cor-

[1] The *Ode on the Morning of Christ's Nativity* will be referred to as the *Nativity Ode* throughout.
[2] Cf. Leslie Parris, 'William Blake's Mr. Thomas', op. cit., and my general Introduction.

responds closely with some of Blake's own notions. In particular, Milton's description of the descent of Christ from the light-filled courts of heaven to the 'darksome house of mortal clay' (l. 14), which is indebted to the Neoplatonist notion of birth as the descent of the spirit to the material world and its incarceration in the flesh, is echoed by Blake in the patently Platonist opening lines of the 'Prophecy' to his *Europe*:

> The deep of winter came,
> What time the secret child
> Descended thro' the orient gates of the eternal day:
> War ceas'd, & all the troops like shadows fled to their abodes.
>   (K 239; pl. 4, 1–4)

In fact *Europe* as a whole was strongly influenced by the *Nativity Ode*. Both poems are concerned with the descent of a spiritual being whose mission it is to transform the world and with the nature of this transformation, and both emphasize the contrast between the latent spiritual power of the Saviour and the physical restrictions that presently beset him.

In the *Nativity Ode* Milton is preoccupied with the significance and complexity of time. He begins by placing the events of the Introduction, and incidentally the occasion of the poem's composition, in time:

> This is the month, and this the happy morn
> Wherein the Son of heaven's eternal King,
> Of wedded maid, and virgin mother born,
> Our great redemption from above did bring
>   (ll. 1–4);

he relates almost all the events described in the main body of the poem to the central episode, the Nativity; and he even concludes with a casual reference to time:

> But see the virgin blest,
> Hath laid her babe to rest.
>   Time is our tedious song should here have ending
>   (ll. 237–9)

This web of temporal relationships has the effect of translating the Nativity into a kind of 'eternal present' according to which all the significant events of theological history from the Creation to the Day of Judgement may be ordered and illuminated. It is this drawing together in Christ of the protracted 'moment' of history, rather than any thread of narrative continuity or any simple celebration of a single event, which governs the construction of the Ode.

Milton's expressed determination to forestall the Wise Men, who in his imagination are drawing ever nearer to Bethlehem during the Christmas morning on which the poem was begun, with his own poetic offering, further increases the temporal complexity of the poem, for it establishes a specific connection between the once-and-for-all 'present' of the poem's composition (and indeed the ever-shifting 'present' in which it is to be read) and the 'eternal present' of Christ's birth. It also enables the reader to appreciate the urgency and paradoxical nature of Christian time and the pressing and personal significance to him of Christ's birth.

The 'Hymn' section of the Ode begins with a brief reference to Christ in the manger, and it ends with a conventional Nativity scene. These opening and closing vignettes provide a 'stable' setting against which to measure the immense sweep of time covered by the central portion of the poem. The time-factor which operates within them is like a gradual but steadily moving flow whose progress is monitored only by the approach of the Wise Men, the laying of the Child to rest, and the appearance of the Star of Bethlehem above the stable.

Milton's preoccupation with the metaphysical simultaneity of all events pertaining to the Nativity is reflected in Blake's *Nativity Ode* illustrations through the use of a constant image[3]—a cross-sectional Nativity stable, which dominates the opening and closing plates of the series and which recurs (with varying dimensions and in various positions) in two and possibly three of the four remaining illustrations of each set. Its repeated use emphasizes the intimacy of the relation between Christ's birth and the other events depicted in the illustrations. The similarity between the opening and closing plates, which are largely devoted to representations of the stable, suggests the sheathing function of the opening and closing passages of the poem. As in the Ode, subtle alterations in detail between the first scene and the last mark the passing of 'time present'.

Throughout the illustrative series the stable is represented diagrammatically and in cross-section. It appears as a single-roomed dwelling, though with lateral extensions in all its manifestations except the first, and it has a steeply-pitched roof. Inside this roof is a frame reminiscent of the delicate reticulated or panel tracery found in many church windows of the Gothic style.

By representing the roof of his stable in the ecclesiastical Gothic style Blake is following a pre-Renaissance tradition according to which the crib of Christ was imaged as the confessional or altar of a church, but as we have already seen, he himself frequently employs the Gothic peak simply in order to signify spirituality. In the context of the *Nativity Ode* illustrations it must have particular reference to the magnificence of Christ's saving gesture of descent.

[3] And through the transference of details and references from one section of the poem to a picture which has another section as its major subject.

On the other hand the living quarters of the stable, with their cramped conditions and lack of apparent exit, appear also to represent the prison of world and flesh that encloses the descended soul—Milton's 'darksome house of mortal clay' (l. 14). So the stable becomes a paradoxical image, conveying both the humility of Christ's coming and the magnificence of his purpose.

The metaphor of the flesh and the world as prisons for the earth-bound soul is common in Neoplatonist and Platonically influenced writings. Milton himself employs it in *Il Penseroso*: 'The immortal mind that hath forsook/Her mansion in this fleshly nook' (ll. 91–2), and in *In Obitum Praesulis Eliensis*:

> cito
> Foedum reliqui carcerem,
> Volatilesque faustus inter milites
> Ad astra sublimis feror
> (ll. 45–8)[4]

Other writers who have used it and who were also known to Blake include Thomas Taylor when describing the Neoplatonists' interpretation of the rape of Proserpine: 'Pluto, then, having hurried Proserpine into the infernal regions, *i.e.* the soul having sunk into the profundities of a material nature, a description of her marriage next succeeds, or of her union with *the dark tenement of body*'[5] (italics mine) ; Jacob Behmen when referring to the Creation: 'Now *Man's* House of Flesh is also such a House as the *dark* Deep of this World is, wherein the seven Spirits of God generate themselves',[6] and Robert Blair in his description of the unprepared man visited by death: 'In that dread moment how the frantuc soul/Raves round the walls of her clay tenement'.[7] Blake himself employs the image several times in his own writings:

> 'Queen of the vales,' the matron Clay answer'd, 'I heard thy sighs,
> 'And all thy moans flew o'er my roof, but I have call'd them down.
> 'Wilt thou, O Queen, enter my house?
> (*The Book of Thel*, K 130; pl. 5, 14–16)

> In this dark world, a narrow house, I wander up & down.
> (*Vala*, K 360; 113)

'I am wrapped in mortality, my flesh is a prison, my bones the bars of death' ('Contemplation', *Poetical Sketches*, K 37).

---

[4] 'Scaping through my prison-wall,/I bade adieu to bolts and bars,/And soar'd, with angels, to the stars' (trans. William Cowper, *Latin and Italian Poems of Milton*, ed. William Hayley; op. cit.).
[5] *A Dissertation on the Eleusinian and Bacchic Mysteries*, 1790, pp. 108–9.
[6] *Aurora*, in *The Works of Jacob Behmen*, 1764–81, i, 263.
[7] *The Grave*, 1808, p. 16. The plates for this edition were engraved by Blake.

The size of the *Nativity Ode* stable varies dramatically throughout the series, expanding from a tiny speck in 'The Choir of Angels' through moderate proportions in the 'Typhon' drawing to dimensions so gross in the first and last illustrations that only its central section can be fitted onto the plate. Its variations in size, as well as its association with the time-dimension and its graceful ornamentation, all suggest that it is an image of Blake's 'atom of space'—a sacred point signifying infinity, and therefore originally without magnitude—in process of extension, and hence an image too of the creation of the fallen or contingent world:

> *Then Eno, a daughter of Beulah, took a Moment of Time*
> *And drew it out to seven thousand years with much care & affliction*
> *And many tears, & in every year made windows into Eden.*
> *She also took an atom of space & opened its centre*
> *Into Infinitude & ornamented it with wondrous art.*
>
> (*Vala*, K 270; 222–6)[8]

In this connection it should be noted that the apparent significance of the stable, as suggested by its size on the plate, is in inverse relation to its true, or spiritual, significance, and that it realizes its least extended form—i.e. its most perfect or 'eternal' state—in the second plate of the series, which is devoted to a representation of eternal harmony, and reaches its most extended or 'debased' form in the two illustrations which are concerned with the passing of contingent time in the fallen world.

NATIVITY ODE I: THE DESCENT OF PEACE (53, 54)

The first illustration of the series is dominated by a cross-sectional representation of the Nativity stable. This contains the Christ-child and other members of the Holy Family, and a couple of oxen instead of the ox and ass of tradition. Above the stable is the inverted figure of Peace, whose arms and wings are held wide so as to catch the Gothic point of the roof in an embrace without contact. At its base lies Nature, naked except for a loin-cloth of snow in the Whitworth version, and gazing upwards with—again only in the Whitworth version—a gesture of prayer. The space to either side of the stable is filled in the Huntington plate by indistinctly represented climbing

---

[8] Cf. also *Jerusalem*, K 678; pl. 48, 30–9. In *Blake and Tradition* (op. cit., ii, 152–66) Kathleen Raine discusses in detail the tradition which conceived of infinity not as unbounded vastness but as a point of no dimension, and which consequently regards the creation of the spatial and temporal world as an opening-out of this point.

plants—a non-personified representation of Nature naked in the winter season—and in the Whitworth plate by a mosaic of falling snow.

While Milton's Christ-child in the opening scene of the 'Hymn' 'All meanly wrapped in the rude manger lies' (l. 31), Blake's is in the Whitworth version cradled in Mary's arms and in the Huntington plate leaping naked into the air in a burst of light while Mary, exhausted by labour, reclines against Joseph. This arrangement brilliantly evokes the Platonic belief that the new-born baby descends mature and perfected into the world from another order of existence, as well as the associated Romantic belief in the independence and vitality of the child and the traditional conception of Christ as the 'light of the world'. Its verse equivalent is to be found in 'Infant Sorrow' from the *Songs of Experience*: 'My mother groan'd! my father wept./ Into the dangerous world I leapt' (K 217; 1–2). The representation also suggests the freedom and the glory that will, thanks to Christ's coming, accrue eventually to mankind.

In the Whitworth plate only Mary and Joseph are with the Child but in the Huntington plate his advent is also observed and acclaimed by members of the extended family—Zacharias, Elizabeth, and the infant John. This version is similar to a tempera Nativity executed by Blake for his Bible series except that there the positions of the onlookers are reversed. The Christ-child himself is enshrined within a brilliant golden aureole that stands out sharply against the dark background of the picture.

Mary, who was to Blake neither blessed nor virginal but merely the bodily vehicle of Christ's divine birth, is clothed not in the blue robes of chastity but in white. Appropriately, if ironically, in the Huntington version it is her husband who is shown wearing the blue.

In both versions of *Nativity Ode* I Joseph is shown stooping beneath the low, gabled ceiling of the stable. In the Whitworth plate his wooden posture emphasizes his discomfort, drawing attention to the narrow confines of his dwelling-place and hence to the prison-like qualities of the world. The symbolic nature of the stable is also apparent through the fact that it provides no space in which the bodies of the oxen, which are not depicted, could possibly have been accommodated.

Nature and Peace, the two figures excluded from the 'bodily house', are both figured as young and attractive women. Nature is drawn to a larger scale than the rest of the figures in the picture, and this as well as her position at the base of the world-stable suggests a comparison with the earth-mother.[9] Her bed and modesty-cloth of snow—Milton's 'saintly veil of maiden white' (l. 42)—suggest that she is

---

[9] Cf. the Eve of *Paradise Lost* XI, whose leaf-mandorla has a parallel in the carpet of snow on which Nature is lying.

under the influence of the puritanical code of sexual restraint, one of the abominations which Blake's Christ has come to overthrow. In his lyrics Blake himself uses snow to represent the repressive moral code:

> I walked abroad in a snowy day:
> I ask'd the soft snow with me to play:
> She play'd & she melted in all her prime,
> And the winter call'd it a dreadful crime.
>> ('Soft Snow', K 176)

> Where the Youth pined away with desire,
> And the pale Virgin shrouded in snow
> Arise from their graves, and aspire
> Where my Sun-flower wishes to go.
>> ('Ah! Sun-flower', K 215)

In *Nativity Ode* 1 Nature's ankles are crossed and her hair is straggling and outspread, as though under water—generally tokens of 'error' to Blake.

The Peace of the illustrative series is a close rendering of Milton's description of her:

> She crowned with olive green, came softly sliding
> Down through the turning sphere
>> . . .
> With turtle wing the amorous clouds dividing,
> And waving wide her myrtle wand
>> (ll. 47–8 and 50–1)

Her gesture of embrace takes in the 'world-stable' and so suggests the universality of her influence. The 'turning sphere' through which she descends is represented by the lower segments of three concentric circles, the outermost of which is pierced by the tip of the Gothic stable-roof. These heavenly spheres do not therefore encompass the world-stable, as they should if the Ptolemaic system were being followed, but are placed in opposition to it. This, and the total inversion of the figure of Peace, indicate that the realm from which she is descending is self-sufficient and moreover one in which the laws and values of the natural world have been reversed. Milton's hint regarding the soundlessness of her coming (see above) is admirably conveyed in Blake's depiction of the flowing grace of her limbs, wings, and swathed robes against the flat background of the 'turning sphere', and by the way in which she embraces the world-stable without actually touching it. Her descent may also owe something to the Neoplatonist notion of birth as descent.

The figures of Nature and of Peace are to some extent in opposition. That of Nature is naked apart from the snow covering her loins, while Peace is clad in a long, flowing robe; Nature is recumbent on the earth (indeed she is the earth) while Peace is descending through the heavenly spheres; and Nature is making an inward-turning gesture while the arms of the spirit of Peace are generously open.

Artistically this opposition or pairing may have been inspired by the genre of the 'debating-picture', in which 'two allegorical figures symbolizing and advocating two divergent moral or theological principles',[10] one figure nude and the other draped, were depicted. Blake must have seen such representations in emblem-books and in illuminated manuscripts. Pairs of figures standing for Nature and Grace or for Eve and the Virgin Mary were comparatively common to the genre, and both are related to the figures of *Nativity Ode* I. The apparent opposition in Blake's picture is of course transcended, for the purpose of Peace's mission is to redeem Nature. It is for this reason that Nature, whose reaction to her descent is not recorded in the Ode, is gazing up at her with rapt devotion.

NATIVITY ODE II: THE CHOIR OF ANGELS (55, 56)

The second illustration of the series is dominated by Milton's 'globe of circular light,/ That with long beams the shame-faced night arrayed' (ll. 110–11). It covers almost half the surface area of the plate and dwarfs the much reduced Nativity stable depicted just beneath it. Its dominance in the illustration is a reflection of its significance in the poem, where it serves as the supreme sign or reflection of the majesty of Christ's birth, and where it is central both in its position (it is evoked in the central stanzas of the Hymn) and in its attributes (it brings together the poem's isolated references to music, light, and order). As its origins can be traced both to the Pythagorean notion that the heavenly spheres produce music and to the account of the Creation that is given in Job 38: 7, it also unites the pagan and the Christian sources of the poem.

In the Ode the globe of light seems merely to surround the angels, but in the illustration they themselves form its very substance—an acknowledgement of one of the secondary meanings of the Latin 'globus', 'a compact body of persons'. It thus becomes a 'humanized sphere', one of Blake's most common images for the Divine Vision. In the Whitworth version the shafts of light that emanate from the globe penetrate dramatically into the surrounding darkness.

The 'circumference' of the globe is formed from a ring of angels, apparently

[10] Erwin Panofsky, *Studies in Iconology*, 1939, p. 154.

female, whose extremities dovetail or overlap, and who are carrying musical instruments that blend unobtrusively with the line of their bodies. Most of the instruments in the Whitworth version are harps, as in the Ode, but in the Huntington picture they are trumpets—perhaps held in readiness for 'The wakeful trump of doom' prophesied at line 156. The central portion of the globe consists of a row of 'helmed' and 'sworded'[11] 'male' angels, with arms appearing as though interlaced on the flat surface of the plate. In the Whitworth version their wings are raised and placed together above their heads—a further indication of their spirituality. Some of them, however, are wearing strangely troubled expressions. This, and their sexual nature, indicate Blake's reservations about the militaristic element in Milton's vision, while still enabling him to acknowledge its essential magnificence.

The source for Blake's pattern of angels has been traced to an engraving on which he may have worked when apprenticed to the master-engraver James Basire:

on plate 2 (of Jacob Bryant's *Ancient Mythology*) is illustrated 'Zor-Aster Archimagus before an altar with a particular covering like a Cupselis or hive; taken from Kaempfer's Amoenitates Exoticae'. Beneath is a frieze of figures with arms upraised and crossed, a theme which was to appear in 1795 in one of the designs for Young's *Night Thoughts*, in 1809 in the third illustration to Milton's 'Hymn on the Nativity', in the watercolour drawing of 'David delivered out of Many Waters' from the Butts collection and finally in the supreme design of 'When the Morning Stars sang together' designed about 1820 and engraved as plate 14 in *Illustrations of the Book of Job*.[12]

In the *Nativity Ode* the description of the 'globe of circular light' is followed directly by an account of the Creation based on Job 38: 4–8. The purpose of the juxtaposition is to suggest a parallel between the Creation and the Nativity as cardinal events in Christian history. Blake later proved himself aware of this parallel by choosing the same design for part of the Job engraving 'When the Morning Stars sang together' as he had selected for his illustration of Milton's choir of angels.

The shepherds—in fact representatives of the 'human family', for women and children are included among their number—are seated with their dog and flocks in the lower part of the illustration. They are gazing up in awe at the angelic globe. Together with the rounded backs of their sheep, which merge imperceptibly into the vegetation depicted behind them, they form a typical Blakean pastoral scene.

---

[11] Only those in the Whitworth version are 'sworded'.

[12] Sir Geoffrey Keynes, *Blake Studies*, 1949, p. 44.

NATIVITY ODE III: THE DEVIL'S IN HELL (57, 58)

Both this and the two illustrations following it are devoted to a representation of the diverse forms of evil. Here Blake concentrates upon its deformity, disunity, and bestiality. He depics a hybrid monster that is based on references in the Ode both to the dragon of Revelation (itself identified with Satan, the adversary of Christ)[13] and to Typhon, the many-headed giant of Greek mythology, who took the form of a serpent below the waist and who was finally vanquished by Zeus, the chief of the Olympian gods:

> The old dragon under ground
> In straiter limits bound,
>> Not half so far casts his usurped sway,
> And wroth to see his kingdom fail,
> Swinges the scaly horror of his folded tail.
>> (ll. 168–72)

> Nor all the gods beside,
> Longer dare abide,
>> Not Typhon huge ending in snaky twine
>> (ll. 224–6)

The two monsters have in common their serpent tails and their many-headedness, both of which are emphasized in Blake's portrait.

The monster of *Nativity Ode* III is shown imprisoned in the bowels of the earth—otherwise hell, where the dragon, Satan, was also confined. The head of the staff which he is carrying suggests the pomegranate, a fruit associated in myth with the classical Hades. Typhon too is associated with the earth and with hell, for he was the son of Earth and of Tartarus, and was finally imprisoned beneath Mount Etna by his adversary, Zeus.

As if to emphasize his relevance to the human condition Blake has depicted the monster in quasi-human form, though with an enormous, scaly tail and several heads but with no body to complement his single set of limbs. In the Whitworth plate he has six heads, in the Huntington version seven—like the dragon of Revelation. All of these heads are gazing in different directions and in the Whitworth illustration all are markedly different in appearance though each of them shows signs of travail. The portrait suggests the disorder and divisiveness of evil as well as the lack of co-ordination in its workings. One of the Huntington monster's heads, which is large

[13] Cf. Revelation 12: 9 and 20: 2.

and bearded, is dominant in size and in position while the others are small and feral, and crowded haphazardly onto the neck around and behind the first. The larger head conveys the tyrannous nature of evil, and the ancillary heads, the way in which tyranny can reduce its subjects to mindless bestiality.

The Whitworth monster's half-dozen heads are arranged in two ranks of three. With their exaggerated facial features—especially the eyebrows—and cranial bumps, they resemble some of the physiognomical diagrams in Lavater's *Physiognomy*.[14] Blake engraved several designs for the 1788 and '89 editions of this work, and in his writings often showed an interest in the 'science' of physiognomy and its relation to character. In a letter to Thomas Butts dated 16 August 1803, for instance, he chides himself for having 'a too passive manner, inconsistent with my active physiognomy' (K 828); and in *A Descriptive Catalogue 1809* he remarks that 'some of the names or titles (of the characters in *The Canterbury Tales*) are altered by time, but the characters themselves for ever remain unaltered, and consequently they are the physiognomies or lineaments of universal human life, beyond which Nature never steps' (K 567). Later in the same work he describes his 'type' of the Ugly man in terms which tally almost exactly with his representation of the monster in the Whitworth illustration:

the Artist has imagined his Ugly man, one approaching to the beast in features and form, his forehead small, without frontals; his jaws large; his nose high on the ridge, and narrow; his chest, and the stamina of his make, comparatively little, and his joints and his extremities large; his eyes, with scarce any whites, narrow and cunning, and every thing tending toward what is truly Ugly, the incapability of intellect.

(K 580)

Many of his portraits, particularly those known as the Visionary Heads, which were executed around 1819 for John Varley the astrologer, resemble the strongly delineated faces in Lavater's *Physiognomy*.

The monster's bestiality is also revealed in the colossal serpentine tail which protrudes above the ground and (thanks to Blake's foreshortening) 'swinges' among the stars in fulfilment of the prophecy made in Revelation 12: 3–4, 9, the passage on which Milton's lines 168–72 are based. The tail's line of motion is further extended by a belt of stars that sweeps around a small Nativity stable represented above the ground, almost—but, significantly, not quite—enclosing it completely. Ironically this tail—potentially a tremendous engine of destruction—prevents the beast from moving at all, as it has wound itself about his legs and, in the larger

---

[14] Trans. Samuel Shaw, n.d., pp. 51 and 58. Cf. especially Lavater's 'foreheads with many angular, knotty protuberances' and 'Wild and perplexed' eyebrows.

version, about his body as well. So, as in the Ode, the beast is impotent despite—even in some measure because of—his fearsome appearance.

The monster is squatting in appropriately ungainly fashion on a narrow outcrop of rock, his ankles crossed. He is surrounded by lesser gods or devils, all of whom are in disarray. Some are submitting listlessly to their fates, one (in the Whitworth version) is fleeing horizontally through the flames, and another is striving desperately to re-enter the world above—a heaven to the devils just as earth is a hell to the gods. Another indication of Satanic pretension is revealed in the Whitworth version through the middle finger of the monster's left hand, the tip of which protrudes above the crust of the earth. Its action is followed by four of the heads. The fact that it is the left hand which is involved suggests that the monster is aspiring to physical but not to spiritual salvation.

All of the lesser devils partake of the human form—a further indication of the relevance of the devils to man—although several of them have vestigial scales on their bodies and one, depicted at the very bottom of the Huntington plate, has an animal head, spiked vertebrae, and webbed hands as well as scales.[15] He suggests the ultimate degradation of the spirit that persists in error.

Several of the devils have mean and swarthy faces; other have vacant expressions that indicate the absence of any capacity for initiative either mental or moral; and one has a rubbery, mask-like visage with thick lips and narrow forehead. The heads to the far left-hand side of the Whitworth plate have apparently been severed from their bodies, and two of the figures in this version are shown clutching their pates in anguish. In the Huntington version one devil is holding aloft a mournful, bearded head—an effigy of the false god whom Blake holds responsible for the wretchedness of the material world—while he attempts to draw the attention of his listless companions to the presence of Christ, the future ruler of the world. Likenesses of the effigy appear again in the Whitworth version as one of the severed heads and as one of the monster's countenances. As the head is the seat of the rational intellect and the rational intellect to Blake the source of evil, it is appropriate that the devils' heads in particular should be shown to be debased. In the Huntington plate one devil clothed in what appear to be a nun's veil and habit constitutes an obscure reference to a church that is in the service of Satan. Two of the Whitworth devils are clutching daggers—an allusion to the violence often employed by evil men.

The turbulence of the lower part of the plate is to some extent offset by the tran-

[15] Besides these scales and webbed hands, the blue colouring of the 'ground' in the Huntington version makes it seem as if the devils are under water. It may be intended to suggest the Sea of Time and Space.

quillity of the conventional Nativity scene above, which with its praying figures, guardian-angels, and slumbering flocks, suggests the harmony of a spiritually percipient universe. The three figures praying outside the stable in the Huntington version may be intended to represent the three Wise Men—a playful hint by Blake that Milton did not manage to fulfil his stated aim of completing the Ode before their arrival in Bethlehem.

NATIVITY ODE IV: APOLLO AND THE PAGAN DEITIES (59, 60)

Like Milton, Blake was bewitched by the classical ideal and remained under its influence long after he had rejected it as a source of spiritual wisdom. The passages in the *Nativity Ode* concerning the flight of the pagan deities contain an elegaic, almost wistful note despite the poem's main 'Christ triumphant' theme, and many other parts of the poem reveal a debt to classical culture.

Of the three vanquished gods in the Blake series only Apollo is attractive. His departing spirit is given lithe, boyish contours and is shown within a downward-sweeping mandorla of flame as it plunges out of its marble form towards the sea. The contrast here is not between the barbarity of some defeated deity and the sweetness and light of Christ but between the immobile beauty of the statue and the fluid grace of the spirit, between the impassivity of the form and the passion of the ghost.

This is the only one of Blake's three 'Expulsion of the Deities' illustrations to be devoted entirely to non-biblical matter. It is therefore appropriate that it should not contain a representation of the Nativity stable—the only illustration of the series not to do so, though in the Whitworth plate the star of Bethlehem is writ large in the sky.

The statue in the Huntington version is a fairly close rendition of a restored Apollo Belvedere—the piece which in the eighteenth century was regarded as the finest known work of antiquity.[16] Blake has not caught its elegant tenseness of stance and of expression and has somewhat altered its proportions but, like the original, his figure has a quiver of arrows strapped to his back and the python is wound about a tree-stump positioned just behind him. His bow has been restored to his outstretched left hand and he is without the Roman-rococo fig-leaf of the Apollo Belvedere—presumably to Blake an irrelevant and prudish excrescence on the body of the naked 'human form divine'.

[16] Winckelmann for instance cited it as his standard of ideal beauty; see *The History of Ancient Art among the Greeks*, trans. G. Henry Lodge, 1850, p. 84.

The stance of the Whitworth statue also echoes that of the Apollo Belvedere, but more faintly, and he is without the distinctive quiver, cloak, and python-entwined tree-stump of the classical statue. The python is, however, depicted here as well, though now wound about and behind Apollo's body in grossly extended form. Its neck is being crushed in the god's left hand and part of its body in his right. His left heel is poised above another section of its body, which terminates in a decorative flourish about his feet. The python-slaying incident is not mentioned in the Ode and the reference to it here is so rendered as to remind the viewer of the promise made by God to the Serpent of Genesis:[17] '[the woman's seed] shall bruise thy head, and thou shalt bruise his heel.' It therefore constitutes a tribute to the tradition which saw Apollo as a 'type' of Christ and hence to Milton's view of him as the least depraved of the pagan deities.

The statue is centrally positioned. To its left and slightly beneath it is a raving priestess imprisoned in a cave—Blake's version of the 'pale-eyed priest from the prophetic cell' whom 'No nightly trance, or breathed spell,/Inspires' (ll. 179–80).[18] This figure, however, far from being denied her preternatural gifts, appears to be undergoing a frenzied and trance-like apprehension of the birth of Christ and of the fall of the god most closely associated with her shrine, for she is gazing up at Apollo as though able to see him through the rock walls of her cavern.

In the Huntington plate she has the lavish curls of a Blakean temptress while in the Whitworth version her hair is spikey and serpentine, suggesting that of the Medusa. The parallel is appropriate, for the departing spirit of Apollo, at whom she is apparently staring, has left him a mere stone effigy. In the Whitworth plate she is seated upon her tripod of prophecy but in the Huntington version she appears to be seated on or enclosed within a tree-trunk—a detail that links her with those classical deities who, when pursued by the gods, were transformed into plants, as well as with Blake's own vegetative universe. The closeness with which the 'prophetic cell' encloses her figure, its lack of apparent exit, and her evident desire to escape from it—she is shown pressing against it with her arms—indicate that, like the cave of 'Satan Rousing his Legions', it represents the constricting material world.

Beneath the statue of Apollo is an altar—in sinister cubic form in the Whitworth plate—upon which a sacrificial fire is burning.[19] The flames of the fire in the Whitworth version are more reminiscent of vegetative growths than of true flame, and

[17] Discussed in connection with the last three illustrations of the *Paradise Lost* series.
[18] Cf. an almost identical figure with the same upraised arms, upstanding hair, haggard features, and wide open mouth, executed by Blake in response to Young's *Night Thoughts*, Night VII, p. 30, ll. 593–4—'*Pride*, like the *Delphic* Priestess, with a Swell,/Rav'd Nonsense'.
[19] Cf. l, 195: 'And the chill marble seems to sweat'.

the fire in the Huntington version is also preternatural, for its flames point downwards as though in sympathy with the fiery mandorla of the departing god. In the same plate a horn—all that remains of a sacrificial beast—protrudes from the flames on the left and serves as a reminder of the bloody pre-Christian custom of animal sacrifice.

Several maidens are doing obeisance before the altar. They may owe their origin to line 188 of the Ode: 'The nymphs in twilight shade of tangled thickets mourn', or to line 204: 'In vain the Tyrian maids their wounded Thammuz mourn', though it is more likely that they are wholly an invention of Blake's, made—like his alteration of the sex of Milton's priest—in order to suggest the susceptibility of the female to influence by tyrannical forces. In the Whitworth version a couple of 'flamens at their service quaint' (l. 194), one of whom is wearing the laurel wreath of Apollo, are visible behind the maidens, evidently aghast at the defeat of their god. The maidens' faces are hidden and the priests have the long, flowing beard and mournful countenance of Urizen, the overlord of the fallen world. By holding his hands to his ears one of them tries to shut out the sounds of lament so elegiacally described by Milton. The originally human form of his body has disintegrated into a pattern of abstract curves.

To the far right of the picture another altar and another fleeing deity can be seen. The deity, a winged and spectral form that is departing the body of a turbaned and bearded man, is hastening upwards amidst thick clouds of smoke[20] to join— amongst other figures, which are unrecognizable—an old man with flowing white beard, a bull, a dog, and a winged sun-disc. Only the bull and the dog have their source in the Ode:

> The brutish gods of Nile as fast,
> Isis and Orus, and *the dog Anubis* haste.
>
> Nor is Osiris seen
> In Memphian grove, or green,
> *Trampling the unshowered grass with lowings loud*
> (ll. 211–15, italics mine.)

The sun-disc, winged and with a serpent rearing up on either side of it, is an emblem recognized in several cultures. Blake himself employed the winged disc with serpents in other illustrations. A quotation from Stukeley's *Abury*, a work with

---

[20] Cf. Matthew 24:29, in which Christ promises that his second coming will be heralded by darkness and disturbances in the heavens.

which he was familiar, will indicate the relevance of the emblem to the 'Apollo' illustration:

By [the circle, snake, and wings the Egyptians] meant to picture out, as well as they could, the nature of the divinity. The circle meant the supreme fountain of all being, the father; the serpent, that divine emanation from him which was called the son; the wings imported that other divine emanation from them which was called the spirit, the *anima mundi*...[21]

Blake, then, has shown Stukeley's abstract Egyptian Trinity ceding to the true divinity—and humanity—of Christ.

In the background to the illustration a cliff—presumably representing the 'steep of Delphos' (l. 178)[22]—descends sharply to the sea. In the Whitworth version it is surmounted by a Doric portico, to an inner pillar of which a male figure is about to apply his strength. Here we may be reminded of the last exploit of Samson, but in any case the downfall of classical architecture, as well as that of classical religion and statuary, appears about to take place.

Much lower on the Whitworth plate, and behind and to the left of the statue, is an Ionic portico. Beneath it a woman is turning away from the statue and making a gesture of rejection. Her posture is similar in reverse to that of the man beneath the Doric portico. By associating a male with the Doric style and a female with the Ionic Blake is epitomizing the reputed chief characteristics of the two civilizations concerned—the toughness and militarism of the Doric, the laxity and sensuousness of the Ionic.

The spectral figure that hovers just above the surface of the sea in the Huntington version, portends an unquiet rest for the spirit of the dying god—for there was according to the heathen religions of ancient Greece no repose for the spirits of those whose bodies remained unburied. Ironically, then, the god is to suffer at the hands of a religion of which he was a leading deity.

In the Whitworth version two sinister shapes, dark and pointed, protrude from the water. They present a mortal threat to the spirit, as his anguished expression suggests, and they demonstrate the 'limits' of 'opacity' and 'contraction' which to Blake mark the farthest conceivable aberration of matter from its spiritual origins. So the frantic spirit is merely fleeing from stone organized in the attractive lineaments of the statue to stone in its most degraded form—'Human majesty and beauty .../ (Condensed) into solid rocks with cruelty and abhorrence' (*Jerusalem*; K 641, pl.

[21] 1743, p. 54.
[22] Though the real Delphi is inland it is on the side of a rocky mountain. The waters in the illustration may represent the Sea of Time and Space. Cliffs descending to water are often associated by Blake with the fallen condition.

19, 24–5). The statue, as Blake's tribute to the former glories of classical civilization, remains unchanged.

The emphasis throughout the illustration is on the rigidity and lifelessness of the petrous forms associated with the culture of the classical world—those of art (the statue and its plinth, and the porticoes depicted in the background) and those of religion (the altars and the cave of the oracle) as well as those that are unorganized and untenanted by man (the two rocks of the reef).

The artistic disarray of the illustration, its crowding and structural imbalance, and its wanton accumulation of detail, reflect the disturbance of the classical ideal that is caused by the coming of Christ. Disarray is also conveyed through the creation of several dramatic centres and through the use of a variable scale: some of the figures and pillars in the background appear to be nearer than their size would warrant, and in the drawing of the olive trees in the Huntington version (Milton's 'thickets'— l. 188—perhaps) three-dimensional perspective is disregarded so that the trees appear as if painted on the cliffs behind.

NATIVITY ODE V: THE FLIGHT OF MOLOCH (61, 62)

Moloch, the ancient Canaanite deity to whom children were sacrificed, is the third and last of the vanquished gods to be depicted by Blake. His idol, a hollow bronze cast filled with flames and blackened by smoke (or by evil), is shown searing the children who are his pathetically trusting victims, while his spirit, naked and bat-winged, flees the scene:

> And sullen Moloch fled,
> Hath left in shadows dread,
> His burning idol all of blackest hue
> (ll. 205–7)

The idol is partially encircled by worshippers, who are dancing and playing percussion and brass instruments—timbrels, trumpets, castanets, and cymbals—in order to drown the children's screams:

> In vain with cymbals' ring,
> They call the grisly king,
> In dismal dance about the furnace blue
> (ll. 208–10)

A mannikin Christ-child is emerging stern but triumphant from the base of the idol.

A range of jagged mountain-peaks has been added to the background of the Whitworth version. These may have been intended to represent the hills surrounding the city of Rabbath, notorious as a centre of Moloch-worship, or simply to emphasize the expressionist drama of the subject.

Both Blake and Milton were familiar with accounts of Moloch-worship[23] and were profoundly distressed by these accounts. Each of them incorporated Moloch into his own catalogue of the fallen deities—Milton in *Paradise Lost*, where the god is characterized as the fiercest of the fallen angels, and Blake in (for instance) *Jerusalem*, K 686; pl. 55, 31–2, where he is identified as the second of the six recusant Eyes of God. He is unquestionably the most depraved of the pagan deities depicted in the *Nativity Ode* illustrations.

The idol of *Nativity Ode* v, with its flame-filled interior, its club (Whitworth version) or sharp stake (Huntington), and its spiked crown, is strongly reminiscent of the deluded and belligerent Spectre of Urthona as he is portrayed in the sixth Night of *Vala*:

> Round his loins a girdle glow'd with many colour'd fires,
> In his hand a knotted Club whose knots like mountains frown'd
> Desart among the stars, them withering with its ridges cold.
> Black scales of iron arm the dread visage; iron spikes instead
> Of hair shoot from his orbed scull; his glowing eyes
> Burn like two furnaces
>
> (K 319; 304–9);

and Moloch's fleeing spirit, which is depicted just above the idol's head in sinister, back-to-back position and with enormous, spiked wings, appears as a typically Blakean Spectre. This means that Moloch has split not into a redeemable personality and an opposing and unregenerate spectre but into two spectres, both of which are by definition illusory and unredeemable. So the fleeing spectre does not leave behind him a redeemable personality but a mere image—fixed, 'opake', and inhuman.

Bat-wings are a common attribute of Blake's Satan-figures, and the horn just visible on the right-hand side of the Huntington spirit's head further suggests his close association, if not identification, with the prince of evil. The Spectres of Adam in the *Paradise Lost* illustrations (and that of Christ in the *Paradise Regained* series, which will be discussed later) also have alternative identities as Satan-figures. The club of the Moloch idol in the Whitworth plate resembles the attributes of many of Blake's Satan surrogates.

[23] Milton from George Sandys's *Relation of a journey*, 1615, p. 186, Blake from Joseph Priestley's *Comparison of the Institutions of Moses with those of the Hindoos and Other Ancient Nations*, 1799, pp. 196–7, and both of them, undoubtedly, from the Bible.

Though the Moloch-spirit is without the weapon and crown of his idol, the spikes of his wings are a reminder of the cruel spikes on its crown. The crown—though that worn by the Huntington idol looks more like a jester's cap—is appropriate, for as Blake had no doubt read in Jacob Bryant's *Ancient Mythology*,[24] 'Melech, or, as it is sometimes expressed, Malech, and Moloch, betokens a king'. In *Paradise Lost* too, Milton alludes three times to the literal meaning of Moloch's name: 'horrid king' (i, 392); 'sceptred king' (ii, 43; and 'furious king' (vi, 357).

The Christ-child is shown emerging triumphantly from a Gothic opening in the frontal façade of the plinth on which the idol is seated. This opening is depicted directly beneath its genitals, always a source of power to Blake. In the Whitworth version there is a clear correspondence between the archway and the cross-sectional frontage of the Nativity stable represented in earlier illustrations, and a correspondence that is less explicit but still worthy of note between the ledge upon which Moloch is resting his foot and the stable's extended wings. So the illustration becomes in part a proleptic vision of the Christ-child breaking out of the 'house of mortality'— something that he will later achieve in reality, through his death and atonement. His freedom of movement—his arms are raised in a gesture of triumph and he is striding forward confidently and with no regard for his natural age[25]—contrasts strikingly with his quiescence in other illustrations of the series, and further emphasizes his unfettering.

But the plinth of the idol is not merely another representation of the 'house of mortality' simple, for here the 'house' has been endowed with a third dimension that is realized not only through the emergence of Christ from its interior but also through the representation in perspective of two additional Gothic arches in either side of the plinth. Physically the addition of a third dimension enables Christ to escape from the 'bodily house' or house of the world; metaphysically it is his release from it that leads to its destruction or transfiguration, for it and the idol as well appear about to be engulfed by fire. The purifying process is also suggested in the triple representation of the divine Gothic arch, and (in the Whitworth version) in the way in which the side arches soar above both the original frontal peak and the general level of the roof-ridge.

It may already have been observed that the plinth in the Whitworth version is a partial optical illusion, for its most elevated portion can appear as a backing for the idol, as the half-closed lid of a chest, or as part of the gabled roof. This disregard

---

[24] 1775–6 (second edn.), i, 70.

[25] Milton attributes a different prodigious feat to the infant Christ—one borrowed from the legends of Hercules: 'Our babe to show his Godhead true,/Can in his swaddling bands control the damned crew' (ll. 227–8).

of conventional object- and space-values is appropriate to a setting in which Eternity is foreshadowed, and to Blake's belief in the contingent nature of space and of material objects.[26]

Christ's triumphant emergence from the fiery belly of evil may also be regarded as an obscure reference to the 'harrowing' of hell—Christ's descent into the Inferno in order to rescue from it the souls of the virtuous pagans. Though not mentioned in the Ode,[27] it is one of the great climactic events of the Christian story. It is supposed to have taken place at some time during the three days of the Entombment and must therefore have been almost contemporaneous with Christ's death and resurrection, though the child protagonist and general context of Blake's illustration suggest that it was metaphorically coincident with his birth.

The traditional 'harrowing of hell' episode and the literal subject of the illustration are closely related, for both centre upon Christ's saving of souls. But whereas the compassionate act of the Harrowing is generally considered to have extended only to the souls of the virtuous pagans who lived and died before the coming of Christ, that of the *Nativity Ode* is being extended to all men, for all men are the children of God. In the Prophetic book *Jerusalem* Blake also associates the harrowing of hell with the overcoming of earthly limitation: 'But Jesus, breaking thro' the Central Zones of Death & Hell,/Opens Eternity in Time & Space, triumphant in Mercy' (K 716; pl. 75, 21–2).

For the Christian Moloch-worship has a traditional association with hell. The valley of the son of Hinnom, according to the Old Testament the chief site of Moloch-worship, became in the New Testament Gehenna, the place of retribution for evil deeds.[28] Gehenna later became associated with the Christian hell.

Whether or not Blake knew that 'Orcus' was one title of the classical god of hell, his own Orc—particularly as represented in the Prophetic book *Europe*—is closely related to the Christ-child of this illustration, for he is generally represented as an infant and frequently depicted within an ambience of fire that is indicative of his revolutionary activity. The Christ-child of the illustration is not, however, accorded

[26] Cf. the drawing known as 'A Vision' (reproduced as plate 58 of *The Blake Collection of W. Graham Robertson*, ed. Kerrison Preston, 1952), in which the poet and his guardian-angel are enshrined within a tiny, light-drenched room which is itself enclosed by a much larger structure. The room may be envisaged as existing either within the larger structure or upon its surface.

[27] Perhaps because it does not receive direct biblical sanction. It is just possible that in *Nativity Ode* v Blake also took as his text lines 216–20 of the poem: 'Nor can he be at rest/Within his sacred chest,/Nought but profoundest hell can be his shroud,/In vain with timbrelled anthems dark/The sable-stoled sorcerers bear his worshipped ark.' Blake's Christ-child, unlike the Osiris of the Hymn, was to be found within his 'ark', and in the illustration is shown emerging from it.

[28] Cf. Jeremiah 19: 6–15.

any of Orc's more sinister connotations—Orc being linked with bloody and ultimately futile revolt rather than with the redemption of the spirit. The armed and apparently troubled angels of the second *Nativity Ode* plate may, however, suggest such an interpretation.

Finally the Moloch-figure and Christ-child may be 'read' as a successful alchemical experiment,[29] with the hollow idol representing the 'athanor' or furnace; the dark, billowing clouds which emerge from it, the sulphureous fumes that would have been exuded during the process; and the Christ-child himself, the precious metal which men have sought so long.

All the pictorial, literary, and theological allusions incorporated into this most complex illustration can be reduced to a single theme—the absolute antagonism between good and evil. This is revealed in the picture through a contrast in size, colouring, and mood between the infant Christ and the idol—the one slight, pure, and exultant, and the other ponderous, dark, and sullen.

The musician-dancers who are represented on either side of the idol are divided into two groups—one of white-bearded old men, the other of youthful and attractive maidens. In a verse account of Moloch-worship Blake refers to how one of the Daughters of Albion was

> Taught to touch the harp, to dance in the Circle of Warriors
> Before the Kings of Canaan, to cut the flesh from the Victim,
> To roast the flesh in fire, to examine the Infants' limbs
> In cruelties of holiness, to refuse the joys of love ...
> (*Jerusalem*, K 706–7; pl. 68, 56–9)

It appears likely that he intended the young women of the *Nativity Ode* illustration to represent the Daughters, sadistic in the rites of death as in the rites of love; and the men, the (equally sadistic) warriors. War to Blake was an occupation of old men, hardened in attitude if not in years, and was frequently associated with the repression of sexual energy. The groups in *Nativity Ode* v are clearly differentiated by position and by age, as well as by sex. The illustration also shows two figures kneeling before the idol. These are turned away from the Christ-child and each is stretching out an arm in a futile attempt to prevent his emergence—for fallen man, though tormented by his divided nature, is unable to recognize and respond to the prospect of regeneration.

When the flames which belch out from the interior of the idol eventually consume it, as they appear likely to do, Moloch will have been annihilated by his own devilish

---

[29] Blake was familiar with some of the writings of Paracelsus, and possibly with those of other alchemists as well.

engine of sacrifice. The downcast expression of the idol, while it belies the impassive metal of which it is composed, indicates that he is aware of his approaching fate. That he hovers on the borders of a macabre consciousness is also suggested in the clutch with which he grasps one of the child-sacrifices.

Moloch's present victims, the children who are reaching up to him with the pathetic trustfulness of the innocent, are thus destined to be saved from his deadly embrace to become citizens of the kingdom of Christ—who is here represented, like them, as a child, and who thus demonstrates the converse of the child's helplessness—the mysterious and majestic power of childlike innocence.

NATIVITY ODE VI: THE STAR OF BETHLEHEM (63, 64)

The last illustration of the series is the visual counterpart to the first. Both are dominated by a large Nativity stable with the Holy Family within and a beneficent guardian-deity above. The differences between the two plates, like those between the first and last verses of the poem, are slight but significant. Those which are taken from the poem—the laying to rest of Christ, the guarding of the stable by angels, and the settling of the Star of Bethlehem above the stable—mark the slow but inexorable passing of 'time present' on Christmas day. Other alterations, which were contributed by Blake, suggest the tightening of the grip of the fallen or generative world upon the child-soul as well as the passing of simple chronological time. These are the extensions to the stable, the falling asleep of Mary, the hooding of Joseph, and (in the Whitworth version only) the addition of an exposed roof-beam and a number of schematic stars, and a mysterious increase in the quantity of straw in the stable.

As already observed, the wings of the stable, which are shown in all its appearances after the first, suggest the spatial extension of the fallen world. The 'sleep' or 'dream' of life and the 'veil' of material existence are metaphorical figures frequently employed by Blake,[30] and schematically-drawn stars are often associated by him with the fallen world.

The illustrator's most striking revision is the raising of the level of straw in the Whitworth stable until it reaches halfway up the walls. The bizarre nature of this detail is emphasized by the fact that the oxen's heads are half covered but their eyes left to stare mournfully out at the viewer. The straw is piled up behind the Christ-child (now laid to rest in the manger) and the body of the Virgin Mary so that they appear on the flat surface of the plate as though engulfed by it.

The figure and situation of the Whitworth Christ are strongly reminiscent of those

[30] The name 'Vala', that of Blake's earth-goddess, is a pun on the word 'veil'.

of a tiny, corpse-like child in plate 9 of Blake's *America*, who has been smitten by the plagues of Albion's Angel—a surrogate for the tyrant Urizen—and stifled beneath a great sea of mown corn. This corn apparently represents the fallen or vegetative world overwhelming the soul. A similarly placed figure is to be found in Blake's illustration to Gray's *Progress of Poesy*, plate 11, and in his illustration to the line, 'Bid Death's dark Vale its Human Harvest yield', from Young's *Night Thoughts* (Night VII, p. 45, l. 914), which shows the human family engulfed in a jungle of corn and gazing up to heaven for assistance. In *Jerusalem* the cradle of grass, a vegetation symbol related to that of the corn, is explicitly identified with the fallen world—although here its function is the merciful one of preserving the soul:

> He who is an Infant and whose Cradle is a Manger
> Knoweth the Infant sorrow, whence it came and where it goeth
> And who weave it a Cradle of the grass that withereth away.
> This World is all a Cradle for the erred wandering Phantom,
> Rock'd by Year, Month, Day & Hour; and every two Moments
> Between dwells a Daughter of Beulah to feed the Human Vegetable.
>
> (K 688; pl. 56, 5–10)

The straw in the Nativity stable also appears to represent the vegetative world. Its rising therefore signifies not any bounty of nature but the overwhelming of the soul by the forces of that world.

The atmosphere of harmony and stability established at the beginning of the Ode is recaptured in its closing verses with the laying to rest of the Christ-child. In the Huntington version the leaning figures of Mary and of Christ support each other in sleep. Blake also conveys this sense of harmony and repose by depicting a personified (and therefore spiritual) Star of Bethlehem, lamp in hand and with the horses of her chariot resting on a belt of cloud:

> Heaven's youngest teemed star,
> Hath fixed her polished car,
> Her sleeping Lord with handmaid lamp attending
>
> (ll. 240–2)

Two of Blake's guardian-angels flank the stable so that their wings rise up against the roof to strengthen and 'humanize' its Gothic crown—just as the angels of *Vala* keep watch over the fallen Albion:

> hovering high over his head
> Two winged immortal shapes, one standing at his feet
> Toward the East, one standing at his head toward the west,
> Their wings join'd in the Zenith over head
>
> (K 341; 6–9)

They serve as a testament to the fact that man will eventually be redeemed—though their instruments of war, which are very prominent in *Nativity Ode* VI, particularly in the Huntington version with its double row of serried spears, remind us that the kingdom of Christ, though it will eventually be realized, is not yet at hand.

V L'ALLEGRO AND IL PENSEROSO

Blake's twelve *L'Allegro* and *Il Penseroso* illustrations exist only in a single series. They are signed but not dated—though as they are executed on paper watermarked 'M & J LAY 1816' they almost certainly belong 'either to that year or the next, for Blake is very unlikely to have bought more than a small quantity of expensive drawing paper at any one time'.[1] They were bought from the artist by Thomas Butts and today form part of the Blake collection at the Pierpont Morgan Library, New York. Their style is delicate and their texture highly worked, and they are more vividly coloured than most of the other Milton water-colours, with visionary reds, yellows, and oranges competing for predominance with the steely greyish-blues and blacks of restricted vision.

Twelve sheets of paper displaying writing in Blake's hand have been preserved with the illustrations. Each of them contains an appropriate quotation from *L'Allegro* or *Il Penseroso* and a note on the illustration concerned, together with, on the verso side, its original title.[2] The Notes, which are purely descriptive, seem a little impertinent, or even perverse, in their refusal to engage with any of the profound mysteries that are intimated by the illustrations.

Milton's companion-poems *L'Allegro* and *Il Penseroso* present a series of charming cameo scenes organized according to the diurnal interests and activities—desired rather than realized—of the contemporary gentleman and around his contrasting moods, the mirthful and the melancholy. This gentleman's identity with the poet has often been assumed but is not explicitly confirmed by the poems.

While preserving the charm of the companion-pieces Blake's illustrative series invests their subject-matter with a new and visionary intensity. It also transforms their elegantly counterpointed contrasts into an urgent antagonism between the saving

---

[1] Sir Geoffrey Keynes in Milton's *Poems in English*, 1926, ii, 274.
[2] These titles will be employed in this chapter, and the relevant Note quoted at the head of each section.

grace of the Divine Vision and the delusions of corrupted or blinkered perceptions. The constraints of the pictorial medium lend added conviction to Milton's invention, for they compel the actual delineation of scenes originally conceived in the hortatory, or wishful, grammatical mood. The poems' subjectivity is emphasized by the inclusion of Milton himself in two of the *L'Allegro* plates and in all except the first of the *Il Penseroso* pictures. His presence as 'perceiver' in illustrations to both poems, and the numbering of the illustrations in the Notes as a single sequence, suggest that Blake subscribed to the view that the poems reveal the different humours of a single man rather than the humours of two separate, and diametrically opposed, personalities.

The series also provides both a celebration and a critique of the life, the works, and the personality of the Poetic Genius Milton, presented in his triple role as Poet, Lover, and Man of God. Each of these roles is shown in the drawings to be intimately related to the others: the Poet takes as one of his major subjects the love of man for woman, his redemption is crucially dependent on his personal relations, and divine love—for which human, sexual love may serve as a symbol—is the motive force behind redemption.

Despite his visionary gifts Milton was also according to Blake the proponent of two signal 'errors'—a belief in tyranny both domestic and personal, and support for self-righteous sexual morality. These 'errors' are exposed in the *L'Allegro* and *Il Penseroso* illustrations, although in the concluding plate he is shown experiencing a vision of regeneration, rejoicing, and renewal in which he appears to overcome them both. This interpretation is similar to that offered in the Prophetic book *Milton*, in which the Puritan poet descends to earth a second time in order to 'correct' the errors of his previous existence, and in so doing becomes the eighth Eye of God, thus causing all eight Eyes to combine in the form of 'One Man, Jesus the Saviour, wonderful!' (K 534; pl. 42, 11). The Prophetic book also has several local points of similarity with the *L'Allegro* and *Il Penseroso* series—reverence for the humblest forms of life, the use of the Lark as a symbol of poetic inspiration, and the portrayal of the maiden Ololon as Milton's lost Emanation, a composite figure representing his three wives and three daughters.

The assumption that the 'I'-figure or observer of the companion-poems is also their author gives Blake the opportunity to explore the complex phenomenon of perception, and in particular to assert his Romantic belief that perception and execution are ideally simultaneous, that simply to envisage Truth should be to realize it. His inclusion of the figure of Milton within the illustrations emphasizes the poet's role as passive observer or perceiver—though this passivity is more apparent than real, for to Blake it is perception and the nature of the perceiver which are the crucial determinants of vision:

The tree which moves some to tears of joy is in the Eyes of others only a Green thing that stands in the way. Some See Nature all Ridicule & Deformity, & by these I shall not regulate my proportions; & Some Scarce see Nature at all. But to the Eyes of the Man of Imagination, Nature is Imagination itself.

(Letter to Dr. Trusler, 23 August 1799, K 793)

If Perceptive Organs vary, Objects of Perception seem to vary:
If the Perceptive Organs close, their Objects seem to close also.
(*Jerusalem*, K 661; pl. 34, 55–6)

The overriding significance to Blake of the 'visionary Moment' in which the dual act of perception and creation takes place led him to organize his poetic works around such moments and therefore to dispense with the representation in narrative of ordered, chronological time, and of much 'incidental' material as well. The structure of the poems *L'Allegro* and *Il Penseroso*—a series of 'moments of vision' loosely arranged around the poet's day and his night—lends itself readily to such an organizing principle, which is in fact that followed in the illustrative series.

The illustrations also reflect the loose organization, complex themes, and counter-pointing relationships of the poems themselves, which appear more preoccupied with the delightful variety of life than with the contrived 'unities' of art. The conventional stylistic oppositions of the opening plates—which are modelled on the introductory portraits of the poems—are quickly discarded in favour of a more flexible vision, and John E. Grant's view that the illustrative series represents an 'integrated progression from innocent poetic visions, through visions of experience, to the culmination in a "peaceful Hermitage"',[3] is an oversimplification which ignores the delusive state revealed in the fifth *L'Allegro* illustration and exaggerates the element of development present in the series.

Emphasis throughout the illustrations to *L'Allegro* and *Il Penseroso* is placed on the integrity and 'vision' of the separate plates, the lack of any narrative thread being offset by the employment of repeated themes, designs, and motifs. Blake has built on Milton's pattern of parallels and contrasts by adding a few of his own: four of his illustrations concern the nature of the inspiration that descends to the earth-bound poet, and his Milton—who is gaily dressed for his own appearance in the *L'Allegro* designs—is (like the Melancholy of the poem) clothed in black whenever he appears in the *Il Penseroso* plates. Edward J. Rose's attempt to pair the corresponding

---

[3] 'From Fable to Human Vision: A Note on the first Illustration' in *Blake's Visionary Forms Dramatic*, ed. David V. Erdman and John E. Grant, 1970, p. xi.

designs for each poem[4] contains some interesting insights but of necessity over-looks others—for example the parallels and contrasts between *L'Allegro* VI and *Il Penseroso* V, between the sun-figures of *L'Allegro* III and *Il Penseroso* IV, and between the third and fourth plates of the *L'Allegro* series—and it attributes to the series a consistency both greater and narrower than it in fact possesses.

Because Blake's illustrations are set in the contingent world and because their agent of vision is prone to err, values are not stable, solutions neither simple nor assured, and forms not immutable. The poet's sleep may be the repose of Divine Vision or the oblivion of Urizenic materialism; love may be tyrannical and sorrowing or blissfully selfless; the composed and beneficent dryad of *L'Allegro* IV has to be opposed by the broken and servile tree-spirits of *Il Penseroso* IV, and the phantasmal Fates of *L'Allegro* VI by the death-spinning sisters of *Il Penseroso* III. This flexibility, this lack of dogmatism, is in keeping with the on the whole tolerant mood of the illustrations and indeed of the poems themselves. It may be related to the fact that the Milton of *L'Allegro* and *Il Penseroso* was himself not encumbered by the strait-jacket of received theology and myth.

As already observed, Blake is primarily concerned not with the contrary aspects of man's nature as they are presented in the companion-poems but with the opposed states of Divine Vision and Urizenic delusion. This raises the question of how far he identifies Mirth and Melancholy respectively with one or other of these states.

On balance Mirth is more closely associated with the state of vision than Melan-choly, and Melancholy more intimately related to corporeal existence than Mirth: the first three plates of the *L'Allegro* series are devoted to the primary attributes of the Divine Vision—its fecundity, its inspirational quality, and its terrible grandeur—and almost all of the *Il Penseroso* plates contain strong evidence of deluded perception. On the other hand the fifth *L'Allegro* illustration is dominated by evil influence, and the final illustration of the *Il Penseroso* series is devoted to the sacred and prophetic aspects of Melancholy.

Blake's other works show a similar bias—and a similar ambiguity. Joy is repre-sented as an admirable, even a spiritual quality: 'I hate scarce smiles: I love laugh-ing' (*Annotations to Lavater*, K 67); 'I'll sing to you to this soft lute, and shew you all alive/The world, where every particle of dust breathes forth its joy' (*Europe*, K 237; pl. iii, 17–18); and in the fifth illustration to Gray's *Ode for Music* the Milton of *Il Penseroso* is shown astray in the fallen world—in contrast to Gray's own Milton, who is in 'celestial transport' (st. 2, l. 6). In the background to *Ode for Music* V is

[4] 'Blake's Illustrations for *Paradise Lost*, *L'Allegro*, and *Il Penseroso*: A Thematic Reading', op. cit., 62–4.

a grove of trees similar to that depicted in *Paradise Lost* VIII and X, and in the left and right foreground two leafless trees, one with exposed roots. The branches of these trees cross overhead to form an enclosed space similar to that of *L'Allegro* VI. The illustration contains a crescent moon as well as the figure of Milton. The sky beneath the branches is blue but that above has been left clear in order to differentiate between the 'corporeal' realm denoted by the enclosed space and the spiritual realm above. A distant church spire rises into the open sky above the branches. Milton's restrictive gesture—his arms are folded and wrapped in his cloak—is paralleled in several of the *Il Penseroso* plates.

On the other hand in a letter to Dr. Trusler (13 August 1799, K 793) Blake goes out of his way to draw a distinction between Mirth and the supreme vision: 'Fun I love, but too much Fun is of all things the most loathsom. Mirth is better than Fun, & Happiness is better than Mirth. I feel that a Man may be happy in This World. And I know that This World Is a World of imagination & Vision'; and in a prose piece entitled 'Contemplation' (*Poetical Sketches*, K 36–7) he presents an attractive portrait of Milton's Melancholy. The *Songs of Innocence and of Experience*, which S. Foster Damon considers to have been modelled on *L'Allegro* and *Il Penseroso*,[5] shows a clear bias in favour of Innocence, and Innocence is associated with joy; yet its delights are not unmixed with sorrow and foreboding, and, as the poem *Tiriel* reveals, Innocence when perpetuated in old age becomes grotesque.

The illustrations are preoccupied not only with the divorce between the divine and the natural worlds but also with the interrelationships between them—the inspiration that descends to the poet, sexual love and the dance as metaphors for the cosmic life (though earthly sexuality is also represented as being opposed to it), the essential, humanized forms of natural objects, and the eventual regeneration of the natural world. The dangers of spiritual impoverishment lie all about the man of genius but the prospect of redemption is never far away. Materialist philosophies, religions, or codes of perception are rejected not because they are yoked to the natural world but because they ignore its spiritual and regenerative essence. The specificities of space and time are accorded due significance, and beauty and divinity inform the meanest aspects of Nature.

The humanized forms of trees, plants, birds, natural features, and even literary and musical devices that throng the *L'Allegro* and *Il Penseroso* illustrations are perhaps the artist's clearest testament to the holiness and vitality of the natural world. They also bear witness to the Poetic Genius of the perceiver—Milton the poet or Blake

[5] See *A Blake Dictionary*, 1965, pp. 274–5, or *The Divine Vision*, ed. Vivian de Sola Pinto, 1957, p. 92.

the artist—for in contemporary times, as in the ancient world, it is only the Divine Vision of the poet which can perceive the sacred humanity of the natural world: 'The ancient Poets animated all sensible objects with Gods or Geniuses, calling them by the names and adorning them with the properties of woods, rivers, mountains, lakes, cities, nations, and whatever their enlarged & numerous senses could perceive' (*The Marriage of Heaven and Hell*, K 153; pl. 11). Even when the poet is in a state of 'error', as in the fifth *L'Allegro* illustration and in several of the *Il Penseroso* plates, his vision remains humanized. According to his own witness Blake too always retained this double, or allegorical, vision:

> For double the vision my Eyes do see,
> And a double vision is always with me.
> With my inward Eye 'tis an old Man grey;
> With my outward, a Thistle across my way.
>
> . . .
>
> May God us keep
> From Single vision & Newton's sleep!
> (Letter to Thomas Butts, 22 November 1802,
> K 817, 27–30, and K 818, 87–8)

By representing such an abundance of personified forms Blake is able to combine fidelity to Milton's highly metaphorical text with a revelation of the nature of his own Divine Vision. His plentiful use of personification is in no way incompatible with the celebrated attacks on allegory which he made in his *Vision of the Last Judgement* (K 604 and 614), for there he was preoccupied not with spiritual forms but with artificial abstractions invented in the interest of moral instruction: 'Allegories are things that Relate to Moral Virtues. Moral Virtues do not Exist' (K 614).

Besides their wholly or partially allegorized figures, which in an artist's hands translate naturally into human shape, *L'Allegro* and *Il Penseroso*—which were described by the Richardsons as 'Exquisite Pictures'[6]—are pictorially biased throughout. They present a series of visual (though generally not visualized) cameo scenes, the manner and ordering of whose leading details are 'imaginable as a painting'[7]—a gift to any artist.

---

[6] *Explanatory Notes and Remarks on Milton's Paradise Lost*, 1734, p. xvi.
[7] Jean H. Hagstrum, *The Sister Arts*, 1958, p. xxii, defining a pictorial description or image.

L'ALLEGRO I and separate engravings: MIRTH (65–7)

> Heart easing Mirth.
> Haste thee Nymph, & bring with thee
> Jest & Youthful Jollity,
> Quips & Cranks, & Wanton Wiles,
> Nods & Becks, & Wreathed Smiles,
> Sport that wrinkled Care derides,
> And Laughter holding both his Sides.
> Come, & trip it as you go
> On the light phantastic toe,
> And in thy right hand lead with thee,
> The Mountain Nymph, Sweet Liberty.

These Personifications are all brought together in the First Design Surrounding the Principal Figure which is Mirth herself.

> *(On the Illustrations to Milton*, K 617–18)

When hailing Mirth and her companions Milton makes Mirth the focal point of his invocation, only referring to her companions by way of their association with her. Jean Hagstrum has identified this organizing principle—'the grouping of subordinate figures around a central one'[8]—as one of the distinguishing characteristics of literary pictorialism, so it is not surprising to find that Blake, as his Note on the first *L'Allegro* illustration indicates, has adopted it himself.

His goddess Mirth is frontally portrayed and shown tripping gaily on 'light fantastic toe' (l. 34) over a grassy hillside. She is represented as an Olympian figure twice the size of the two companions depicted on either side of her. Her significance is reflected in her size and centrality, her urgency in the fact that she appears about to dance right out of the frame of the picture and into the world of the viewer. Her left hand is raised and seems to be beckoning to all who would see or hear to accompany her and experience her delights. The figures of the five dancers collectively form a shape that swells outwards and upwards from their feet to suggest the rounded forms of burgeoning life.

The air is filled with 'joys' whose numbers and whose communicative gestures reflect the bounty and the companionable nature of Mirth. Some are nearly as big as the goddess's dancing companions, others so tiny that their activities can barely be discerned with the 'natural' eye although they clearly have a rich and self-sufficient existence of their own.

The delicacy, buoyancy, and exuberant gesturing that are common to all the

[8] *The Sister Arts*, p. 28.

figures suggest a freedom from gravitational forces which in turn implies spiritual emancipation. So tentative is the contact that they make with each other and with the ground—generally it is made, if made at all, with the tips of the fingers or toes—that it too may be construed as evidence of immateriality.

Besides the water-colour drawing which is the first plate of the *L'Allegro* series, the design also exists as the first and second states of an engraved plate. The first state of the engraving is delicately executed in line and stipple; the second, which is in fact the first largely rubbed down and re-executed, is vigorously drawn but in line only. Both of the engraved states and the water-colour are similar in design though there are some differences between them in detail and in their conceptions of the central figure. Each engraving survives only in a single print.

The Mirth of the water-colour conveys the sweetness and ethereal delicacy of a Botticelli figure; that of the first engraved state, a restrained and somewhat conventional beauty. In the other engraving she appears as a truly 'debonair' young girl making an impetuous sally towards the viewer. In the water-colour and the first engraved state she wears a coronet of roses, in the second engraving a headband. In all three versions her hair cascades down her back in a flood of luxuriant curls. In the second engraved state these reach right down to her ankles. The curls on either side of her face are jerked upwards by the motion of her steps, and the circle thus begun is completed by a band of tiny figures that form a humanized halo as they rise and fall. In the engravings the halo consists only of four figures; the upper pair are blowing trumpets and the lower pair shaking tambourines. The infants depicted within a glory surrounding the throne of Christ in Blake's 'Vision of the Last Judgment' represent 'Eternal Creation flowing from The Divine Humanity in Jesus' (*Description of a Vision of the Last Judgment*, K 444): the figures that glorify the head of Mirth appear likewise to be the product of a quasi-divine vitality. The goddess's robes are fashionably diaphanous and fully reveal the countours of her 'buxom' figure.

On either side of Mirth are a sprightly lad and lass, the 'Jest and youthful Jollity' coupled in line 26 of the poem. They are dressed respectively in decorative waistcoat and breeches and in trim bodice and swathed skirt, and are communicating through gesture. In the water-colour they are also glancing flirtatiously at each other behind the goddess's back.

With the thumb and forefinger of her right hand Mirth is lightly touching the raised hand of an attractive girl dressed in a loose, knee-length robe and with a quiver of arrows strapped to her back: 'And in thy right hand lead with thee,/The mountain nymph, sweet Liberty' (ll. 35–6). In the engravings Liberty has a bow as well, though the casual elegance with which she is drawing an arrow from its quiver suggests that the violence which she threatens is metaphorical. Her expression is both grave and gentle. In the engravings her right breast is bared: this hints at an association with the fabled warrior race of Amazons and at sexual rather than purely military or political freedom.

'Laughter holding both his sides' (l. 32) is figured as the quaint youth hovering in mid-air to the left of the goddess, Mirth evidently making him airborne—and tilting him sideways as well. A 'wreathed smile' (l. 28) is spread across his face. In the second state of the engraving the line 'LAUGHTER holding both his sides' is somewhat superfluously inscribed above him.

The pair of figures in the upper left-hand corner—a maiden pointing downwards with both index fingers and glancing gleefully up at her companions, and a careworn old man with darkened figure, whose own hands are open and raised to shoulder height and who is the object of her gesture—are also labelled in the second state of the engraving, as 'SPORT that wrinkled CARE derides'.

Launched in the water-colour and in the first engraving from the tip of Mirth's index finger is a tiny trumpeter who has just expelled three bubbles—minute 'globes of vision'—from his instrument. Beneath the bubbles hover a man and a woman in the water-colour, and a man, woman, and child in the engraved versions. The child is apparently being handed from father to mother. These tiny figures, who are all positioned about the gesturing left hand of Mirth and making distinctive gestures of their own, are the Becks of line 28.

The four figures who share Sport's joke with her in the upper left-hand corner of the plate mimic both severally and combined, and with their arms and bodies, the 'wreathed smiles' which they represent, and the tiny beings that trace a halo about Mirth's head are the Nods of the poem. 'Nods, and becks, and wreathed smiles' (l. 28), are also represented directly in the movements and expressions of almost all of the figures in the picture.

The farthest right of the earthbound figures is a female with hair (or a headpiece) coiled on either side of her head and a toupée that is wafted upwards by motion or by a breeze. In the engravings she has feline whiskers. Springing from beside or behind her left shoulder and pointing down at her is a dragon-winged figure, and balancing on its back with the tip of a pointed toe is a grotesque contortionist with animal ears, his right arm wrapped about what appears to be his right knee and his left arm raised straight up in the air. The animal attributes of this trio suggests that the delights it offers may not be unqualified.

In the engraved states the chain continues further: a diminutive figure holding a hand-mirror is perched on the contortionist's open palm, and hovering above it are two more figures of comparable size, one pouring a libation from a pitcher and the other receiving it in his goblet. They suggest the charity that may be associated with Mirth. John E. Grant[9] draws a comparison between them and two planetary spirits drawn by Blake for Young's *Night Thoughts* (Night VI, p. 32), in which one figure also pours from a pitcher and the other holds out a flat basin, this time in response to the following couplet: 'The Planets of each System represent/Kind Neighbours; mutual Amity prevails' (ll. 728–9). The equivalents of these tiny 'joys' are also present in the water-colour, though there their exact postures and activities are indistinct.

The dragon-winged figure almost certainly represents a Quip; the earthbound female at whom he is pointing, his butt. Her hair, which is coiled about her ears, protects them from the barbs of his sharp wit. The contortionist is an ingeniously represented Crank—tentatively defined by Thomas Warton as 'CROSS-PURPOSES, or some other similar conceit of conversation, surprising the company by its intricacy, or embarrassing by its difficulty',[10] and with more confidence by W. Bell as 'literally a crook or bend; ... a form of speech in which words are twisted away from their ordinary meaning'.[11] The diminutive figures above the contortionist are Milton's 'wanton wiles', to be understood in their slightly archaic (and milder) significance as 'playful tricks'. So it can be seen that Blake preserves a close pictorial association between figures that were originally associated in the text—in this case the 'Quips and cranks, and wanton wiles' of line 27.

The negative potential of these figures and of 'Sport that wrinkled Care derides' (l. 31) is controlled by the humanizing and optimistic vision of the poet so that the figures appear more whimsical than subversive, though they do herald the sexual antagonisms that are dramatized later in the *L'Allegro* series. They also serve to warn us that the bounties of Mirth do not represent the ultimate ecstasies of the spirit but the qualified bliss of the Divine Vision on earth. However, it should be remembered that a similarly ambiguous scene, 'With trees & fields full of Fairy elves/ And little devils who fight for themselves', described by Blake in a letter to Butts (22 November 1802, K 816; ll. 5–6), terminates in the intensities and the unsurpassable magnificence of 'fourfold vision'.

Beneath the second state of the engraving is an inscription that runs: 'Solomon

---

[9] 'The Meaning of Mirth and Her Companions in Blake's Designs for "L'Allegro" and "Il Penseroso"', *Blake Newsletter*, v, iii (Winter 1971–2), 201.

[10] John Milton, *Poems Upon Several Occasions*, ed. Thomas Warton, 1791, p. 44.

[11] John Milton, *Nativity Ode, Lycidas, Sonnets and Comus*, ed. W. Bell, 1929, p. 27.

says, "Vanity of Vanities, all is Vanity," & What can be Foolisher than this?' (K 773). Its inclusion by Blake testifies to the faith he placed in the spirituality of Mirth. The mirror-gazing figure of the engravings may suggest an irreverent play on Solomon's words. Years earlier, when illustrating Young's *Night Thoughts*, Blake had represented those worldly beings who 'see no further than the Clouds; and dance/ On heedless Vanity's phantastic Toe' (Night VI, p. 32, ll. 624–5)—clearly an echo of line 34 of *L'Allegro*—as an attractive maiden very similar to his Mirth. In ironic obedience to Young's lines he shows her poised unawares at the edge of the grave—but as innocent victim rather than as vain and pleasure-seeking hoyden.

The natural setting of *L'Allegro* I has been reduced but not entirely suppressed. It is shown in a tiny fringe of grass, woodland, hamlets, and a stretch of water at the very foot of the picture. The contrast in scale between the comparatively Olympian stature of Mirth herself and the minuteness of the landscape emphasizes Blake's Berkeleyan belief that the nature of the physical universe is crucially dependent on that of the man or woman who perceives it. The presence of the landscape, though reduced, indicates that the natural world—dismissed in some of Blake's works—does have a place in Mirth's redeeming vision. The colouring of the dawn sky—vivid orange above the horizon, light and luminous overhead—suggests that this Nature hovers on the threshold of transfiguration into spirit. This promise of transfiguration is perhaps the greatest of Mirth's gifts.

L'ALLEGRO II: THE LARK (68)

The Lark is an Angel on the Wing. Dull Night starts from his Watch Tower on a Cloud. The Dawn with her Dappled Horses arises above the Earth. The Earth beneath awakes at the Lark's Voice.

> (*On the Illustrations to Milton*, K 618)

In the splendid second illustration of the series the great Lark is shown soaring freely above the confines of the natural world. Though described in Blake's Note as 'an Angel on the Wing', he is conceived in the picture as a naked boy-child with delicate features and a flame-like peak of hair. His magnificent golden wings indicate his spirituality while his human body asserts his relevance to man.

Just beneath him, and watching his ascent with some apprehension, is the shrunken figure of Night—shrunken because his influence is already on the wane. He is peering around the edge of his battlemented 'watch-tower in the skies', the top of which protrudes from a horizontal band of cloud. Only his head and right shoulder are visible but his white hair and beard are sufficient to identify him as Blake's tyrant of the fallen world—here less fearsome than usual, for he has already ceded the hour to youth.

In the lower sky a wraith-like maiden with the Morning Star trapped in her streaming veil is gliding across the plate. Her arms are outstretched and her dappled horses straining before her. Visually she is an avatar of the charioteer-goddess who also figures as Diana in the fourth plate of the *Comus* series; iconographically she represents the dawn. The brief duration of the dawn is conveyed by her insubstantial appearance and diaphanous robes, and by the pink flowers—presumably roses, traditional symbols of ephemeral beauty and inextricably linked since Homer with the dawn—which are caught in her robe. The rest of her figure, but especially her veil, is also touched with pink. Her four dappled horses—taken over perhaps from the quadriga of the sun, for the goddess of the dawn was normally represented driving a pair—derive from the animating of a poetic epithet—the adjective 'dappled', which in the poem simply qualifies the dawn itself.

At the foot of the picture the veiled spirit of Earth, appropriately clothed in brown, is shown rising from her dewy couch and gazing in adoration at the golden Lark. Their relationship, and her position and significance, are similar to those of Nature and Peace in *Nativity Ode* I. Textually the portrayal is indebted not to the cameo-description of the Lark's rise but to a slightly later scene in which reference is made to

> how the hounds and horn
> Cheerly rouse the slumb'ring morn,
> From the side of some hoar hill
> (ll. 53–5)

In the Prophetic book *Milton* a succession of larks—all bodily forms of the same 'eternal identity'—mounts through the twenty-seven 'Heavens' of the natural world and into the heaven of heavens beyond. This Lark is explicitly associated with poetic inspiration:

> Mounting upon the wings of light into the Great Expanse,
> Reecchoing against the lovely blue & shining heavenly Shell,
> His little throat labours with inspiration; every feather
> On throat & breast & wings vibrates with the effluence Divine.
> (K 520; pl. 31, 32–5)

As if affirming the connection between the Lark of *Milton* and that of *L'Allegro* II, Blake describes the former as appearing in the shape of a 'mighty Angel' (K 527;

pl. 36, 12) and as 'Los Messenger' (K 526; pl. 35, 63),[12] and locates its nest as the 'eastern/Gate' (K 526; pl. 35, 66–7), which is cited also at line 59 of *L'Allegro*.

The lark is a felicitous symbol for poetic inspiration, for it suggests the lofty and inspired flights of the Romantic poet as well as the beauty and apparent spontaneity of his utterances. The Lark of *L'Allegro* 11 is associated as well with a preternatural reconciliation of oppositions—humanity and divinity, motion and fixity, minuteness and sublime proportions, fleeting appearance and duration. His size on the plate indicates his true grandeur but it also reveals the discrepancy between the way in which he appears to mortal eyes and his 'visionary' dimensions. Both his size and his 'divine humanity' affirm that he has been perceived and depicted by an artist (Blake? Milton?) who is possessed of that Divine Vision which he himself embodies. Some critics have conjectured that the Earth-figure who is gazing up at him may also be intended to represent the poet Milton.

The Lark of the Prophetic book *Milton* is to Kathleen Raine an image of that 'minute center in which eternity expands'.[13] As far as the category of Time is concerned, the expansive moment of the Lark's soaring flight is equivalent to that of poetic inspiration:

> Every Time less than a pulsation of the artery
> Is equal in its period & value to Six Thousand Years,
> For in this Period the Poet's Work is Done, and all the Great
> Events of Time start forth & are conciev'd in such a Period,
> Within a Moment, a Pulsation of the Artery.
>
> (K 516; pl. 28, 62–pl. 29, 3)

The ambiguous nature of this 'instant', momentary and yet equivalent to the fabled duration of the world, is suggested in the *L'Allegro* Lark's frozen but still soaring posture.

The 'lovely blue & shining heavenly Shell' (*Milton*, K 520; pl. 31, 33) of the material world is reproduced in the sky against which the Lark rises. This is studded with the stars of materialism and coloured a deep and impervious, Urizenic blue on the left-hand side of the picture, where 'Dull Night' raises his melancholy head, though more luminous tones are visible in the direction towards which Dawn is moving. At one point in *Milton* the earthbound deity Los is represented as a fledgling trapped within the Mundane Egg—a symbol of the material world and one borrowed by Blake from the Hindu and Orphic mythologies:

---

[12] The Greek word from which 'angel' is derived means 'messenger'.

[13] *Blake and Tradition*, ii, 162. Cf. also the Introduction to my discussion of the *Nativity Ode* plates.

> ... Los heard them [i.e. the Eternals], as the poor bird within the shell
> Hears its impatient parent bird, and Enitharmon heard them
> But saw them not, for the blue Mundane Shell inclos'd them in.
>
> (K 504; pl. 21, 28–30)

The ecstatic flight of the Lark of *L'Allegro* II suggests the release of this imprisoned being.

In *Milton* Blake also speaks of the twenty-seven 'eras' of the Christian church, which he compares to 'twenty-seven-folds of opakeness' (K 498; pl. 17, 26). This 'fold' metaphor is preserved in *L'Allegro* II, which is arranged in four roughly horizontal layers.[14] These are occupied (from top to bottom) by the Lark himself, by old Father Night, by the Dawn, and by the spirit of Earth. Despite the basically horizontal arrangement of the design the diagonal thrust that is set in motion by the rising figure of Earth runs disturbingly through each of the layers. The horizontal pattern is finally ruptured and the diagonal stress exalted by the Lark, who soars, with arms and wings uplifted, towards the heavens.

The awakening of Earth at the Lark's song suggests that she is at last fulfilling the role allotted to her in the *Songs of Innocence and of Experience*:

> In futurity
> I prophetic see
> That the earth from sleep
> (Grave the sentence deep)
>
> Shall arise and seek
> For her maker meek;
>
> ('The Little Girl Lost', K 112; 1–6)

> O Earth, O Earth, return!
> Arise from out of the dewy grass;
> Night is worn,
> And the morn
> Rises from the slumberous mass.

So the moment which heralds a new day is analogous to that in which inspiration is born to the poet; and this in turn is reminiscent of, and indeed helps to create, the apocalyptic moment in which the regeneration of the world takes place. Within the space of this moment Earth is to be redeemed by Spirit, by one who is at once artist, youthful lover, and Divine Humanity.

[14] Cf. the concept of 'four-fold vision', discussed in connection with the following illustration.

L'ALLEGRO III: THE SUN AT HIS EASTERN GATE (69)

The Great Sun is represented clothed in Flames, Surrounded by the Clouds in their Liveries, in their various Offices at the Eastern Gate; beneath, in Small Figures, Milton walking by Elms on Hillocks green, The Plowman, The Milkmaid, The Mower whetting his Scythe, & The Shepherd & his Lass under a Hawthorn in the Dale.

(On the Illustrations to Milton, K 618)

The third illustration is dominated by the great globe of the sun. Within it stands the sun-god—a handsome, naked youth who is poised to begin his 'state', or stately progress, round the earth. He is shown standing erect and gazing straight ahead, with arms extended sideways and body frontally positioned—a posture which enables him fully to display that 'Naked Beauty' without which 'Art & Science cannot exist' (*Jerusalem*, K 663; pl. 36, 49).

His attributes are appropriately majestic. He is enclosed within a fiery mandorla— the 'flames, and amber light' (l. 61) with which he is 'robed' in the poem, and which is itself set within the golden sphere of the sun, though the mandorla's flames break out of the sphere at its topmost point: Energy retains its vital nature even when controlled and directed by the 'bound' of Reason.[15] A smaller sun with spear-sharp rays is placed behind and slightly to the right of the god's head and serves him for a halo. He is wearing a spiked crown (also reminiscent of sunbeams) and holding a sceptre with a fleur-de-lis head. The sceptre points downwards, indicating the direction of his rays.

With his prophetic gaze, his spiked crown and halo, and his splendid regalia, the sun-god appears a rather fearsome figure. This quality derives partly from the nature of the sun itself. In Blake's juvenile lyric 'To Summer' the estival spirit is requested to 'curb (his) fierce steeds, allay the heat/That flames from their large nostrils!' (K 1, 2–3); and in 'Day' (*Poems from the Note-book 1793*, K 177) the sun is described (arising)

> ... in the East,
> Cloth'd in robes of blood & gold;
> Swords & spears & wrath increast
> All around his bosom roll'd,
> Crown'd with warlike fires & raging desires.

Another sun-god and agent of prophecy, the Apollo of classical Greece, who was himself associated with occasional barbarities like the flaying of Marsyas, is with

---

[15] Cf. *The Marriage of Heaven and Hell*, K 149; pl. 4: 'Energy is the only life, and is from the Body; and Reason is the bound or outward circumference of Energy.'

his golden locks and 'ideal male figure, which has reached its full growth, but still has all the suppleness and vigour of youth',[16] reminiscent of the sun-god of *L'Allegro* III.

In *Milton* the sun-god is represented as Los, the Zoa of poetry and of the Imagination. Blake describes his own terror and exultation as the god descends right into his soul:

> And Los behind me stood, a terrible flaming Sun, just close
> Behind my back. I turned round in terror, and behold!
> Los stood in that fierce glowing fire, & he also stoop'd down
> And bound my sandals on in Udan-Adam; trembling I stood
> Exceedingly with fear & terror, standing in the Vale
> Of Lambeth; but he kissed me and wish'd me health,
> And I became One Man with him arising in my strength.
> 'Twas too late now to recede. Los had enter'd into my soul:
> His terrors now posses'd me whole! I arose in fury & strength.
> (K 505; pl. 22, 6–14)

The abundant curls of the god of *L'Allegro* III also relate him to Los, and especially to Los in his aspect as the spirit of time:

> Los is by mortals nam'd Time ...
> But they depict him bald & aged who is in eternal youth
> All powerful and his locks flourish like the brows of morning
> (*Milton*, K 509; pl. 24, 68–70)

In Blake's system, as in the Christian religion, it is only through time that man may be redeemed: 'Time is the mercy of Eternity; without Time's swiftness,/Which is the swiftest of all things, all were eternal torment' (*Milton*, K 510; pl. 24, 72–3). It is therefore appropriate that Los the redeemer should represent time—in particular time present, that perpetually renewed moment in which all thoughts are thought and all actions acted out. This aspect of time is manifested by Blake's Chronos, who is the embodiment of youthful vigour:

The Greeks represent Chronos or Time as a very Aged Man; this is Fable, but the Real Vision of Time is in Eternal Youth. I have, however, somewhat accomodated my Figure of Time to the common opinion, as I myself am also infected with it & my Visions also infected, & I see Time Aged, alas, too much so.

> (*A Vision of the Last Judgment*, K 614)[17]

In *Milton* the Lark, who of course precedes the Sun in the *L'Allegro* sequence of

---

[16] H. J. Rose, *A Handbook of Greek Mythology*, sixth edn., 1958, p. 134.

[17] The painting referred to here has been lost but the 'accomodation' which Blake confesses to having made can also be seen in several of his *Night Thoughts* illustrations—for example those for Night II, pp. 12 and 16.

plates, is described as 'Los's Messenger' (K 526; pl. 35, 67), and the 'awful Sun'
is described 'Stand(ing) still upon the Mountain looking on this little Bird [i.e. the
Lark]/With eyes of soft humility & wonder, love & awe' (K 520; pl. 31, 36–8).

Blake frequently uses the sun as a touchstone for determining whether or not an
individual is possessed of the humanizing Divine Vision or of the blinkered and prosaic vision of fallen man: ' "What," it will be Question'd, "When the Sun rises,
do you not see a round disk of fire somewhat like a Guinea?" O no, no, I see an
Innumerable company of the Heavenly host crying "Holy, Holy, Holy is the Lord
God Almighty" ' (*A Vision of the Last Judgment*, K 617). The humanized sun of *L'Allegro* III, like the Lark of the preceding plate, is evidently being viewed by an agent
of the Divine Vision.

In the visionary context of the illustration there is scarcely a form that remains
unhumanized. Around the upper hemisphere of the sun's globe for instance personified clouds are to be seen performing their 'various Offices'. The females on the
left are pouring decanters of rain-water down the margin of the plate; three of them
are also offering up harvest fruits, the product of their labours. They may represent
the three Fates harnessed to the beneficent cycle of nature. The diminutive figures
hovering above them are the spirits of the water and the fruits. Two of the clouds
on the right are also offering up harvest fruits, and one who is not, a quiffed and
woebegone, head-clutching figure placed against a dark background, is being
rejected or pushed away by the sun-god's left hand. He must surely stand for the
storm-clouds which ruin the harvest and which form no alliance with the sun.

The 'figure in the sun' presides not only over the seasonal transformation of flowers
into fruits but also over its human analogue, the resurrection of the soul. The three
figures depicted beneath the god's outstretched right arm are newly risen souls still
clutching their cinerary urns. Their transformation is heralded by trumpeter-angels
shown both within and below the sphere of the sun, and prefigured by two winged
insects, probably butterflies, depicted in the trees below. Two of the angels within
the sun are wearing spiked haloes. Depicted beneath the god's left arm is a boy
who is bearing a flat wicker basket of fruits on his head: he may be either a cloud-
spirit or a figure who is being regenerated.

It comes as something of a shock to realize that the sun-god, who dominates the
plate so completely, is in fact balancing on tiptoe upon the highest mountain of
a whole world, which is represented in miniature as a pastoral landscape at the foot
of the picture. The mountain is wreathed in trailing cloud, clouds in the world beneath appearing merely as clouds. Not only the feet of the sun-god but also his
extremities at the other three points of the compass—his extended left hand, the

tip of the staff held in his right hand, and his topmost lock of hair—fall outside the circumference of the sphere. These breaches of his own element suggest his ability to penetrate, and hence to redeem, all quarters of the world.

While the god's left foot is poised upon the mountain-top his right foot rests on a line that stretches across the width of the plate, just above the top of the mountain, to form a kind of false roof to the world. Beneath this line is the pastoral landscape, which is peopled with tiny figures representing the ploughman, the milkmaid, the mower, the shepherd with his lass,[18] and Milton himself, 'walking not unseen' (l. 57) on the hillocks. Upon either extremity of the false 'roof' stands an angel with a trumpet. A second 'roof' is drawn above the first and just below the level of the angels' waists. To either side of the landscape is a tree containing a winged figure. These trees are the only objects of the lower world to extend above the false horizon. The winged figures within them are depicted just above the level of the second 'roof'.

The three territories formed by these 'roofs'—the rural landscape, the area between the two horizons, and the area above the upper horizon which is not occupied by the sphere of the sun—together with the sphere itself, represent the four 'levels' of vision to which Blake frequently refers in his poetry. His most concise description of them is contained in a verse letter to Butts dated 22 November 1802:

> Now I a fourfold vision see,
> And a fourfold vision is given to me;
> 'Tis fourfold in my supreme delight
> And threefold in soft Beulah's night
> And twofold Always. May God us keep
> From Single vision & Newton's sleep!
>   (K 818, 83–8)[19]

The sun-god is largely contained within the sphere or region of 'fourfold vision[20] but he penetrates the other three levels as well. It is characteristic of the tolerant mood of the series that even the normally debased state of 'Single vision' should be represented as a land of pastoral tranquillity, and that even it should be included in the sun-god's blessing.

The sizes of the figures depicted in each of the four areas vary according to

---

[18] Cf. *L'Allegro*, ll. 63–8, and Blake's Note on the illustration.

[19] The same letter again represents Los as the god of the sun, and uses the sun as a touchstone of multiple, spiritual vision: 'Then Los appear'd in all his power:/In the Sun he appear'd, descending before/My face in fierce flames; in my double sight/'Twas outward a Sun: inward Los in his might' (K 818, 55–8).

[20] Cf. *Jerusalem*, K 666; pl. 39, 12–13: 'Los was the friend of Albion who most lov'd him. In Cambridgeshire/His eternal station, he is twenty-eighth & is four-fold.'

whether the figures belong to a state of greater or of lesser vision. The layered presentation of the three lower states suggests the gradational nature of Blake's universe and also preserves the metaphor of the 'folds' of vision, for each state marks a fold, as it were, in the painting. It is fitting that the fourth state, being different in kind as well as in degree from the others, should be represented not by a fourth 'layer' on a plane surface but by a sphere—a traditional symbol for eternity.[21] The sphere can in fact be 'read' as a two-dimensional disc, a kind of backdrop for the god, as well as a three-dimensional globe upon whose rotund surface the trumpet-playing angels and the urn-carrying cherubs enact their two-dimensional existences: that which is three-dimensional to the lower, appears as two-dimensional to the higher.

L'ALLEGRO IV: A SUNSHINE HOLIDAY (70)

In this design is Introduced,

> Mountains on whose barren breast,
> The Laboring Clouds do often rest.

Mountains, Clouds, Rivers, Trees appear Humanized on the Sunshine Holiday. The Church Steeple with its merry bells. The Clouds arise from the bosoms of Mountains, While Two Angels sound their Trumpets in the Heavens to announce the Sunshine Holiday.

> (*On the Illustrations to Milton*, K 618)

This illustration is preoccupied with earthly, sexual love and with the possibility of its translation into adoration of the divine. The foreground of the picture is devoted to the holiday-makers described in lines 94 to 98 of *L'Allegro*. They are divided by Blake into two groups, one on the left of lithe and fashionably dressed young people dancing around a maypole to the strains of a rebeck, and the other on the right of a family group—mother, children, and grandparents. The absence of a father from this group may be significant. An area of dark shading covers the onlookers, the strip of ground on which they are standing, and the tree above them, and an area of intense, orange-green radiance illuminates both the dancers and the foliage to their rear—Blake's free rendering of Milton's 'chequered shade' (l. 96).

This distribution of light and shade suggests that the onlookers are separated from the revellers by more than the figure of the dance, and the diptych structure of the plate and its rural setting recall some of the 'illuminations' and verses of the *Songs*

[21] And therefore a fitting residence for Blake's god of time: cf. *Milton*, K 510; pl. 24, 72; 'Time is the mercy of Eternity'; and the Letter to William Hayley, 6 May 1800, K 797: 'The Ruins of Time builds Mansions in Eternity.'

of Innocence and of Experience.[22] It is possible that a juxtaposition of the values of Innocence and Experience, as well as of Mirth and Melancholy and of the various stages of human life, is intended—although it is not clear whether the allusion might be to the purity of Innocence and the corruption of Experience or to the frivolity of the former and the wisdom of the latter. In any event the dancers, who are taking part in the ancient fertility ritual of the maypole dance, suggest the preoccupation of youth with the polarities of social courtship and sexual potency; and the group on the right appears to have experienced the joys and sorrows of family life, matters by which the dancers are as yet untouched.

The 'unseen genius of the woods' (*Il Penseroso*, l. 154), whose solemn visage blends harmoniously with the foliage of the trees on the right, is gazing at the dancers and pointing upwards with the index finger of his right hand—apparently in an attempt to recall them from the transient summertime of their delight to the trials and values of eternity. His gesture is balanced by a non-human reminder of eternity, a Gothic steeple which rises out of the foliage on the left. Both the manner in which the tree-spirit is represented and the context in which he is placed suggest that he is to be associated with the Jack-in-the-Green, one form of the beneficent vernal spirit of vegetation, who was impersonated in May-day revels by a chimney-sweep dressed in a leaf-covered wicker frame. An association of the chimney-sweep with the spiritual quality of Innocence is made in the 'Chimney Sweeper' poems from Blake's *Songs of Innocence and of Experience*.

In the middle ground of the picture is a stream, which disappears from view for a short time before broadening out into a wide stretch of water. On the edge of this is a reclining figure. The arrangement suggests the 'Shallow brooks, and rivers wide' (l. 76) of Milton's description, but it also recalls Socrates' description of the River Acheron in the *Phaedo*:

flowing through other solitary places, and under the earth, (Acheron) devolves its waters into the Acherusian marsh, into which many souls of the dead pass; and abiding there for certain destined spaces of time, some of which are more and others less extended, they are again sent into the generation of animals.[23]

The figure on the margin of Blake's sheet of water may be that of a soul waiting to be reborn.

---

[22] As do some of the individual figures: cf. the elderly cripple and the child with similar figures represented on the 'London' plate (also with *Jerusalem*, K 729; pl. 84, 11–12: 'I see London, blind & age-bent, begging thro' the Streets/Of Babylon, led by a child; his tears run down his beard'), and the boy piper with the piper of Innocence.

[23] *The Works of Plato*, trans. T. Taylor and F. Sydenham, 1804, iv, 334–5.

At the apparent source of the river reclines a voluptuous river-goddess, her right arm resting on an overturned tub from which the head-waters of the river appear to flow. She is drinking from a conical goblet, the shape of which suggests the enchanted glass of *Comus* I and Rahab's 'Poison Cup/Of Jealousy' (*Jerusalem*, K 698; pl. 63, 39–40), and therefore that the goddess herself also has sinister connotations—presumably those of sexual tyranny.

Above the Acherusian 'lake' is a small hill with a figure reclining at its foot. The straight sides of the hill recall those of a pyramid, and the reclining figure that of the Sphinx. If the resemblance is more than coincidental then it is significant, for things Egyptian are insistently associated by Blake with the fallen world.

In the background to the illustration are a couple of mountains, personified as a reclining giant and giantess. The male is wearing a coronet of leaves, the woman a turreted crown. She is harbouring one of Milton's 'upland hamlets' (l. 92) in her lap and another is laid out before the man. A third is situated on the river-bank.

The position of the first hamlet is a reminder of Blake's belief that the material world has its only reality in the perceiving human mind:

> For all are Men in Eternity, Rivers, Mountains, Cities, Villages,
> All are Human, & when you enter into their Bosoms you walk
> In Heavens & Earths, as in your own Bosom you bear your Heaven
> And Earth & all you behold; tho' it appears Without, it is Within,
> In your Imagination, of which this World of Mortality is but a Shadow.
> (*Jerusalem*, K 709; pl. 71, 15–19)

In the fallen world, where such truths are no longer readily accessible, the arrangement also constitutes a call to action, for

> unless we plant
> The seeds of Cities & of Villages in the Human bosom
> Albion must be a rock of blood
> (*Jerusalem*, K 728; pl. 83, 54–6)

The turreted crown worn by the woman identifies her as Cybele,[24] the great fertility-goddess who according to myth destroyed or mutilated the sacred king after mating with him on a mountain-top. Cybele is also known as the spirit of mid-summer—a title appropriate to the seasonal setting of the illustration. In *L'Allegro* IV the body of the man is not visible and both figures convey a lassitude that approaches exhaustion.

[24] In the masque *Arcades* (ll. 21–2) Milton mentions 'the towered Cybele,/Mother of a hundred gods'; and in *Comus* (ll. 933–4) his Attendant Spirit blesses Sabrina, a gentler manifestation of the goddess of fertility, with another reference to Cybele: 'May thy lofty head be crowned/With many a tower and terrace round'.

A procession of tiny figures—the teeming issue of Cybele and perhaps the product of a recent orgy—is progressing from behind the goddess's right breast (one or two appear from behind the 'king') past the face of the 'natural' sun and into the upper sky. The figures are bearing musical instruments, chalices, and wicker baskets—the emblems and vessels of divinity—and are heralded by two angels with clarion trumpets: 'Every scatter'd Atom/Of Human Intellect now is flocking to the sound of the Trumpet' (*Milton*, K 510; pl. 25, 18–19). So the children of nature are shown to have their home in the world of the spirit. Their impulse towards ascent is strengthened by the struggles of several creatures still caught in the toils of the generative cycle. All of them are shown within or against the tree in the lower right-hand corner of the plate, attempting to take their place with the regenerating spirits. One is holding a trumpet to its lips and another is represented as a butterfly emerging from a chrysalis.

Despite her teeming fecundity Cybele herself is clearly unable to nurse her brood: though she is shown touching the nipple of her left breast it remains obstinately dry. As if to emphasize her aridity, a stream of water descends from the cloud that garlands her shoulders. It runs down her side to join the river in the middle ground of the picture. These details offer a whimsically literal representation of Milton's personification, 'Mountains on whose barren breast/The labouring clouds do often rest' (ll. 73–4), and suggest that female tyranny and natural fecundity are both, ironically, impotent.

L'ALLEGRO V: THE GOBLIN (71)

The Goblin, crop full, flings out of doors from his Laborious task, dropping his Flail & Cream bowl, yawning & stretching, vanishes into the Sky, in which is seen Queen Mab Eating the Junkets. The Sports of the Fairies are seen thro' the Cottage where 'She' lays in Bed 'pinchd & pulld' by Fairies as they dance on the Bed, the Ceiling, & the Floor, & a Ghost pulls the Bed Clothes at her Feet. 'He' is seen following the Friars Lantern towards the Convent.

(*On the Illustrations to Milton*, K 618)

In the fifth *L'Allegro* illustration 'she' and 'he', who in the poem figure only as the tellers of fragmentary, and unrelated, drinking stories—'She was pinch, and pull'd she sed,/And he by friers lantern led'[25]—are depicted as Everyman and Everywoman

[25] From the 1645 text of *L'Allegro*. This was used by Thomas Warton in his edition of Milton's *Poems upon Several Occasions*, the collection of the minor poems which Blake is most likely to have known. The later, 1673 text, which was used by Carey and Fowler, omits the 'he' of line 104 and attributes that and succeeding lines to the woman.

in the throes of serious sexual discord. The lad is shown at centre foreground, between a thatched cottage and a shed, and is following a ghostly figure with a lantern; the lass, who is alone in bed inside the cottage and plainly visible through its lattice windows, is being tormented by a lean and malevolent ghost and tweaked by tiny sprites 'on the Bed, the Ceiling, & the Floor' (Blake's Note, K 618). Other sprites are emerging from the ground to join in the sport. 'He' has the gait and the broad-brimmed hat of Blake's lost-traveller figure; 'she' is clutching her head with both hands—a sign of 'error' to Blake though here it is clearly a gesture of self-protection and despair as well.

The 'friar's lantern' which the lad is following is Milton's version of the Jack-and-lantern or will-o'-the-wisp of rural folklore. In the illustration it is shown in the possession not of a friar but of a ghost, though Blake manages to incorporate Milton's ecclesiastical allusion into his picture by including in the background the gate-house and part of the wall of a convent. The Note makes it clear that the convent is the lad's destination. The left-hand tower of the gate-house takes the form of a Gothic spire surmounted by a cross; that on the right, a rounded and possibly battle-mented Norman tower. The association of the tower with secret female delights may owe something to one of the cameo-scenes described in *L'Allegro* itself:

> Towers, and battlements it [i.e. mine eye] sees
> Bosomed high in tufted trees,
> Where perhaps some beauty lies,
> The cynosure of neighbouring eyes.
>
> (ll. 77–80)

The architectural medley hints at the common cause of state and established Church, an old point of grievance to radical Blake.

The plate is dominated by the colossal figure of the goblin rising up against the sky. To Milton he is a lumbering but well-meaning drudge—one who may be com-pared with the hobgoblins and Robin Goodfellows of folk superstition: Blake has transformed him into a grotesque and malevolent figure with flaps of skin over his ears and vestigial horns on the upper part of his forehead,[26] and a spectral body. This exists in outline only: through it the darkened, Urizenic sky and its schematic stars are clearly visible.

Having just emerged from a barn that could never have contained his grossness, the goblin is shown leaping vigorously into the air, his body, arms, and legs bent slightly backwards—an admirable rendition of Milton's verb 'flings'. He has just dropped his flail and cream-bowl, the instrument and the reward of his night's servile

---

[26] The animal comparison is subtly conveyed in the poem as well.

labours, and his unprepossessing features are contorted into a yawn that 'reads' more like a howl of rage. Significantly, he is positioned immediately above the retreating figure of the country lad.

Directly above the lass is the figure of Queen Mab—here a small and inconspicuous deity enthroned within the white sphere of the moon and placed at the top of a flight of steps that, as they lead nowhere, serve merely to emphasize her authority. Her 'junkets' are being served by a devotee bearing a tray on its head. The textual reference for this detail is 'How Faëry Mab the junkets eat' (l. 102)—in the poem the subject of yet another drinking story.

So the innocent folk superstitions and cosy story-telling of the text have been transformed into a grim drama of sexual discord and mental 'error'. Queen Mab, traditionally regarded as the bearer of lovers' dreams, is figured as a tyrannical ruler and as an image of the chaste moon-goddess, and the 'pinching' and 'pulling' of the text—according to tradition a punishment administered by the 'little people' to lazy and sluttish country servants—have become sexual torments, specifically the frustrations of unfulfilled sexuality, which are here meted out by the 'Ghost' and 'Fairies' but may also be self-inflicted. In following the friar's lantern Blake's lad is pursuing a will-o'-the-wisp of illusory happiness—the male fantasy that the delights of sex must be seized by force, the female fortress (here represented by the convent) taken by storm.

Both the goblin and Queen Mab may be regarded as subjective extensions of the states of mind of the figures below them: these have in turn fallen victim to their creations. Queen Mab's influence upon the Lady is realized in her determination to preserve her chastity and thus to make a timid and enfeebled servant of her mate. The goblin's rejection of the tools and fruits of labour dramatizes the lad's similar though less ostentatious denial of the labours and 'sweet delights' of love, and his— the goblin's—nakedness and unprepossessing appearance indicate the waywardness of the lad's mission. The form and position of the goblin as well as the context in which he is placed suggest that he is the lad's Spectre. Both the size of the goblin and the minuteness of the deity emphasize the gap between their pretensions and their true, or spiritual, significance: both figures are denied the proportions of Blake's 'human form divine'.

Though for lad and lass alike the 'sweets' of sexual fulfilment lie close at hand in a fulfilled and fulfilling relationship with each other, they have both rejected this, the gift of open-hearted and ever accessible Mirth—'he' for forbidden fruits, and 'she' for the illicit power of chastity. Their 'errors' are of course crucially interdependent.

L'ALLEGRO VI: THE YOUTHFUL POETS DREAM (72)

The youthful Poet, sleeping on a bank by the Haunted Stream by Sun Set, sees in his dream the more bright Sun of Imagination under the auspices of Shakespeare & Johnson, in which is Hymen at a Marriage & the Antique Pageantry attending it.

(*On the Illustrations to Milton*, K 618)

This illustration incorporates almost all the themes and motifs of the poem's last twenty-seven lines in a masterfully intricate design whose purpose is to glorify the splendour of the poet's vision. It depicts the 'youthful Poet' as Milton himself, asleep on a river-bank between two shallow-rooted trees and beneath their enclosing foliage. Just above him is an enormous globe that reveals the subject of his visionary dream. Its wisdom is being mediated to him by the spirits of Jonson and Shakespeare, who hover in mid-air on either side of it. The globe, the most striking detail of the picture, is entirely of Blake's invention.

Milton is represented in pastoral attire, with his broad-brimmed hat encircling his head like a halo and his slippers recalling the 'sock' of the comic actor. His body appears to be placed against a background of the river-bank rather than to be lying upon it—an indication that the spirit of Mirth is obeying the request to 'Lap (him) in soft Lydian airs' (l. 136). His position is relaxed and his eyes closed, and his expression is one of rapt and sensuous languor appropriate to a devotee of the Lydian mode. He appears to be greeting the gift of inspiration with his gesturing left hand while with his right he is transferring that inspiration to an enormous volume that lies open on a mound beside him.[27] The fact that his eyes are closed emphasizes that his inspiration is not derived from the external world and that his writing is 'automatic'. It may also be a reference to, in a sense a granting of, his plea in the invocation of Book III of *Paradise Lost* that he should be permitted to 'see and tell/ Of things invisible to mortal sight' (iii, 54–5).

Like Milton, Blake characterizes Jonson as the 'learned' artist and Shakespeare as 'fancy's child,/Warbl[ing] his native wood-notes wild' (ll. 133–4). His Jonson is staring into the distance and holding an open book and a quill pen while his Shakespeare is gazing at the viewer and holding a set of pan-pipes. He is also gesturing towards the natural world, the source of his inspiration. As Blake considered the works of Shakespeare, along with those of Milton, Michelangelo, Raphael, and 'the finest specimens' of ancient art, to reveal the 'extent of the human mind' (K 579), it is not surprising that he should have endowed him with the more prominent halo

---

[27] Anne Kostelanetz Mellor in *Blake's Human Form Divine*, 1974, p. 277, points out that he repeats on the horizontal plane the gestures of the Mirth of *L'Allegro* i.

and the more youthful visage of the two, nor that he should have bestowed upon him the 'peak of flame' hair-style worn by the Lark and by the sun-god of *L'Allegro* II and III.

Shakespeare's creative genius infuses the illustration in another way, for the well-known lines from *A Midsummer Night's Dream*[28] which describe the inspired poet at work provide it with an appropriate secondary referent:

> The poet's eye, in a fine frenzy rolling,
> Doth glance from heaven to earth, from earth to heaven;
> And, as imagination bodies forth
> The forms of things unknown, the poet's pen
> Turns them to shapes, and gives to airy nothing
> A local habitation and a name
>
> (v, i, 12–17)

Blake obviously knew the passage well, for he echoed it in *Milton*, plate 28, lines 1–5,[29] though Alexander Gilchrist records in his *Life* of the poet that he objected to the words 'and gives to airy nothing/A local habitation and a name' on the grounds that 'the things imagination saw were as much realities as were gross and tangible facts'.[30]

The notion of mediation is fundamental to Blake's theory of poetic creation. He claimed to have 'received' his own poetry through spiritual dictation: 'I may praise it [a long poem recently completed], since I dare not pretend to be any other than the Secretary; the Authors are in Eternity' (Letter to Thomas Butts, 6 July 1803, K 825);

> when I came
> Into my parlour and sat down and took my pen to write,
> My Fairy sat upon the table and dictated Europe.
>
> (*Europe*, K 238; pl. iii, 22–4)

He even sketched the spirit 'who instructed [him] in Painting &c. in [his] Dreams',[31] and in the drawing known as 'A Vision' he depicts the Poet inside a tiny, light-filled room at the centre of what appears to be a crystal, with his Angel of Poetry before him. In the letter to Dr. Trusler dated 16 August 1799 Blake called Milton himself to witness as a supporter of his theory of mediation: 'tho' I call [my Designs]

---

[28] One of the Shakespeare plays which is frequently echoed in *L'Allegro* and *Il Penseroso*.

[29] And also probably at plate 30, ll. 21–5.

[30] *Life of William Blake*, 1880 (2nd edn.), i, 364.

[31] Reproduced in *Pencil Drawings by William Blake*, ed. Geoffrey Keynes, 1956, pl. 48. The quotation is from an inscription added by Blake to one version of the drawing.

Mine, I know that they are not Mine, being of the same opinion with Milton when he says That the Muse visits his Slumbers & awakes & governs his Song when Morn purples the East' (K 792).[32]

The sun of this world, a tiny, orange-red sphere that hovers just above the horizon, is dwarfed by the globe of vision. It is without enlivening detail, though it floods the whole upper portion of the illustration, including the lowest sector of the globe, with the glowing colours of sunset. The juxtaposition between the two suns indicates the superiority of the 'Sun of Imagination' (K 618) over the sun of this world, and hence of imaginative over 'natural' vision. We may be reminded of Swedenborg's comparison between the 'spiritual' and 'natural' suns:

the Sun of the natural World is perfectly dead, but the Sun of the spiritual World is alive, inasmuch as it is the first Proceeding of the Divine Love and the Divine Wisdom ... The Sun of the natural World is pure Fire from which all Life is abstracted; but the Sun of the spiritual World is Fire in which there is Divine Life.[33]

Blake must have been well acquainted with this conception for he had read and annotated a copy of the work from which it is taken. Two of the passages he annotated also concern the doctrine of the two suns.[34]

The globe of vision itself is divided into an upper and a lower hemisphere, each of which is peopled with shadowy figures—nine in each section. Both of the central figures are standing full-face to the viewer. In the upper hemisphere those to either side of him—one apparently a man, the other a woman wearing a veil—are facing each other but their equivalents in the lower hemisphere, though touching heels and keeping their faces turned towards each other, have both taken a step away from the centre. At either extremity of the upper hemisphere are six shadowy figures who seem to be waiting their turn to move into the centre. Those directly beneath them are babies that are attempting to rise from a swirl of flames emanating from the 'floor' of the globe but are held back by chains.

Not all the details within the globe are clearly visible, and this makes categorical identification of them all impossible. It is evident, however, that the world of the globe is hierarchically organized and that there is a parallel between the events and figures depicted in each hemisphere. It also appears that there is a tentative movement from the lower hemisphere to the upper, and that the six babies below are regenerated by fire to reappear as the shadowy figures waiting in the wings of the

---

[32] The Miltonic passage to which Blake is referring is *Paradise Lost*, vii, 28–31: 'thou/Visit'st my slumbers nightly, or when morn/Purples the east: still govern thou my song, Urania'.

[33] *The Wisdom of Angels, concerning Divine Love and Divine Wisdom.* 1788, pp. 127–8.

[34] Cf. K 92 and 94.

upper hemisphere. The man and woman in the centre are being united by the figure who stands between them. So the globe appears to depict two typically Blakean subjects—the movement of the spirit from the lower world to the upper, and the final 'marriage' or reunion of the disparate male and female entities. The 'saffron robe' of the god Hymen, who officiates at the ceremony, is clearly visible, and so too is his 'taper clear' (l. 126), though it is apparently being held by the woman rather than by the god himself.

The contents of the globe also have a referent in the text of the poem—the formation of celestial music described in lines 136–44. According to this interpretation the central figure of the lower hemisphere, who is holding a long-stemmed trumpet in each hand,[35] is the 'meeting soul' which 'pierces' the music; the figures to either side of him, who are holding a lyre and a tambour, are 'wanton heed' and 'giddy cunning' drawing out the music 'with many a winding bout [i.e. turn]/Of linked sweetness long drawn out', their heels touching as they separate; the babies in the lower hemisphere are the 'tied' soul(s) of harmony being 'untwisted' by the music; the figures above them, these souls made free; and the central figures in the upper hemisphere, 'airs' or music being married by Hymen to 'immortal verse'. As far as the mediation of the vision to Milton is concerned, it is Shakespeare who purveys the music and Jonson, the verse; Shakespeare who provides the inspiration and Jonson, the 'auctoritee'.

Milton's vision has perhaps been strengthened through a correspondence with Blake's own, for the globe of inspiration conveys the essence both of Milton's vision and of Blake's. Indeed Blake appears in the illustration to be asserting the common nature of all creative vision and the corresponding unimportance of its individual and distinctive features, whether they result from authorial personality, from period, or from genre.

The tiny demon in the lower right-hand corner of the plate, who is fleeing, with arms raised, away from the poet, must be one of the 'eating cares' expelled by the spirit of Mirth. It is generally accepted that some of Blake's tiny beings are 'Joys'; it should therefore surprise no one that he should have chosen in an illustration for a poem based upon the allegorical figure of Mirth to depict the expulsion of Misery, the inappropriateness of its presence being suggested in the minuteness of its dimensions. John E. Grant points out that the 'care', as he calls him, 'seems to have a wooden right leg';[36] it is therefore pertinent to note that in a letter to William Hayley, Blake once gave it as his opinion that 'Happinesses have wings and wheels; miseries

[35] Cf. the double trumpet of Fame.
[36] 'Blake's Designs for *L'Allegro* and *Il Penseroso*', p. 127.

are leaden legged, and their whole employment is to clip the wings and to take off the wheels of our chariots' (26 November 1800, K 807).

The 'haunted stream' mentioned both in *L'Allegro* and in Blake's Note flows across the foreground of the illustration. Three spectral figures are hovering just above it and two slender forms are embracing on its near side. The latter must be Orpheus and Eurydice, the implication of their reunion being that the melodies of Mirth have indeed persuaded Pluto to 'quite set free/[The] half-regained Eurydice' (ll. 149–50)—further proof of the power of art and something which the poem only contemplates as a past (and therefore unrealizable) possibility. The stream separating Milton, who is still imprisoned within this world, from the lovers, who are reunited in the next, must be the Styx, which in classical mythology divided the earth from the underworld; and the three figures hovering above the stream are presumably the Fates, whose chief function was to determine the limit of a man's earthly life. The several directions which they are indicating suggest their different roles as Time Past, Time Present, and Time Future: the one on the right is gazing back in the direction from which they have come, the central one is staring at the viewer, and the one on the left is pointing up at Milton—thus either giving his visions the status of prophecy or marking him in his very moment of illumination for mortality.

Milton's disquisition on Mirth in Society has been transformed into an essay on poetic vision: inspiration is spiritual, though not wholly divorced from the natural world; it is conveyed through mediation; and its nature is common to all ages and all true artists. Yet Milton, though as a poet possessed of the Divine Vision, will remain a descended being until he can embrace his Emanation as another supreme artist, Orpheus, embraces his Eurydice: redemption requires harmony of the life as well as a perfecting of the vision.

IL PENSEROSO I: MELANCHOLLY (73)

> Come pensive Nun, devout & pure,
> Sober, steadfast, & demure,
>
> . . .
>
> And join with thee calm Peace & Quiet,
> Spare Fast, who oft with Gods doth diet,
>
> . . .
>
> And add to these retired Leisure,
> Who in trim Gardens takes his pleasure;
> But first, & chiefest, with thee bring,
> Him who yon soars on golden Wing,

> Guiding the Fiery wheeled Throne,
> The Cherub Contemplation.

These Personifications are all brought together in this design, surrounding the Principal Figure Who is Melancholy herself.

(On the Illustrations to Milton, K 618–19)

In the illustrations as in the poems themselves, the contrasting portraits of Mirth and Melancholy lend depth and definition to each other through contrast. Where Mirth was a liberated maiden tripping gaily over a hillside and beckoning to all comers, Melancholy is a 'pensive nun' (l. 31) standing rapt in contemplation, her arms by her sides and her fingers spread out in a kind of world-dismissing gesture. Where Mirth was clad in a filmy, sleeveless gown and wore her hair cascading down her back, Melancholy is dressed in the black habit and wimple of her calling, and her wimple all but hides her hair. Where Mirth was gazing straight at the viewer Melancholy's 'looks [are] commercing with the skies' (l. 39). And while Mirth's rosy cheeks asserted her commitment to the active outdoor life her sister's pallor testifies to the life of devoutness and self-denial.

In place of the countless companions of Mirth, who filled the air and the ground about her, suggesting the plenitude of nature and displaying an exuberance that resists control, Melancholy has only a select band of companions, who form themselves into an ordered arrangement on the plate. Most of them are depicted in solitary contemplation and there is little if any physical contact, even between those who are paired. In *L'Allegro* 1 the energy of Mirth and her companions was expressed in activity that extended even to their fingertips and seemed about to carry them out of the flat surface of the plate; Melancholy and her associates are confined to stationary poses and restrained gestures. In *L'Allegro* 1 the dominant lines of force were the full, rich curves formed from the bodies of the revellers; in the first *Il Penseroso* plate the figures form sober vertical lines which are emphasized by the sweep of Melancholy's gown, the crook held by one of her companions, and the trunks of the trees in the background.

Like her sister Mirth, Melancholy dominates her portrait-picture both in size and in position. Tendentiously, her figure separates—at least on the flat surface of the plate—the women from the men. At her right hand an attractive female pair, 'calm Peace, and Quiet' (l. 45), are engaged in conversation. One is making a gesture of prayer and the other is carrying a staff, an emblem of pastoral care. Both are haloed.

At the goddess's other hand is

> Spare Fast, that oft with gods doth diet,
> And hears the Muses in a ring,
> Ay round about Jove's altar sing.
>
> (ll. 46–8)

He is gazing upwards at his vision, which is depicted just above his head and as though housed in the bosom of an oak tree, the oak being for the ancients sacred to Jove. His arms are crossed and his fingers outspread over his chest—a gesture suggesting the denial of worldly pleasures.

Behind and to the right of Fast is 'retired Leisure,/That in trim gardens takes his pleasure' (ll. 49–50). He is wearing an expression of coy piety and standing with arms loosely folded. A stylized plant is depicted on either side of him—a rose-bush to his left and a lily to the right.[37]

Directly above Melancholy's head, and perhaps serving as her presiding genius, is he

> that you soars on golden wing,
> Guiding the fiery-wheeled throne,
> The cherub Contemplation
>
> (ll. 52–4)

The 'cherub' conveys none of the splendour in motion that is suggested by Milton's description. He is an insignificant, kneeling figure whose arms, wings, and hair are extended sideways in a manner that recalls the Jupiter-Pluvius image familiar from the *Paradise Lost* illustrations. Even the coiled flames emerging from around the base of his throne are subject to this horizontal pull.

In the lower sky beneath and to the left of the 'cherub' is a tiny, humanized Philomel ascending with upraised hands to '[Smooth] the rugged brow of night' (l. 58). Night, a female figure appropriately dark in colouring, is bending down towards the naked Philomel. Her arms are wrapped around her head and her wings folded above her arms, presumably in order to suggest repose. The minute and unadorned Nightingale contrasts markedly with the Lark of *L'Allegro* ii, his counterpart in the companion poem.

Directly opposite Night the virginal moon-goddess 'checks her dragon yoke,/ Gently o'er the accustomed oak' (ll. 59–60)—and, incidentally, directly above the self-denying figure of Fast. The crescent moon serves her as a chariot. Her dragon-

[37] Though sometimes juxtaposed as emblems of innocence and of virtue respectively, the rose and the lily are often employed by Blake simply as examples of the world's natural beauty. It is with this latter significance that they are depicted here.

pair with their spiked wings and spindly tails are, like those of *Comus* IV, fanciful rather than fearsome.

The natural world receives more attention than it did in *L'Allegro* I, for a row of sturdy oaks (cf. the 'accustomed oak' of the poem) now looms behind the figures and beneath a darkening and star-studded sky. Despite its apparent overtones of spirituality the picture details a state of restricted vision in which the characters are placed in a Urizenic setting and isolated from each other in their own self-communing and essentially unilluminating private worlds.

IL PENSEROSO II: THE WANDERING MOON (74)

Milton, in his Character of a Student at Cambridge, Sees the Moon terrified as one led astray in the midst of her path thro' heaven. The distant Steeple seen across a wide water indicates the sound of the Curfew Bell.

(On the Illustrations to Milton, K 619)

Here the moon is personified not as the mythological charioteer of the previous illustration but as a youthful and attractive maiden exploring the territory of the sky. Her lunar crescent, now set within a globe which is itself encircled by a ring of light with rays streaming from it, is placed just above and behind her head, thus serving her for a halo and incidentally also suggesting a pair of horns.

To either side of the maiden is figured a constellation with lines linking the stars of each group, as in astronomical charts—though here the effect is to suggest celestial flowers still attached to their stems, a fitting attribute for a virginal planetary deity and a kind of triumph of the organic over the Newtonian universe.

Milton himself is shown in the right-hand foreground of the picture, standing on a 'wide-watered shore' (l. 75) and gazing up in the direction of the maiden. He is wearing a gown and trencher and is portrayed with long hair and delicate features, which suggest Dr. Johnson's description of him at Cambridge: 'Milton has the reputation of having been in his youth eminently beautiful, so as to have been called the Lady of his college. His hair, which was of a light brown, parted at the foretop, and hung down upon his shoulders.'[38]

The moon-maiden's inquiring expression, her raised arms, and perhaps even her oblique position on the plate—she is placed at an angle to the 'floor' of the picture— suggest unease. The notion of the moon astray derives originally from *Il Penseroso* itself:

[38] 'The Lives of the English Poets' in *The Works of Samuel Johnson LL.D.*, 1810, ix, 143.

> the wandering moon,
> Riding near her highest noon,
> Like one that had been led astray
> Through the heaven's wide pathless way
>
> (ll. 67–70)

but the terror which Blake ascribes to her (see his Note on the illustration, quoted above) does not originate in the poem. It may however be attributed to the threatening, blade-like forms that protrude from the portion of cloud upon which she is treading, and which presumably stand for the maiden's fearful view of male sexuality: one of the blades between her feet has even transfixed a straying star-flower on its tip.

The Prophetic book *Milton* provides a striking analogue to the illustration. In it Ololon, a collective entity representing the poet's three wives and three daughters—his 'Sixfold Emanation'—is described gazing down from heaven into the descended world:

> And Ololon looked down into the Heavens of Ulro in fear.
> They said: 'How are the Wars of man, which in Great Eternity
> 'Appear around in the External Spheres of Visionary Life,
> 'Here render'd Deadly within the Life & Interior Vision?
> 'How are the Beasts & Birds & Fishes & Plants & Minerals
> 'Here fix'd into a frozen bulk subject to decay & death?
> 'Those Visions of Human Life & Shadows of Wisdom & Knowledge
> 'Are here frozen to unexpansive deadly destroying terrors
>
> (K 524–5; pl. 34, 49–pl. 35, 1)

Despite her fear Ololon determines to descend in order to seek out Milton. This she does in a dawn moment which 'renovates every Moment of the Day if rightly placed' (K 526; pl. 35, 45), thus opening up 'a wide road ... to Eternity' (K 525; pl. 35, 35) by which others will be able to ascend—the divine equivalent of the path to hell that is constructed by Sin and Death in *Paradise Lost*. She makes her appearance on earth in the form of 'a Virgin of twelve years' (K 527; pl. 36, 17). Soon afterwards Milton's Spectre also descends. His domain is associated by Blake with

> ... the Chaotic Voids outside of the Stars [that] are measured by
> The Stars, which are the boundaries of Kingdoms, Provinces
> And Empires of Chaos invisible to the Vegetable Man.
> The Kingdom of Og is in Orion: Sihon is in Ophiucus.

> Og has Twenty-seven Districts: Sihon's Districts Twenty-one.
> From Star to Star, Mountains & Valleys, terrible dimension
> Stretch'd out, compose the Mundane Shell, a mighty Incrustation
> Of Forty-eight deformed Human Wonders of the Almighty[39]
>
> (K 528–9; pl. 37, 47–54)

Like the Ololon of the poem, the moon-figure of *Il Penseroso* II is a young maiden 'who has just reached the point of fertility'[40]—a detail which her near-translucent dress does nothing to conceal. Both are searching for Milton and both are distraught. The portrayal of the poet in academic dress accords with the description in *Milton* of how his Spectre, 'clothed in black, severe & silent' (K 529; pl. 38, 8), descended, and the colour of his gown links him also with the Melancholy of the first *Il Penseroso* illustration, with whom he must in his 'error' be to some extent identified. The icy blades which protrude from the cloudbelt may be compared with the deadly, frozen forms of earthly life which threaten the descended being (cf. pl. 34, 52–5, quoted above), and the two constellations with those of Orion and Ophiucus, which make up the 'shell' of the mundane world through which the descending Ololon must travel. Their resemblance to the originals is not particularly close, though the constellation on the right does suggest the compactness of Orion and that on the left, the straggling form of Ophiucus the Serpent-Bearer. Blake conveys his view, expressed in *Milton*, that 'Satanic [i.e. Cartesian] Space is delusion' (K 527; pl. 36, 20) by drawing Ololon, who is still in the sky, according to the same scale as the earthbound Milton, though the belt of cloud that encloses her serves to suggest the distances that lie between them.

The poem *Milton* concludes with a contrite Ololon renouncing her independence even to the point of her separate existence and fleeing into 'the depths/Of Milton's Shadow' (K 534; pl. 42, 5–6). Immediately afterwards Blake has a vision of Milton regenerated in the form of Christ the Saviour 'clothed in Clouds of blood' (K 534; pl. 42, 20).

The second *Il Penseroso* illustration does not presume so much. It leaves us with the poet still in his Spectral form and still separated both from his Emanation and from his redemption, symbolized here by the church steeple which rises above the foliage on the opposite bank and which itself has a textual origin in the 'far-off curfew sound' that the Milton of *Il Penseroso* hears from 'Over some wide-watered shore'

---

[39] Og and Sihon, in the Bible chieftains defeated by the Israelites, are to Blake giants who threaten man's imaginative life. There are forty-eight constellations in the Ptolemaic universe. Blake unites twenty-seven of them under the great 'southern' constellation Orion and the remainder under the 'northern' constellation of Ophiucus.

[40] S. Foster Damon, *A Blake Dictionary*, p. 279.

(ll. 74–5). Thematically and pictorially it contrasts with the many cruel, slanting blades within Ololon's cloud. The small red roses depicted on Milton's side of the water[41]—a reminder of the unobtrusive delights of the natural world and of the 'sweets' that emanate from the centre of vision, and perhaps also of Milton's own sexuality—are drooping: their moment of 'renovation' and regeneration is yet to come.

IL PENSEROSO III: THE SPIRIT OF PLATO (75)

The Spirit of Plato unfolds his Worlds to Milton in Contemplation. The Three Destinies sit on the Circles of Plato's Heavens, weaving the Thread of Mortal Life; these Heavens are Venus, Jupiter & Mars. Hermes flies before as attending on the Heaven of Jupiter; the Great Bear is seen in the Sky beneath Hermes, & The Spirits of Fire, Air, Water & Earth Surround Milton's Chair.

(On the Illustrations to Milton, K 619)

Plato's spirit, or ghost, is clad in a long white robe and appears as a bearded old man. A mandorla of smoke or flame encloses his lower parts and interposes itself between his feet and the ground, while his form from the waist upwards is framed by a large sphere.[42] He is indicating either this sphere or the heavens above with the index finger of his right hand while with his left hand he is pointing to a volume— no doubt containing some of his 'Dialogues'—which lies open before his disciple, Milton.

Milton, who is again dressed in black, is seated sideways on to the viewer. His hand is clasped wearily to his forehead and a swarm of tiny, listless figures is laboriously describing a circle about his head—a whimsical rendering of a head 'going round in circles' and a mocking reminder of the ethereal figures that formed a halo about the head of Mirth in the first *L'Allegro* illustration.

The Platonic spirit of *Il Penseroso* III is ignoring the question regarding the nature of the afterlife that the Milton of the poem wishes to put to him:

> What worlds, or what vast regions hold
> The immortal mind that hath forsook
> Her mansion in this fleshly nook
>
> (ll. 90–2)

and revealing instead those supernatural beings which in his view govern the

---

[41] Perhaps to Blake, with his Milton in academicals, the River Cam.

[42] Leaving the lower portion of his body literally 'unsphered'—cf. *Il Penseroso*, l. 88.

material world—the deities of love, war, and reason, the three Fates, and the elemental spirits.[43]

The sphere to which Plato is pointing is the left-hand one of three. Two of the three are shown side by side and the other is placed behind and between them so that only a small portion of it is visible. This multiple vision of error opposes the single spheres of truth displayed in the third and sixth *L'Allegro* illustrations.

From left to right the spheres contain the figures of Aphrodite, Ares, and Zeus. The functions of these deities correspond roughly with the three aspects into which Plato divides the human animal—the deliberative, the passionate, and the appetitive.[44] These are located respectively in the head, the heart, and the belly. In his own writings Blake incorporates a three-part division of the mortal body which is clearly based on Plato's:

> the Vegetated bodies which Enitharmon wove
> Open'd within their hearts & in their loins & in their brain
> To Beulah
>
> (*Vala*, K 342; 54–6)

The left-hand sphere of *Il Penseroso* III is under the domination of Aphrodite, goddess of love and of generation. Her body appears to be emerging from a tree-trunk[45] and leaves and twigs are sprouting from her left arm, which is extended like a branch. With her right hand she is trying half-heartedly and after the manner of the Venus pudica[46] to cover her breasts. At the base of the globe, and ignored by the upward-gazing Aphrodite, are two pairs of tiny figures who demonstrate the wretchedness of what the world calls love. The pair on the left are bound back-to-back by serpents, and a man on the right has rejected a weeping female.

Blake's justification for making this very earthly Aphrodite a significant element in Plato's philosophy may have been the passage in 'The Symposium' in which Pausanius discourses on the two Aphrodites—the heavenly Aphrodite, who inspires man to love nobly, and her common sister, who counsels him to be without discrimination.[47] The common Aphrodite is traditionally associated with vegetation and the processes of generation.

[43] No mention is made of Aphrodite, Ares, or Zeus, or of the three Fates, in *Il Penseroso*.
[44] Cf. e.g. 'The Timaeus', in *The Works of Plato*, ii, 544–6.
[45] Cf. the various stories in Ovid's *Metamorphoses* of the transformation of nymphs into plants.
[46] A cast of the most famous example of the Venus pudica, the Venus de' Medici, was bought for the young Blake by his father—cf. Benjamin Heath Malkin, *A Father's Memoirs of his Child*, 1806, pp. xviii–xix.
[47] 'The Banquet', in *The Works of Plato*, iii, 459–61. Cf. Blake's apostrophe in *Jerusalem*: 'O Venus! O Double God of Generation!' (K 706; pl. 68, 18).

Fleshly love and the existence of the 'Vegetative Universe' are to Blake intimately related, so it is appropriate that the Aphrodite of 'The Spirit of Plato' should be portrayed as a tree-spirit and that the scenes in the lower half of the globe should be conducted in terms of the Fall: the posture of the weeping woman is identical to that of Eve in the 'Judgement' illustration from the *Paradise Lost* series, and the serpent-bonds of the couple on the left also recall the Fall. In *A Vision of the Last Judgment* Blake speaks of 'Vegetable Life & Death with its Lusts' (K 609), and there are numerous points of correspondence between Vala, his own nature-goddess, and Aphrodite.

It is likely that the binding depicted within the globe of Venus is intended primarily to recall Aristophanes' comic theory on the origin of the attraction between the sexes as it was recounted in Plato's 'Banquet'.[48] The notion bears some resemblance to Blake's own belief in the hermaphroditic nature of prelapsarian man— with the crucial difference that Blake treats his own myth with full seriousness, even with awe, whereas Aristophanes' tale is unashamedly and exuberantly bawdy.

It may also be that Blake considered the binding of lovers back-to-back to suggest the way in which a vindictively moralistic society takes vengeance upon adulterers. If this is so then by depicting such a pair in 'The Spirit of Plato' he is probably implying a criticism not of Plato but of Milton, to whom chastity was both a virtue and an ideal.

The right-hand sphere contains a listless and rather mournful Zeus, seated with his left foot trailing below his right in an attitude similar to that adopted by the Moloch idol in the Huntington version of the fifth *Nativity Ode* illustration. He is holding a sceptre in one hand and with some diffidence manipulating a pair of compasses with the other. Behind him a naked slave is turning a large wheel, and a sector of the shadowy, created world is visible beneath his footstool. He is Plato's 'God of Gods, who governs by law'[49]—a tyrannical supreme being who, like the classical Zeus, Blake's own Urizen, and the Jehovah of the Old Testament, is preoccupied with abstract modes of creation and systems of law.

The central sphere contains a bust of Ares, who is helmeted and shown with a spear alongside him. A bat hovers just above his right shoulder and part of the Mosaic tablets of stone are to be seen beneath him, perhaps suggesting an association between physical aggression and repression through the force of law. War is accorded a prominent place in the 'Dialogues', for to Plato strife is a fundamental aspect of the

[48] *The Works of Plato*, iii, 475–8.
[49] 'The Critias', in *The Works of Plato*, ii, 592.

human condition: 'the body and its desires cause wars, seditions, and contests, of every kind: for all wars arise through the possession of wealth; and we are compelled to acquire riches through the body, becoming subservient to its cultivation'.[50] For Blake the greatest flaw in the classical civilization was its martial attitudes: 'The Classics! it is the Classics, & not Goths nor Monks, that Desolate Europe with Wars' (*On Homer's Poetry & On Virgil*, K 778). Somewhat unfairly perhaps, he associates this belligerence with Milton as well: 'Shakespeare & Milton were both curb'd by the general malady & infection from the silly Greek & Latin slaves of the Sword' (*Milton*, K 480; pl. 1).

Blake often uses the bat to represent the attitudes of the eighteenth-century establishment.[51] Its inclusion within the sphere of Ares is probably in part a reference to the besetting militarism of that establishment. (It must be remembered that the *L'Allegro* and *Il Penseroso* series of illustrations was executed only a couple of years after the end of the Napoleonic wars.) The bat, because it 'emerges at dusk and lives in lonely, dark and decaying places',[52] is a traditional emblem of melancholy, and may also have been included in an illustration to *Il Penseroso* for that reason. A bat appears in Dürer's 'Melencolia I', a reproduction of which Blake kept by him in his work-room.[53]

Seated in acrobatic postures astride the three spheres are the Fates, who appear in the Myth of Er from Plato's 'Republic'[54] and whom Blake sometimes identifies as the daughters of Urizen. One is unwinding the thread of life from her distaff, the second is measuring a length off from it, and the third—even more malign in appearance than her sisters—is snipping off the length with a pair of shears. Their positions on top of the spheres indicate that it is they and not the Olympians who are rulers of the world. The snipping of the cord of life raises—only to ignore— Milton's inquiry concerning the afterlife.

Neither the Parcae nor any of the classical deities are mentioned at this point in *Il Penseroso*. By associating them with Plato and with details that are relevant to the life and works of Milton—sexual strife, Fall and Judgement, militarism, and abstract rule—Blake implies that Milton was strongly influenced by Plato, and that

---

[50] 'The Phaedo', in *The Works of Plato*, iv, 269.
   In Blake's system the portion of the body that corresponds to Ares is the loins, and it is from the loins that the spirit of war emerges—cf. e.g. *Jerusalem*, K 650; pl. 27, 37–8: 'Albion's Spectre from his Loins/Tore forth in all the pomp of War'; and K 677; pl. 47, 4–5: 'Luvah tore forth from Albion's Loins in fibrous veins, in rivers/Of blood over Europe'.
[51] Cf. Jean H. Hagstrum, *William Blake: Poet and Painter*, pp. 7–8.
[52] Erwin Panofsky, *Albrecht Dürer*, 1948, i, 162.
[53] Alexander Gilchrist, *Life of William Blake*, i, 347.
[54] *The Works of Plato*, i, 477.

this influence was a harmful one. Though in his youth impressed by the works of Plato, Blake came in later life to regard him as a mistaken prophet.

To the right of the picture Hermes, a youthful figure armed with his caduceus and with tiny wings sprouting from his head, is depicted alongside his master, Zeus. He is pointing downwards in the direction of the constellation of the Great Bear and appears to be attempting to deliver a message to his master. He is of course the Hermes of Greek mythology and not his namesake, the Hermes Trismegistus or 'thrice great Hermes' mentioned in *Il Penseroso*. As Blake would have known, the Great Bear was regarded by this other Hermes as an emblem of the unchanging perfection of eternity because it perpetually describes an exact circle around Polaris. Blake has sketched the body of a bear about the stars of the constellation, thus transforming it into an 'animated' emblem. It may be that Hermes, the guide of souls, is here attempting to recall Zeus from his preoccupation with a lower, debased world by drawing his attention to the eternal values represented by the Great Bear.

Sections of the illustration about the chair of Milton are devoted to the spirits of the four elements—which the poet of *Il Penseroso* appears to associate with Plato.[55] Blake, who must have known that the elemental spirits originated not with the 'Dialogues' but with the writings of the alchemists and Neoplatonists, also chooses to associate them with Plato.[56] It is difficult to avoid the suspicion that he is here, as in his substitution of the classical Hermes for Hermes Trismegistus, revising the text in order that it should better reflect one of his own prejudices—a tendency to associate Plato with materialism. A desire to dissociate Hermes Trismegistus from it may also be involved.

In Blake's own works these spirits are personified forms of the physical forces of the material world. They are ceaselessly engaged in the strife of the natural cycle and remain eternally unregenerate:

> they know not of Regeneration, but only of Generation:
> The Fairies, Nymphs, Gnomes & Genii of the Four Elements,
> Unforgiving & unalterable, these cannot be Regenerated
> But must be Created, for they know only of Generation:
> These are the Gods of the Kingdoms of the Earth, in contrarious
> And cruel opposition, Element against Element, opposed in War
> Not Mental, as the Wars of Eternity, but a Corporeal Strife
>
> (*Milton*, K 520; pl. 31, 19–25)

[55] The syntax is ambiguous at this point—perhaps intentionally so.

[56] In fact Plato is careful to stress the inanimate nature of the elements—cf. e.g. 'The Laws', in *The Works of Plato*, ii, 298.

In *Il Penseroso* III each of the four elements represents a different aspect of the material world: air, the futility of the never-ending generative cycle; earth, the cramping and vegetative aspects of the world; water, the world's cruelty and tyranny; and fire, the false hope of redemption in the body.

The spirits of air are shown rising and falling about the head of a mind-weary Milton. The ineffectiveness of their gestures and the confined nature of their cycle indicate their imprisonment within the 'nightmare of recurrence'.[57]

The spirits of earth are represented within a strip of soil beneath the floor of Milton's 'tower'. Leaves, flowers, and roots are springing from the extremities of a prostrate maiden in the centre—leaves from her feet, and roots from her head; a doleful figure on the left is emerging from a large leaf or vegetable; a crouching mother is looking intently at her child's right hand, which appears to have adopted either a vegetative or a serpent-headed form;[58] and the lower portions of two figures on the far right, one of whom is lying face downwards, are embedded within the earth. Only the right arm of the maiden in the centre protrudes above this earthy strip— and that arm discovers only the enclosed area beneath Milton's chair.

Another rigidly defined rectangular space, this time behind the chair, represents the element of water. Within it a bat-winged nymph holds a clam-shell from which hangs a large net containing an inverted male figure. The voluptuousness of the nymph suggests that it was a sexual snaring that Blake had in mind.

Behind Plato are three recumbent stone effigies. One apparently represents a helmeted warrior and a second, a bearded man. The third is indistinct. Above them are their souls, encased within a sheet of flame. Two, who are figured as females, are gazing fearfully at the third, a male spirit hovering above them in kneeling position and with arms raised in order to beat them down again. So while fire, the least 'corporeal' of the elements, may seem to contain the promise of regeneration, that promise proves to be delusory—because the spirits of fire are themselves the prisoners of the material world. This part of the illustration counterpoints the sexual tyranny exhibited by the ensnaring nymph, by showing the male principle on the offensive.

The cumulative message of this most complex illustration is that Plato, who after all expelled the poet—for Blake the saviour of the world—from his ideal republic, is a false prophet obsessed with the harsher aspects of the generative material world and with an afterlife that promises only re-entry into the generative cycle. As the scenes within the globes suggest, Milton has for the moment fallen under the influence of the philosopher, though the Puritan poet's perplexity indicates that he may

---

[57] Morton Paley, *Energy and the Imagination*, 1970, p. 123.
[58] Similarly, its arm and leg are bound either by a tendril or by the body of a serpent.

be about to reject his master's teachings. In doing this he will move closer to his own redeeming self.

IL PENSEROSO IV: THE SUN IN HIS WRATH (76)

Milton led by Melancholy into the Groves away from the Sun's flaring Beams, who is seen in the Heavens throwing his darts & flames of fire. The Spirits of the Trees on each side are seen under the domination of Insects raised by the Sun's heat.

(On the Illustrations to Milton, K 619)

Here the sun-god is shown wresting solar arrow-heads from the sky and flinging them down about the head of Melancholy, who is leading the young Milton along a path and into a 'close covert by some brook' (l. 139). The trees between which they are passing, are shown to the right and left foreground of the picture. Each contains a listless and dejected tree-spirit or 'Sylvan' 'under the domination of Insects' (Blake's Note)—enormous, winged forms that hover in the trees above them. The brook is depicted in the background with other trees—all, like those in the foreground, suggesting oaks—lining its banks. The illustration is an imaginative reconstruction of the following lines:

> And when the sun begins to fling
> His flaring beams, me goddess bring
> To arched walks of twilight groves,
> And shadows brown that Sylvan loves
> Of pine, or monumental oak,
> Where the rude axe with heaved stroke,
> Was never heard the nymphs to daunt,
> Or fright them from their hallowed haunt.
> There is close covert by some brook,
> Where no profaner eye may look,
> Hide me from day's garish eye,
> While the bee with honied thigh,
> ... at her flowery work doth sing
> (ll. 131–43)

As in *L'Allegro* III the sun-god is shown as a comely, naked youth with hair ascending in a 'peak of flame', but the ball of the sun has shrunk dramatically and instead of being contained by it the sun-god is shown astride it in a position which signifies sexual potency, an abundance of that 'Energy [which] is Eternal Delight' (*The Marriage of Heaven and Hell*, K 149; pl. 4). His arms are raised in order to pluck his arrows out of the sky, and his body, taut with exertion, is leaning to one side—probably a reference to the angle of the sun's rays.

The arrows reinforce the sexual reference, although they must be regarded primarily as 'Mental' weapons:

> Los flam'd in my path, & the Sun was hot
> With the bows of my Mind & the Arrows of Thought—
> My bowstring fierce with Ardour breathes,
> My arrows glow in their golden sheaves
> (Letter to Thomas Butts, 22 November 1802,
> K 818; 77–80)

They have their source in a metaphor from *Il Penseroso*: 'And when the sun begins to fling/His flaring beams . . .' (ll. 131–2), which itself derives from the ancient custom of endowing solar gods with arrows that originally represented the beams of the sun—a tradition which Blake himself followed when he depicted Hyperion armed with a many-stringed bow, in his sixth illustration to Gray's *Progress of Poesy*.

Prim Melancholy, who is the primary target for the sun-god's arrows, is still dressed in her nun's habit and wimple, and has in addition been endowed with a small plate-halo. She is wearing the slightly pained expression of long-suffering authority. Milton, whom she is leading by the hand, is also dressed in black. He appears as a youthful, tractable, and effeminate figure who might at first glance be mistaken for a novice under her tutelage. In his left hand he is clutching a large tome. The religious references are supported in the text by Milton's description of the grove as a 'hallowed haunt' (l. 138) and by his expressed desire to escape the sight of the 'profaner eye' (l. 140).

The tree-spirits, which bear no resemblance to the beneficent figure of *L'Allegro* IV, have fallen under the influence of the 'Vegetative Universe'. They are accompanied by distressed and servile minions—by no means 'undaunted', as are the nymphs of Milton's text, though they may still be Blake's version of them. The tree-spirit on the left is holding the sceptre of power and appears to be an avatar of tyrannical rule; that on the right is being transmogrified into wood degraded into a vegetable form. His features have become indistinct and his only visible arm, which is serpent-entwined, is without a hand and already resembles a branch more than a human limb. The serpent is hissing and forking its tongue at Milton.

The winged insect on the right has spiked wings and a head that terminates in a spiked crown or fringe. The other is more conventional, with shapely wings and large antennae. Their presence derives initially from lines 142–3 of *Il Penseroso*: 'While the bee with honied thigh,/That at her flowery work doth sing', but their primary function in the illustration is to 'externalize' the guilt that might otherwise have accrued wholly to the tree-spirits, who in their original state would have revealed the 'divine humanity' of the poet's world.

So the wood into which Melancholy is leading the poet,[59] and which is rendered with dark and threatening shadows—'artist's licence' for the 'twilight groves,/And shadows brown' (ll. 133–4) of the poem—is filled with omens of evil. Milton is being introduced to the paths of error by a representative of the female Will—repression that poses as holiness and purity. It is against this attitude that the sun-god, himself an agent of masculine potency and of true spirituality, is launching the mental arrows of his anger. Some of the arrows are also intended for the insect on the left: when Blake describes the insects as 'raised by the Sun's heat' (Note) it is the natural sun and not the spiritual solar god depicted in the illustration, of whom he is speaking.

IL PENSEROSO V: MYSTERIOUS DREAM (77)

Milton Sleeping on a Bank; Sleep descending, with a Strange, Mysterious dream, upon his Wings, of Scrolls, & Nets, & Webs, unfolded by Spirits in the Air & in the Brook; around Milton are Six Spirits or Fairies, hovering on the air, with Instruments of Music.

(*On the Illustrations to Milton*, K 619)

This illustration is visually and thematically similar to the last illustration of the *L'Allegro* series, though it lacks the earlier illustration's clarity of conception and is too programmatic to be artistically successful. Milton is again shown sleeping on a river-bank beneath a large globe or disc of vision that is mediated to him by a third party. Here however he is in a state not of divine inspiration but of mortal error. Both the vision and its mediator, in this case Sleep, are contaminated, and Milton is lying with his hands crossed over his lap—a position which suggests the repression of sexual desire.

A personified Sleep—a form of Blake's descending god—is shown ministering to the poet. His posture is thematically conceived and his inverted figure clumsily drawn. His large and solidly-built wings, which are dotted with the 'eyes' of the peacock, are cupped about the body of his charge. One wing is hovering in mid-air and the other trailing dismally in the water. The figure has a finely drawn head and legs with feather-encased thighs, but apparently no arms or torso. His face is bent solicitously over Milton's and he is sharing part of his disc-halo with him. In turn the poet has inclined an ear towards his mentor.

[59] In *Il Penseroso* it was Milton who requested to be taken there.

As requested in the poem, Sleep is bearing 'at the wings' a dream to lay upon Milton's delicately drawn eyelids. One of the wings appears to have cracked under the burden. The 'lively portraiture' (l. 149) of the dream is composed of 'Scrolls, & Nets, & Webs, unfolded by Spirits in the Air & in the Brook' (Blake's Note). Three large spirits are gliding forward upon a scroll depicted just above Sleep's air-borne wing, and a second scroll is being carried aloft by smaller spirits. The other wing contains a downward-gliding figure encased within a scroll, a pair of lovers trapped within its folds, numerous smaller nymphs, and (half immersed in the water) several struggling figures caught in nets and webs. The spirits may owe their origin to Milton's plea in *Il Penseroso* that Sleep should let a dream 'Wave at his wings in *airy stream*' (l. 148; italics mine). The scrolls, nets, and webs are entirely of Blake's invention. They are emblems which appear frequently in Blake's poetry and paintings, and always in association with the fallen world—with false religion and with fallen sexuality in particular.

The 'globe of vision' above the poet has shrunk to a two-dimensional disc—the unilluminating 'sun of this world'. It is divided into concentric circles, of which the outermost is red and yellow, the two in the middle blue, and the innermost light pink: the white light of vision has disintegrated into its prismatic colours. Part of the disc is obscured by overhanging foliage but at its centre a tiny, bearded old man can be seen. In front of him are three figures who are depicted above another scroll. They appear to be moving outwards from the bosom of the disc. The central figure is an old man with raised eyes, a long white beard, and an attenuated body clad in a long, flowing robe. His arms are raised at the elbows and tucked in to his sides. The naked figures on either side of him are bent double and clutching their heads.

The trio quite closely resembles a group depicted in a pencil drawing of 'A Vision of the Last Judgment' and described by Blake as

Noah ... Canopied by a Rainbow, on his right hand Shem & on his Left Japhet; these three Persons represent Poetry, Painting & Music, the three Powers in Man of conversing with Paradise, which the flood did not Sweep away

(*A Vision of the Last Judgment*, K 609)

though in the drawing the figures are bearing emblems of the arts they represent—Noah a scroll, Shem a harp, and Japhet, an artist's palette. The group in *Il Penseroso* v may also stand for 'Poetry, Painting & Music', though in the fallen world, so that instead of carrying tools of their trade, Painting covers his eyes and Music, his ears. Only Poetry, the prophetic figure in the centre, manages to hold himself erect and gaze heavenwards, for he has a redemptive mission to fulfil—the keeping of 'the Divine Vision in time of trouble' (*Jerusalem*, K 742; pl. 95, 20).

The figure in the centre of the disc must if we follow this interpretation be the tyrant-god Jehovah, who controls the destinies of Noah and his sons and who stands in the same relation to the fallen arts as the Christ of 'A Vision of the Last Judgment' does to the resurrected arts. In *Il Penseroso* v the Arts, if such they be, appear to be attempting to escape from his influence.

Apart from this possible hint of the artist's ripeness for redemption, it may augur well for the Milton of the illustration that the 'eyes' on Sleep's wings recall to us those of the sublime Vision of Ezekiel, and that there are seven of them. In Blake's writings the seven Eyes of God will when joined by the eighth—almost certainly Milton himself—be transformed into the sacred image of Christ.

The guardian spirits that hover about the sleeping form of Milton are a more certain sign that he is to be regenerated. In the Prophetic book *Milton* similar immortal spirits sustain the poet's immortal self with nectar, thus preserving it for eternity, after his Spectre has assumed independent form:

> for when he enter'd into his Shadow, Himself,
> His real and immortal Self, was, as appear'd to those
> Who dwell in immortality, as One sleeping on a couch
> Of gold, and those in immortality gave forth their Emanations
> Like Females of sweet beauty to guard round him & to feed
> His lips with food of Eden in his cold and dim repose
>
> (K 496; pl. 15, 10–15)

These immortals are almost certainly Blake's Daughters of Beulah, the guardians of man's spirit. Those portrayed in *Il Penseroso* v have the same function but their number, six, suggests that they are also to be associated with the 'Sixfold Emanation' that was represented in the eighth illustration of the series by the composite figure of Ololon. The association is significant, for it suggests that Milton's rift with his womenfolk is ripe for repair. The musical instruments which the spirits are carrying may in the first place owe their origin to a reference in the text to the 'consort' or musical harmony made by the murmuring waters of the brook, but for Blake they serve primarily to indicate that the poet's Divine Vision remains potentially whole even in times of trouble, and there will ultimately be no division between the life and the work, his womenfolk and his art.

IL PENSEROSO VI: MILTON: OLD AGE (78)

Milton, in his Old Age, sitting in his Mossy Cell, Contemplating the Constellations, surrounded by the Spirits of the Herbs & Flowers, bursts forth into a rapturous Prophetic Strain.

(On the Illustrations to Milton, K 619)

Finally Milton is depicted as an aged hermit, dressed in a hair shirt and contained within his 'mossy cell' (l. 169—a cavern formed from the trunks, foliage, and intertwined branches of trees[60] and illuminated only by the light of a candle. The meanness of his condition cannot conceal his new status as Prophet-poet or man of God. His arms are outstretched in a gesture of universal blessing, and light appears to be streaming from his head. He has at last put his tome aside and is gazing with awe and rapture into the heavens, where stars and zodiacal signs—many of them in redemptive, 'humanized' form—are thronging the sky. His private vision has at last become a universal reality: the airborne forms are not here contained within any perfect, but subjective, sphere, and Nature, particularized as 'the Spirits of the Herbs & Flowers' (Blake's Note), is rejoicing with him.

Dr Johnson once observed that, 'For the old age of Cheerfulness [Milton] makes no provision; but Melancholy he conducts with great dignity to the close of life.'[61] Blake's concluding illustration for *Il Penseroso* shows the Puritan poet in the final stage of his life—the period after 1660 in which, his public career having ended and his sight gone, he lived modestly and devoted himself to the writing of his greatest poems. The 'cell' or cavern of the illustration is an emblem for the world-cave within which the descended soul is trapped but it also suggests both the modest circumstances and the blindness of the ageing poet.

Despite his 'natural' blindness, or perhaps in part because of it, Milton is endowed with 'spiritual' vision. His gazing eyes and alert expression call attention to the paradox that, although his eyes were closed when sighted (as in the previous illustration and in *L'Allegro* VI), when blind he was privileged to see. We are reminded again of the celebrated Invocation to Book III of *Paradise Lost.*

The vision itself is composed of the zodiacal signs from Cancer to Aries and, beneath them, the constellation of Orion—all in humanized form. Aries and Ram, clasped firmly under the arm of a shepherd with broad-brimmed hat and crook, is shown on the far right. Beside him Taurus the Bull is plunging recklessly down through the sky. Only his head and front legs are visible, and he has stars for eyes. Below and to the left of him is the warrior Orion, brandishing a sword and wearing

---

[60] Cf. the less emphatically confining spaces of *L'Allegro* VI.
[61] 'Lives of the Poets' in *The Works of Samuel Johnson,* ix, 157.

a starry belt. He is shown lunging in the direction of Taurus—no doubt a reference to the legend of his vain pursuit of the Pleiades, who are companions of Artemis in the mythological world but in the zodiacal universe part of the constellation of the Bull. (The astronomical basis for this legend is the fact that the Pleiades rise above the horizon just before Orion.) He is represented beneath the other figures and appears to be sinking beneath the trees. This detail also has an astronomical origin, for the constellation that he represents disappears beneath the southern horizon for two months every spring, the season that is indicated by the presence of the particular zodiacal signs that are shown above him.

Opposite Taurus are Gemini—the Twins—and on the far left is Cancer the Crab with human figure seated back-to-front on it shell, presumably in order to suggest the crab's sideways motion,[62] and apparently engrossed in a book. These charmingly whimsical figures are depicted against a background of schematically drawn stars. All of them with the exception of the sword-bearer appear to be progressing in an anti-clockwise direction.

The zodiacal signs represented in *Il Penseroso* VI are those that were associated by the Neoplatonists with the descending soul.[63] As we have already seen, the Milton of *Milton* returns to earth in order to correct the 'errors' of his first existence. Here we see the 'original' form of the poet nearing the end of his life and overcome by a vision of his own redemptive return. He is also reading in the stars of the second coming of Christ, which he glorifies in *Paradise Lost*: life and works have become one, the Poet has become a Prophet, and the Prophet is himself to become a Saviour. By rhapsodizing spontaneously about his vision (cf. Blake's Note) the Milton of the illustration has attained the ideal mastered effortlessly by the Lark—the identification of the moment of perception with the moment of artistic creation. (Orion, whose sightlessness links him with Milton, was also believed by the ancients to have been raised from the dead.)

The season of spring has regenerative implications of its own, which are confirmed by the joyful rising of the humanized vegetation-spirits on the ground and in the trees around Milton: the natural world is included in the poet's saving vision.

While the spirits in the trees are rejoicing with Milton and stretching their arms towards the heavens, those within the cell are embracing or succouring each other. In the right-hand corner of the cell a mother, her own body still trapped in the

---

[62] Cf. Spenser's description of the spirit of June, from the 'Mutability Cantos': 'Upon a Crab he rode, that did him bear/With crooked crawling steps an uncouth pace,/And backward yode, as bargemen wont to fare/Bending their force contrary to their face' (Canto VII, stanza 35).

[63] Cf. Porphyry's 'Cave of the Nymphs' in *Thomas Taylor the Platonist: Selected Writings*, ed. George Mills Harper and Kathleen Raine, 1969, pp. 309-10.

earth, is nursing two children while a third looks on. Beneath Milton's right arm a male and a female placed between two rose-bushes are embracing, their bodies flowing about each other like flame. Two cherubic soul-figures meet above their heads, thus indicating that their union is of the spirit as well as of the flesh. In the far left-hand corner another female spirit, whose head appears as though framed by lilies growing on a bush behind her, is helping a companion to wrest himself free of the imprisoning earth.

The spirits within the cell of the world are identified by Edward J. Rose as the poet's three wives:

Jane Powell (with children), Katharine Woodcock, and Elizabeth Minshull. Milton's short-lived but happy second marriage is portrayed idyllically and we see Milton and Katharine embracing. Milton's third marriage, which took place in the last years of his life, is portrayed so as to indicate Milton's proximity to the grave. We see him with only head and arms above ground.[64]

So the perfected vision of the poet incorporates his 'Sixfold Emanation' and includes a recognition of the regenerating qualities of his wives—the maternal affection of Jane, the womanly love of Katharine, and (apparently) the saving grace of Elizabeth.

[64] 'Blake's Illustrations for *Paradise Lost, L'Allegro*, and *Il Penseroso:* A Thematic Reading', p. 65.

VI PARADISE REGAINED

The *Paradise Regained* series comprises twelve drawings—significantly, perhaps, an 'epic' number. They are not dated but were probably executed in 1816 or shortly afterwards, as the watermarks, 'M & J LAY 1816', which are found on the *L'Allegro* and *Il Penseroso* plates, are also discernible on three of the *Paradise Regained* sheets.[1] The set was bought from Blake by John Linnell in 1825 and is now the property of the Fitzwilliam Museum, Cambridge, England.

Some critics have commented on a difference in tone between *Paradise Regained* and *Samson Agonistes* on the one hand, and Milton's earlier poems on the other: 'A certain Miltonic note very much present in the companion pieces, in *Comus*, in "Lycidas", and still at the forefront of *Paradise Lost* is no longer heard in *Paradise Regained* and *Samson Agonistes*. Milton's ever available lyricism is gone.'[2]

This change is reflected in Blake's *Paradise Regained* illustrations. The finely wrought detail of the earlier sets has given way to simple forms boldly outlined and elaborately shaded, and their evocation of the sensuous delights of the natural world to austere and formalized renderings of the human figure. Figure-drawing predominates throughout, particularly in the eleventh illustration, in which all trace of background detail has been eliminated so as to leave only an harmonious arrangement of figures against a plain wash of blue, yellow-green, and crimson.

Many of the figures in the *Paradise Regained* series retain the Grecian or Michelangelesque 'lineaments' of those in the earlier sets, but their monumentality, their combining of intensity with remoteness, their hieratic gestures, their prominent disc-haloes, and (in Christ's case) devout upward gaze, are all more reminiscent of the Byzantine style. The association is appropriate to a work preoccupied with the triumph of the Christlike mind over the Satanic passions.

---

[1] The first, sixth, and eleventh illustrations. Cf. my note on the dating of the *L'Allegro* and *Il Penseroso* illustrations (Introduction to Chapter V).

[2] William J. Grace, *Ideas on Milton*, 1968, p. 146. Grace obviously accepts the late dating usually assigned to *Samson Agonistes*. However, this has been convincingly challenged by William Riley Parker in *Milton: A Biography*, 1968, ii, 903–17.

Milton associates his Christ with Platonic idealism, with the 'Mental Fight', and with the soul; his Satan with scientific empiricism, with physical violence, and with materialist ends. It is therefore appropriate that Blake should have interpreted the poem in terms of his own vision of a cosmic struggle between 'truth' and 'error', spirit and matter, Imagination and Ratiocination—the agencies of Los and those of Urizen.

The dialectical slant of his subject leads Milton to emphasize through incident, physical description, and imagery the contrasting natures of Satan and of Christ. It also leads to the characters themselves defining, even realizing, each other's natures through dialectical opposition. This is particularly true of the effect that Satan has upon Christ. As Don Cameron Allen observes, 'It is amazing how strongly the undefined expectations of the human Christ flare into divine certainty whenever he is confronted by the subhuman enticements of the mind of evil.'[3] In this of course lies the ultimate absurdity of Satan—that all his efforts for evil only help to determine the shape of the good.

Blake conveys the poem's debating character by employing a high degree of symmetry (especially in figure-drawing) within individual plates, by the repeated use of identical or similar detail, and in particular by emphasizing the opposed figures of Christ and Satan, who dominate the illustrations in which they appear. Both of them are represented in six of the twelve plates, and one of them in four of the others. The arrangement of the second and seventh illustrations, in which they are depicted alone together, strongly suggests the ritualized nature of their opposition.

Milton's Christ is associated with light and with the steadfastness of rock; his Satan with darkness and with the insubstantiality of air. The forms and postures of Blake's antagonists are likewise opposed, and symbolize forcefully and succinctly their bearers' states of mind and soul. The pictorial Christ is an elegant and attenuated figure clad for all his 'entrances' after the first in a long white robe that amply reveals the contours of his 'Eternal Body' (*The Laocoön*, K 776). He is generally shown motionless, in a dignified and upright position, and with a countenance both solemn and serene. Though he is not invested with any of the insignia of earthly power he is endowed with a nimbus—generally a brilliant white disc—and in the climactic eleventh illustration he is associated with the 'humanized' Gothic arch, Blake's supreme symbol of divinity.

By contrast the Devil is usually shown naked, and—as befits Milton's 'Prince of Darkness'—with darkly shaded body. His expression is anxious and his brow furrowed throughout, and he is frequently depicted in postures that suggest frenzied

[3] Don Cameron Allen, *The Harmonious Vision*, 1954, p. 119.

or futile activity. For all of his appearances except two he is shown hovering in his own dominion, that of the air[4]—though, significantly, it is in the air that he is finally conquered.

Satan is not portrayed standing upright at any stage in the series; indeed he is only once shown standing, and even then in a slightly hunched position that contrasts with the stately carriage of his 'adversary'. He is twice (three times if we include a rejected design for 'The Temptation of Bread') shown upside down, and on one occasion—that of the banquet-scene—in the sinister Jupiter-Pluvius position, an indication of the inverted nature of his values and the absurdity of his aims. His deviations from the normal standing position are on the whole artist's additions: in the banquet-scene for instance the text indicates simply that 'a man [Satan] before him [Christ] stood' (ii, 298). Upright posture is a clear indicator of steadfastness of vision: not only is Satan never shown upright but the only two plates in which Christ is not so depicted are the eighth and the ninth, in which he is shown undergoing and then recovering from the most violent of Satan's assaults.

In *Paradise Regained* Satan appears in different disguises for the first two biblical temptations[5] but 'in wonted shape' (iv, 449) for the third. Elizabeth Pope points out that the phrase is ambiguous: it may mean that he appeared in his original form or in 'the shape in which he usually appeared in the wilderness'[6]—if the latter, then the 'courtier' of the second day must be the 'aged man' of the first, for there would have been no point in referring to the Devil's accustomed shape if he had not actually assumed more than one.

Blake appears to compromise on this point: he shows Satan in all three of his encounters with Christ as the white-bearded old man of this world—certainly disguised when compared with his 'natural' youthful form in the first and fifth illustrations but on all three occasions differently dressed. For the first temptation he is clad in a garment reaching almost to his knees; for the second he is wearing only a loin-cloth, having somehow managed to change out of the robe that he was wearing in the banquet-scene;[7] and for the third he appears naked. This progressive disrobing, which is thematically the most significant aspect of Blake's renderings of the 'disguises', enables the darkened 'lineaments' of evil to be fully exposed in the scene in which Satan is finally defeated. It is paralleled in the poem by Christ's gradual

---

[4] Cf. Ephesians 2:2, in which he is described as the 'prince of the power of the air'.

[5] Cf. i, 314: 'an aged man in rural weeds'; and ii, 298–300: 'When suddenly a man before him stood,/Not rustic as before, but seemlier clad,/As one in city, or court, or palace bred'.

[6] *Paradise Regained: the Tradition and the Poem*, 1947, p. 49.

[7] No doubt an oversight on Blake's part: the Satan of the poem is onstage, engaged in verbal duelling with Christ, for all of the intervening period.

demolishing of Satan's arguments—a process which leaves him morally and spiritually naked.

At the beginning of *Paradise Regained* Milton emphasizes Christ's 'merely' human nature, and particularly his typological relation to Adam; by the end of the poem he has revealed the full significance of the title 'Son of God' by showing Christ as the 'True image of the Father .../... enshrined/In fleshly tabernacle, and human form' (iv, 596 and 598–9).

Blake too asserts Christ's human nature—though more radically than Milton—by casting doubts on the immaculateness of his conception, by insinuating that in one of his ordeals he was in some physical and even spiritual danger, and (most blasphemously of all) by asserting that his implacable adversary, Satan, is in fact his Spectre—the debased portion of his own human nature.[8] However, for Blake Christ's humanity was in no way opposed to his divinity: it was the essence of it. The climax of his illustrative series emphasizes this 'Divine Humanity' by showing a victorious Christ balancing on the pinnacle of the temple in the Crucifixion posture, the Crucifixion being the episode from his life which best demonstrates his humanity.

PARADISE REGAINED I: THE BAPTISM OF CHRIST (79)

The first illustration of the series establishes Blake's familiarity with literary and pictorial tradition regarding the Baptism. Its general design is that of many biblical illustrations of the subject: Christ is depicted frontally, with John the Baptist on his right, onlookers to either side,[9] and the Holy Spirit 'in likeness of a dove' (i, 30) descending from the sky.[10] The lightning shown on either side of the Dove is not mentioned by Milton and is seldom found in illustrations of the Baptism though it may be justified by reference to the prophecy of the Baptist at Matthew 3:11: 'he that cometh after me is mightier than I, whose shoes I am not worthy to bear: he shall baptize you with the Holy Ghost, and *with* fire'. The long-haired pelt and girdle worn by John the Baptist are also taken from Matthew: 'John had his raiment of camel's hair, and a leathern girdle about his loins'.[11] The bareness of the figure's arms and exposed right shoulder is sanctioned by pictorial tradition, for the typical

[8] For a full discussion see my analysis of *Paradise Regained* I.
[9] They are usually shown only on Christ's left.
[10] The schematic appearance of the Dove sorts oddly with the more realistic appearance of the human figures and is reminiscent of the style of pre-Renaissance biblical illustrations.
[11] iii, 4.

Baptist of Western art wears 'une peau de mouton ou de chèvre qui laisse à nu les bras, les jambes et même une partie du torse'.[12] The left hand of Blake's John is raised, with the palm open towards the sky and the thumb widely separated from the four fingers—a gesture similar to that of many baptizing Johns found in biblical illustrations from the Middle Ages onwards.

Milton does not particularize the witnesses of the ceremony: 'to his great baptism flocked/With awe the regions round' (i, 21–2). In traditional renderings of the Baptism they are generally apostles or angels but in Blake's they are common people and include representative figures from four main stages of man's life—infancy, childhood, parenthood, and old age. The hands of the old man and those of the baby are raised in prayer, and the children—to Blake vessels of divine energy and spiritual vision—are exuberant in the expression of their joy. Through the presence of these common people Blake stresses the particular relevance to the humble of Christ's mission, and perhaps also the humble origins of the Son of God himself.

Christ is shown naked except for a loin-cloth. His carefully worked Michelangelesque torso and calves, the disproportion of his body—larger in the legs and torso, smaller in the chest and head—and the statuesque rigidity of his stance are typical of many of Blake's nudes. His feet are immersed in the waters of a narrow channel—presumably a diagrammatic representation of the River Jordan—at the point where it opens out into a lake, and his hands are displayed with palms towards the viewer, as if to indicate that the stigmata are not yet imprinted upon them. The figure's eyes are raised heavenwards but his nimbus is only adumbrated in the faint rays of light that emanate from his head. As a perplexed Satan later observes to his henchmen, 'man he seems/In all his lineaments, though in his face/The glimpses of his father's glory shine' (i, 91–3).

Satan himself is portrayed in flight and in his own element of the air. He is shown naked and from the rear, his hands raised above his head and his figure foreshortened. Unlike the Satan of the fifth illustration, he displays none of the traditional iconographical attributes of the Devil though the Serpent, 'Glittering with festering Venoms' (*The Everlasting Gospel*, K 755; 84) of red, yellow, and blue, is draped across his chest and is presumably being carried along or fleeing with him. Its presence suggests the 'well-couched fraud, well-woven snares' (i, 97) which are to characterize all of Satan's confrontations with Christ. Though Milton does not mention the Serpent in his Baptism-scene, he later refers to it by describing Satan as 'girded with snaky wiles' (i, 120), 'collecting all his serpent wiles' (iii, 5), and once as 'the

[12] Louis Réau, *Iconographie de l'art chrétien*, 1955–9, ii, 439.

old serpent' (ii, 147). The Devil's presence at Blake's Baptism and the manner of his portrayal are justified by the text:

> The Spirit descended, while the Father's voice
> From heaven pronounced him his beloved Son.
> That heard the adversary, who roving still
> About the world, at that assembly famed
> Would not be last, and with the voice divine
> Nigh thunder-struck, the exalted man, to whom
> Such high attest was given, a while surveyed
> With wonder, then with envy fraught and rage
> Flies to his place...
>
> (i, 31–9)

In his poetry Blake sometimes identifies Satan with the Spectre of Christ and even portrays him emerging from Christ's body:

> ... at length an awful wonder burst
> From the Hermaphroditic bosom. Satan he was nam'd,
> Son of Perdition, terrible his form, dishumaniz'd, monstrous,
> A male without a female counterpart, a howling fiend
> Fo(r)lorn of Eden & repugnant to the forms of life
>
> (*Vala*, K 347; 250–4)[13]

> Then Roll'd the shadowy Man away
> From the Limbs of Jesus, to make them his prey,
> An Ever devouring appetite
> Glittering with festering Venoms bright
>
> (*The Everlasting Gospel*, K 755; 81–4)

The Satan of *Paradise Regained* i, who is represented without demonic attributes and in the company of the Serpent, and who is depicted behind and above Christ's left shoulder as though he, like the Spectre of Los, had emerged from the back of his principal,[14] was almost certainly also regarded by Blake as Christ's Spectre. So the illustrative Temptations, involving as they apparently do the confrontation of Christ by an aspect of himself, inevitably take on an internal, psychological significance.

---

[13] It is clear from the context that the 'Hermaphroditic bosom' is in this case Christ's and not that of Albion, Blake's 'original' man.

[14] Cf. *Milton*, K 483; pl. 3, 34–6: 'all the while from his Back/A blue fluid exuded in Sinews, hardening in the Abyss/Till it separated into a Male Form howling in Jealousy'; and *Jerusalem*, K 624; pl. 5, 68, and pl. 6, 1–2: 'But Westward, a black Horror,/His Spectre driv'n by the Starry Wheels of Albion's sons, black and/Opake divided from his back'; also the vanquished gods fleeing from their idols in the *Nativity Ode* series.

This has its counterpart in the close, almost intimate relationship that develops in the epic between Christ and Satan, and in an extreme theological view which held that the Christ of the Temptations was tempted inwardly, 'by his own corruption'.[15] It is however sharply opposed to the orthodox doctrine, fundamentally that of Milton himself, which stresses the absolute disparity between the nature and origins of Christ and those of Satan.

Though Blake's writings on the subject are fragmentary and somewhat obscure, it appears that to him the 'separation' of the Satan–Spectre from Christ was concomitant with Christ's own assumption of a 'vegetated body', and that this body could itself be associated with, or serve as a symbol for, his human sinfulness. Similarly, the Devil is vanquished only with the death of Christ's body—that is, at the Crucifixion, an event depicted in the penultimate illustration of the *Paradise Lost* series and prefigured in the tenth *Paradise Regained* plate. So Blake's Christ took on not only the punishment that was demanded for man's sins but also those very sins themselves.

By endowing his Christ with an originally erring nature, Blake was not, according to his own view, tarnishing the Son of God's divinity but adding a vital element to his saving grace. It is this propensity to sin which emancipates the Blakean Christ from the inhibiting meekness of the Saviour of Christian tradition; which strengthens his identity with those whom he came to save; and which supports the antinomian doctrine, to which Blake adhered, of the identity between divinity and humanity: 'Thou art a Man, God is no more,/Thine own Humanity learn to Adore' (*The Everlasting Gospel*, K 750; 41–2). Christ's sinfulness is also used by Blake to support his own belief that 'error' has to be known in order to be overcome. It has only a distant parallel in Milton's emphasis at the beginning of *Paradise Regained* on the human nature of Christ, something which may itself be reflected in the barely discernible nimbus with which the artist endows the Christ of *Paradise Regained* I—a dramatic contrast to the clearly delineated disc-haloes of the later plates.

So in his opening illustration to *Paradise Regained* Blake interprets the Baptism as a kind of bodying forth of Christ's mortal sinfulness. The great sheet of water which stretches out behind the figures is presumably intended to represent the Galilean lake, which lies at the northern end of the River Jordan, but also the waters of materialism. On its further shore is depicted a walled city with dome and spire—emblems similar to those used in *Jerusalem*, plate 57, to represent the opposed (as Blake saw it) cities of fallen London and the New Jerusalem. The manner of their

---

[15] The theologian Diodati (who himself opposed this position), quoted by John Carey, *The Poems of Milton*, eds. John Carey and Alastair Fowler, p. 1063.

depiction suggests the youthful Christ's uncertainty regarding his destiny and identity.

The trumpet-shaped vessel from which John is pouring the baptismal water on to the head of Christ derives in part from Milton's description of the voice of the prophet:

> Now had the great proclaimer with a voice
> More awful than the sound of trumpet, cried
> Repentance, and heaven's kingdom nigh at hand
> To all baptized
>
> (i, 18–21)

The trumpet in question does not however resemble the elegant, straight-stemmed clarions of Blake's 'Last Judgement' illustrations. It is a squat vessel with coiled stem and curling lip—a cousin to the trumpets of doom which in *Europe*, plate 9, blow plague-seeds into the corn and to the trumpet of the wind which in Young's *Night Thoughts*, Night v, page 24, dispels figures representing fleeting bliss. Its curled stem is reminiscent of the coils of the Serpent and of the vegetation of the natural world.

The Baptism, traditionally conceived as a 'second birth', as the bestowal of the power and virtue of the Father upon the Son, and as the ceremony which marks the beginning of Christ's ministry, is interpreted by Blake as an essential first stage in the redemptive process—the giving of the 'vegetated body/To be cut off & separated, that the Spiritual body may be Reveal'd' (*Vala*, K 348; 265 and 267), or as the objectifying of sin in order that it may be confronted and overcome.

PARADISE REGAINED II: THE TEMPTATION OF BREAD (80, 81)

Here Blake depicts the first encounter between Christ and the Devil. Both are shown pointing to their mouths with their right hands. With his left hand Satan is indicating a small rock that lies at his feet:[16]

> But if thou be the Son of God, command
> That out of these hard stones be made thee bread;
> So shalt thou save thyself and us relieve
> With food, whereof we wretched seldom taste.
>
> (i. 342–5)

and in reply Christ is pointing heavenwards: 'Man lives not by bread only, but each word/Proceeding from the mouth of God' (i, 349–50). While keeping his eyes

[16] The first part of my discussion refers to the Fitzwilliam version only.

fixed on his antagonist each figure is therefore indicating with his left hand the source of the values which he expounds and defends in debate—heaven and things spiritual in the case of Christ, obdurate earth and things material in the case of Satan.

Christ is presented as an upright figure clothed in long and semi-translucent robes. He is standing with his back to the viewer but with his face in profile. His head is set within a white disc-halo and he is gazing steadily and sternly at Satan.

By contrast the Prince of evil appears sly and cringing. His brow is furrowed and his expression downcast. As in the poem, he is disguised as 'an aged man in rural weeds' (i, 314). The 'weeds' hang down behind him in a manner suggestive of the folded wings of the Devil but are drawn up in front to reveal his muscular, Michelangelesque legs. He sports the beard of Blake's old man of the fallen world.

The gestures and appearance of the two figures resemble those of Plato and Aristotle in Raphael's wall-painting 'The School of Athens', which Blake must surely have known from engravings. The similarity is appropriate, for the Christ of *Paradise Regained* is associated with certain tenets of the Platonist philosophy and Satan with the Aristotelian method of experimental investigation. In *Jerusalem* (K 685; pl. 54, 19–24) Blake represents the Temptation of Bread as a taunting challenge by the Spectre of Albion to his original to perform a scientific experiment as confirmation of his belief:

> Where is that Friend of Sinners? that Rebel against my Laws
> Who teaches Belief to the Nations & an unknown Eternal Life?
> Come hither into the Desart & turn these stones to bread.
> Vain Foolish Man! wilt thou believe without Experiment
> And build a World of Phantasy upon my Great Abyss,
> A World of Shapes in craving lust & devouring appetite?

In his later years Blake often emphasized his belief in the superiority of the teachings of Christ to those of Plato, but he had earlier annotated Lavater's Platonic sixteenth Aphorism:

The greatest of characters, no doubt, was he, who, free of all trifling accidental helps, could see objects through one grand immutable medium, always at hand, and proof against illusion and time, reflected by every object, and invariably traced through all the fluctuation of things

with, 'This was Christ' (K 66).

As has already been noted, rocks are associated by Blake with the Satanic material world. For this reason they are contrasted in his poetry with Christ and with the Christian values of Imagination and brotherhood:

> those combin'd by Satan's Tyranny, first in the blood of War
> And Sacrifice & next in Chains of inprisonment, are Shapeless Rocks
> Retaining only Satan's Mathematic Holiness, Length, Bredth & Highth,
> Calling the Human Imagination, which is the Divine Vision & Fruition
> In which Man liveth eternally, madness & blasphemy against
> Its own Qualities...
>
>   (*Milton*, K 521; pl. 32, 16–21)

The background to the illustration is formed from closely ranked trees whose burgeoning foliage suggests that of the 'oak groves' of Albion, which Blake frequently links with the fallen world. Their presence is justified, if barely, by a reference in the text of *Paradise Regained* to Christ taking shelter 'Under the covert of some ancient oak' (i, 305). The outline of the trees is broken by the nimbus of Christ but it rises to a curious, pyramid-shaped peak above the head of Satan.

Sir Geofrey Keynes has identified a water-colour in the Frick Collection, New York, as a rejected design for 'The Temptation of Bread'.[17] He suggests that it was rejected 'because another quite different version, which agreed more closely with the text, was eventually included in the series'.[18] It is similar in conception, style, colouring, and size to the illustrations of the *Paradise Regained* series, though its design is quite different to that of *Paradise Regained* II. It shows a profile figure of Christ in a long white robe and with a star-shaped nimbus turning his back on a Satan who is descending naked from the sky, his body inverted and set within a mandorla of flames and smoke. Hs is depicted lifting a stone from the ground. Several spectral heads, which Keynes identifies as 'Spirits of Hunger',[19] are shown within the upper part of the mandorla, and the top of a pillar is visible behind Satan's feet.

PARADISE REGAINED III: ANDREW AND SIMON PETER SEARCHING FOR CHRIST (82)

The plate is dominated by the figures of Andrew and Simon Peter, who are standing together at centre foreground, and by those of their guardian-angels, who are hovering at shoulder height beside them. The disciples are making stylized gestures of despair at their failure to seek out Christ. The disc-haloes which encircle their heads are translucent, unlike the radiant nimbus borne by Christ. The angels' heads and backs are framed by mandorlas. Their presence is not mentioned in the text.

[17] John Bunyan, *The Pilgrim's Progress*, ed. G. B. Harrison and Introduction by Geoffrey Keynes, 1941, pp. xxviii, xxxi.
[18] Ibid., p. xxviii.   [19] Ibid., p. xxviii.

The scene in which Andrew and Simon Peter reveal their doubts about Christ's whereabouts and intentions is one of several at the beginning of Book II in which the disciples themselves, Mary, and then Satan all display anxieties and doubts of various kinds concerning Christ. These doubts are counterpointed by the certitude of Christ himself, who, though also without the surety of certain knowledge regarding his own nature, is quite 'Without distrust or doubt' (iii, 193).

Blake too placed great importance on the doubt theme, devoting five illustrations (*Paradise Regained* II to VI) to it and concluding his series with an illustration in which Andrew, Simon Peter, and Mary are all shown overcoming their anxieties. In his writings it is associated particularly with the Baconian school of experimental science, which in turn is contrasted with the rule of Christ: 'To teach doubt & Experiment/Certainly was not what Christ meant' (*The Everlasting Gospel*, K 752; 49–50).

The walled city in the background to *Paradise Regained* III is flanked by palms and must surely represent 'Jericho/The city of palms' (ii, 20–1), one of the places visited by the disciples in their search for Christ. It is broken into three sections on the plate by the intervening figures of the two disciples. The section on the left contains a square-topped tower surrounded by a castellated wall, that on the right a domed roof, and that in the centre a spire. The outermost structures suggest the forces of the secular and (anachronistically) the Moslem worlds; the central spire, the power and promise of Christianity.

PARADISE REGAINED IV: MARY LAMENTING CHRIST'S ABSENCE (83)

Much of the appeal of this illustration resides in its delicate and harmonious use of colour. It is executed in blue, light brown, and green, and is imbued with light. It shows the Virgin Mary veiled and seated at home, her distaff propped up against the wall beside her. Her thatched house or shelter, which is drawn schematically and in cross-section, fills most of the plate. Two guardian-angels, who have adopted mirror positions on either side of the house, are shown in profile peering down at Mary through the ridged roof. She is gazing up at the one on her left and making a gesture of ignorance or of despair.

The symmetry of the design is enhanced by two palm trees that grow one on each side of the house, their branches framing the angels' heads, and by two small plants that are straggling up either wall. One has a few small, lozenge-shaped leaves; the other is without foliage. Their positions suggest a symbolic significance. They may be intended to indicate man's dual nature—his propensity for 'error' and his genius for salvation[20]—or they may be related to the tradition of Baptism illustration in which a tree with leaves is juxtaposed with a withered tree. They could also be taken as a reference to the typological belief that the rod of Aaron was 'a type of the Priesthood of Christ, who in the world seemed a dead branch and drie, but after his death and resurrection beganne again to flourish'.[21]

Blake's Mary is dressed not in her traditional robes of blue but in white, although her halo is blue. Her distaff and veil indicate her role as earthly mother, spinner of Christ's mortal body, and relate her to other Blakean female figures who are also corporeal 'guardians', like Vala and Rahab.

The cross-sectional 'house' of *Paradise Regained* IV is very similar to the stable of the *Nativity Ode* series. The resemblance is appropriate for, apart from the pictorial Mary's role as spinner of the earthly body, the Mary of the poem herself recollects the Nativity in lines which form part of the text for the illustration:

> scarce a shed
> Could be obtained to shelter him or me
> From the bleak air; a stable was our warmth,
> A manger his ...
>
> (ii, 72–5)

PARADISE REGAINED V: SATAN ADDRESSING HIS FOLLOWERS (84)

This illustration shows Satan holding one of his Infernal councils. In design and in detail it forms a contrast with the eleventh illustration of the series, in which Christ is ministered to by angels after his victory over the Devil. In both pictures the protagonist is shown at centre and surrounded by his followers, but whereas Christ stands calm and upright and is supported by two of his 'companions', Satan is distraught and perches in ungainly isolation on his throne. He is holding the sceptre of power in his left hand (where the Christ of the eleventh illustration wields none) and making grandiose, if unacknowledged, gestures—a reflection of his empty rhetoric in the poem. The angels of *Paradise Regained* XI form a living mandorla about Christ's body; the devils, a kind of horseshoe around Satan. Apart from the devils in the foreground,

[20] Cf. plate 4 of the illustrations to Gray's *Ode for Music*, in which Milton himself is shown seated between a bare tendril on one side and a large sunflower and lily on the other.
[21] Taylor, 'Christs Combate', pp. 161–2; quoted by Barbara Kiefer Lewalski, *Milton's Brief Epic*, 1966, p. 310.

whose bodies form the centre-piece of the 'shoe', only their heads are visible. This is appropriate, as to Blake the rationalizing intellect of fallen man was at the service of the devil. Most of the heads appear melancholy, and several have bestial features. Their number includes two old men and a couple of temptresses. At either extremity of the horseshoe the faces of the devils fall victim to lassitude and melt into the flames, which appear ready to liquidate the rest of the lesser devils and finally to engulf the Prince of Evil himself. They serve as a reminder of that hell-fire which awaits the devils and which Satan blusteringly implies that he can ignore:

> much more willingly I mention air,
> This our old conquest, than remember hell
> Our hated habitation
>
> (i, 45–7)

The subdued colouring of the flames—yellow, with hardly a touch of red—denies the fiery energy which to Blake was concomitant with spirituality. The row of raised spears in the background indicates Satan's obsession with violence and his lust for power.

The illustration is relieved by several comic touches. Satan is posturing absurdly, and one of the foremost devils has stabbed the toe of his opposite number with his spear, causing the injured devil to glare malevolently back at him—an unexpected note of humour.

The demons display several of their traditional iconographic attributes—nudity and, in the case of Satan, ruffled hair, an expression of anguish, and reptilian wings. Scales are shown on the body of one of the lesser devils, and bestial facial characteristics can be seen in the demons in the upper left-hand portion of the horseshoe.

As in the poem Satan is presented as a callow and commonplace fellow who has 'lost/Much lustre of [his] native brightness' (i, 377–8). His throne, which is not mentioned in *Paradise Regained* yet which appears as an ironically over-elaborate edifice in Book II, lines 1–4, of *Paradise Lost*, consists merely of a flight of stone steps that rise ponderously out of the flames. The small flames visible between two of the steps suggest that Satan is about to be engulfed by the hell-fire that already surrounds his fellows.

PARADISE REGAINED VI: CHRIST REJECTING SATAN'S BANQUET (85)

Texturally this illustration is the richest of the series, though its 'pompous delicacies' (ii, 390) are perhaps overblown to the artistic as well as to the moral sense. In the middle ground it shows the banqueting table, with two voluptuous naked females reclining at it on couches. Before it stand Christ and a trio of shapely and seductive young women who brush the ground near him with the tips of their toes and whose bodies rise sharply away from his and as one, like a shadow from its source. Christ's head is turned, and his body tilted, away from them, and he is gesturing rejection. The Devil appears to be offering him a false, triple version of his Emanation.

Satan is hovering with inverted body above his handiwork. He is again disguised as an old man, and his beard, his outstretched arms, and his elevated position on the plate all suggest the old Jupiter-Pluvius image familiar from two of the *Paradise Lost* illustrations. However, his expression of alarm as he sees his offering rejected by Christ, and the impression of motion—and of impermanence—created by his sideways-streaming beard, by the swirling, dog's-tooth mandorla which surrounds him, and by the motion-charged position of his inverted body, may be contrasted with the impression of impassivity and assured incumbency conveyed by the presiding deity of 'The House of Death' and by the Jehovah of *Paradise Lost* v (2). Where both of the latter figures were secure in their dominion, Satan's rule is here being threatened by the constancy of Christ.

Satan is dangling the crown of worldly dominion just above Christ's head but, ironically, it is depicted beside the Saviour's radiant halo and so appears as the puny, even contemptible, reward that it is. No crown is mentioned in the banquet-scene of the poem though one is alluded to by Christ in the debate that follows:

> What if with like aversion I reject
> Riches and realms; yet not for that a crown,
> Golden in show, is but a wreath of thorns,
> Brings dangers, troubles, cares, and sleepless nights
> To him who wears the regal diadem,
> When on his shoulders each man's burden lies;
>
> . . .
>
> Yet he who reigns within himself, and rules
> Passions, desires, and fears, is more a king . . .
>
> (ii, 457–62 and 466–7)

The three women in the foreground of the illustration presumably derive their presence from a reference by Milton to 'Nymphs of Diana's train, and Naiades/ With fruits and flowers from Amalthea's horn,/And ladies of the Hesperides, that seemed/Fairer than feigned of old' (ii, 355–8), who 'Under the trees now tripped, now solemn stood' (ii, 354). By moving to the centre of his plate a group that was of marginal significance in Milton's banquet-scene Blake alters the emphasis of the temptation from one of gluttony to one of lust.

Together the three figures form a closely integrated group reminiscent of traditional representations of the three Graces. The two seductresses furthest from the viewer are clasping hands above their heads, thus forming a controlling arch above the group. The figure of the foremost of the three falls within the boundaries established by the other two. One is making amorous overtures to Christ, the second is skittishly kicking her leg back towards him, and the third is clasping the second just under her left breast. Two are gazing at Christ, the other is glancing coyly at the viewer. The foremost of them is wearing a scaly bodice decorated—like the hem of her dress—with tassels. The other two are naked. They appear to be forms of the three sinister women who, as the Fates or the daughters of Urizen, dominate man's terrestrial existence in the universe as it is conceived by Blake.

The seductresses of *Paradise Regained* vi have their immediate origin in the fertile mind of Belial, the 'dissolutest spirit that fell,/The sensualest, and after Asmodai/ The fleshliest incubus' (ii, 150–2):

> Set women in his eye and in his walk,
> Among daughters of men the fairest found;
> Many are in each region passing fair
> As the noon sky; more like to goddesses
> Than mortal creatures, graceful and discreet,
> Expert in amorous arts, enchanting tongues
> Persuasive, virgin majesty with mild
> And sweet allayed, yet terrible to approach,
> Skilled to retire, and in retiring draw
> Hearts after them tangled in amorous nets.
>   (ii), 153–62)

The paradoxical charms of the women of Belial's imagination have been precisely rendered, even down to the 'retiring' but alluring curve of their bodies.

In the poem Satan makes 'a quick answer' (ii, 172) of fifty-one lines on the follies of executing such a stratagem as Belial's. That he should nevertheless proceed to adopt it is telling evidence of his slyness, his insecurity, and his own poverty of imagination.

As at Comus's banquet the food does not appear particularly enticing and is unattractively displayed. The many-branched candlesticks perhaps suggest (falsely) that the feast conforms to Mosaic dietary law[22] and the seats take the form of reclining Roman couches—an acknowledgement of Milton's comparison of the banquet of *Paradise Regained* with the orgies of the Romans. Leaves and berries are depicted

---

[22] Cf. ii, 344–5: 'all fish from sea or shore,/Freshet, or purling brook, *of shell* or fin' (italics mine).

on the sides of the couches. These, and the olive-leaves in the upper left-hand corner of the plate, are a reminder of the grove in which the banquet was conjured up.

On the far side of the table above the reclining female guests are a pair of angels, shown in profile with their faces almost touching and their wings placed together behind them. The motif is repeated both to the left of Christ and to the right of the maidens. Textually the angels derive from Christ's reply to the Devil—a scene represented in the eleventh illustration of the series:

> I can at will, doubt not, as soon as thou,
> Command a table in this wilderness,
> And call swift flights of angels ministrant
> Arrayed in glory on my cup to attend ...
>
> (ii, 383–6)

Visually the juxtaposition of angels with the saw-toothed edge of Satan's mandorla is reminiscent of the design for plate 22 of *Jerusalem*, in which a band of angels with interlocking arms, feet, and wings is shown hovering above the cruel wheels and cogs of industrial England. The text for this detail is also appropriate to *Paradise Regained* VI, for it exalts what to Blake was Christ's supreme quality—forgiveness:

> Why should Punishment Weave the Veil with Iron Wheels of War
> When Forgiveness might it Weave with Wings of Cherubim?
>
> (K 645; 34–5)

PARADISE REGAINED VII: THE TEMPTATION OF THE KINGDOMS (86)

This illustration has Satan revealing the kingdoms of the world to Christ. Christ is standing on a large, flat-topped rock, and Satan is hovering in mid-air with a symbolic vision of the three major kingdoms depicted just beneath his right hand.

As in Blake's illustration of the first temptation, the contrast between Christ and his adversary, Satan, is presented in terms of an opposition between classical and Renaissance styles of figure-drawing. Christ is portrayed in profile as a small-headed, long-limbed, and full-bellied Grecian figure. He is gazing sternly down at Satan, who is again shown with beard and with furrowed brow, and is naked apart from a green loin-cloth, the colour of which serves to suggest his association with the natural world.

Christ is robed in white and has a radiant disc-halo; Satan has a darkened body and a black spiked halo. The positions and appearances of the two figures reflect the dominant image-patterns in the poem, according to which Christ is associated with a rock and Satan with the 'power of the air', Christ with light and Satan with darkness; and according to which the steadfast stillness of Christ is contrasted with the futile bustling of Satan. The rock upon which Christ is standing does not evoke Milton's 'mountain high' (iii, 252) and may in part owe its presence to a subsequent reference by Christ to Nebuchadnezzar's vision of a stone which smashed the metal image of the kingdoms and 'became a great mountain, and filled the whole earth' (Daniel 2:35).

The gestures of the two figures are also contrasted. Both are using the index fingers of both hands but Satan is pointing skywards with his left hand and to the kingdoms with his right, Jesus skywards with his right hand and to the kingdoms with his left. By indicating heaven with his 'corporeal' hand and the kingdoms with his 'spiritual', Satan is revealing the distortion of his values; by indicating the opposite Christ is affirming his own set of values and the 'natural order' of the universe.

The three kingdoms of Parthia, Rome, and Athens are shown in an 'allegoric' (iv, 390) manner quite divorced from Milton's cumbersome but quasi-realistic presentation of them as an actual 'sight'. They are depicted within three concentric elliptical arcs that hover in the air just beneath Satan's right hand, and are coloured yellow and orange but fringed—portentously—with black rays. The lowest 'kingdom' contains an enthroned figure wearing a helmet and holding a spear, and two others worshipping on their knees at an altar. The central arc also contains a despot worshipped by two kneeling minions. The topmost 'kingdom' is largely given over to chaos but a flaming altar and a kneeling figure can be discerned within it.

Milton's manner of presenting the kingdoms conveys the immense expanse of the territories over which their rulers presided (Parthia and Rome) or their architectural glories and the splendour of their sites (Rome and Athens): Blake's denies them even the dubious prestige of physical expanse by stressing the way in which they appear to the eye of true vision—despotic, disordered, and barbaric. Their worthlessness is also revealed in *Paradise Regained*, however, for at Book iv, line 86, Satan admits that, apart from Parthia and Rome, all 'thrones' are barbarous; at lines 94 and 100–2 he describes the 'monster' Tiberius with his 'horrid lusts', who made his throne a 'sty' and enslaved his people; and at lines 209–10 he concedes that 'The kingdoms of this world' 'are transitory'.

PARADISE REGAINED VIII: CHRIST'S TROUBLED DREAM (87)

Milton does not commit himself as to the extent of Satan's responsibility for the storm that overwhelms the sleeping Christ:

> at his head
> The tempter watched, and soon with ugly dreams
> Disturbed his sleep; and either tropic now
> 'Gan thunder, and both ends of heaven, the clouds
> From many a horrid rift abortive poured
> Fierce rain with lightning mixed, water with fire
> In ruin reconciled ...
>
> (iv, 407–13)

though traditionally the weather was under the control of the 'prince of the power of the air'. By figuring him as Jupiter Pluvius Blake makes the Devil directly responsible for the storm.

The outstretched arms and wings, bodiless nature, and straggling beard of this figure are all familiar. As is traditional in representations of Jupiter Pluvius, thick lines of driving sleet descend from his arms and hands. The fact that his arms and wings are extended suggests the apparent universality of the catastrophe: 'either tropic now/'Gan thunder, and both ends of heaven ...' etc. It is appropriate to his roles both as god of the storm and as 'Prince of Darkness' (iv, 441) that Satan's wings should be dark and his head surmounted by a black disc-halo, and the glint in his eye, which combines desperation with malice, indicates the futility of his action: he has no new tricks left to play and is simply venting through the storm the rage and frustration which he feels at his failure to vanquish Christ.

Christ is shown sleeping on a grassy bank, his figure draped diagonally across the plate. His position stresses the attenuation of his figure, his lack of intimacy with his surroundings, and the physical discomfort of his situation. The light emanating from his halo is considerably dimmer than it was in previous plates. Through this detail, and through the awkwardness of his posture, Blake may be attempting to suggest that it was here—in an episode that was not to Milton even a temptation but merely an expression of unbridled demonic despair, and throughout which Christ remained 'patient' and 'unshaken'—that Satan came near to achieving his purpose.

The lightning mentioned in the *Paradise Regained* storm-scene is represented in the illustration by spirals of brightly coloured venom unleashed from Satan's hands. The spiral on the right terminates in serpents' heads, which are menacing the head of the sleeping Christ. Besides these, several other vermicular forms are in evidence. Two describe decorative flourishes about Christ's feet and legs, one appears to be emerging from the ground beneath him, and a third rears itself over his body to flick its tongue at his head. They all appear rather fantastical, as might be expected of dream-serpents or serpents that are the product of a subjective, and temporarily deluded, vision. The heads of a couple of lions, which appear to be closing in on Christ, are also visible. Though they are largely the product of the Satanic imagination, the lions and serpents may in part owe their presence to lines from Book I of the poem which describe Christ inviolate in the wilderness:

> his walk
> The fiery serpent fled, and noxious worm,
> The lion and fierce tiger glared aloof
> (ll. 311–13)

or even to Psalm 91:13: 'Thou shalt tread upon the lion and adder: the young lion and the dragon shalt thou trample under feet'—a passage which is traditionally allegorized as the defeat of the dragon, which is Satan, by Christ. The equivalents of the lions and serpents in Milton's storm-scene are the vaguely conceived 'Infernal ghosts, and hellish furies' (iv, 422).

PARADISE REGAINED IX: MORNING CHASING AWAY THE PHANTOMS (88)

The lyricism and engaging humour of this illustration are more characteristic of the *L'Allegro* and *Il Penseroso* plates than of the rest of the *Paradise Regained* series. The personified figure of Morning—an attractive maiden with free-flowing locks whose left foot is poised on a miniature hillock—bears some resemblance to the Mirth of *L'Allegro* I, and the cloud-figures whom she is dispelling with 'radiant finger' (iv, 428) are similar to the 'devils' of that illustration:

> morning fair
> Came forth with pilgrim steps in amice grey;
> Who with her radiant finger stilled the roar
> Of thunder, chased the clouds, and laid the winds,
> And grisly spectres, which the Fiend had raised
> To tempt the Son of God with terrors dire.
> (iv, 426–31)

The clouds are imaged as naked boy-children with light-blue bodies framed within fluffy clouds. They are shown fleeing without ceremony from the advancing spirit of Morning. The last of them, who has tripped and whose feet almost brush against the body of Morning, is being whisked away by a darker, bat-winged companion who is already airborne. The 'winds,/And grisly spectres' (iv, 429–30) are represented as phantom heads and arms, with one partially exposed body that is covered in scales sinking back into the ground. Arms are clasping heads, and heads, at least one of which is that of a bearded old man, are wreathed about with vermicular forms. These are considerably less substantial, and less threatening, than they were in the storm-scene of the previous illustration. The creations of the Prince of Darkness are being vanquished by the spirit of Morning.

Christ, in a more relaxed and more nearly horizontal position now that the ordeal of the storm is over, has awakened and is gazing upwards. The contrast with the earlier scene is emphasized both by the radiance of his figure and by the fact that it is now shown pointing in the opposite direction. In the previous plate, in which he was surrounded by illusion, he had to touch his own body for reassurance; here he is shown touching the ground. Blake has endowed him with a golden disc-halo which is so positioned that it appears to be rising like a sun from behind the greenery at his back. This derives perhaps from the traditional Son-sun figure that is employed by Milton at lines 431–2 of Book iv: 'To tempt the Son of God with terrors dire./ And now the sun with more effectual beams . . .'

Morning, whom we might have expected to be the herald of the sun, is shown not with a golden halo but with a blue one—a tribute perhaps to the hood or 'amice grey' (iv, 427) which she wears in the poem. Her long, high-waisted robe is also blue, and her locks are without colour. She is carrying a staff, which probably derives from a reference in the poem to her 'pilgrim steps' (iv, 427).

Through the figures of Christ and Morning Blake may again be invoking the concept of the 'spiritual' and 'natural' suns. In *L'Allegro* vi the relative significance of these two suns was conveyed through size and by filling the greater sun with figures: here the key is one of colour. It is the greater or spiritual sun—Christ, who is also the Son of God and the redeemer of the world—that is golden; the lesser sun, whose function is limited to expelling the terrors of the night, is blue, the colour most frequently associated by Blake with the material world.

PARADISE REGAINED X: THE TEMPTATION OF THE PINNACLE (89)

What exactly the pinnacle was that is mentioned in the Gospels in connection with the third temptation was a question much debated by biblical exegetes.[23] Milton supported the view that it was a sharp point or spire. The implication of his temptation was therefore not the straightforward, 'I dare you to cast yourself down', but the more devious, 'In order to save yourself you must perform a miracle—either by balancing on top of the pinnacle or by casting yourself down and then saving yourself.' So the only way in which Christ can defeat the wily Satan is to balance upon the pinnacle through natural skill, thus neither injuring himself nor being forced to invoke divine assistance.

Blake's illustration conveys the magnitude of this feat. It shows the tips of a whole nest of ornate Gothic spires—the 'golden spires' (iv, 548) of Milton's Temple. The highest of them is tipped by a fleur-de-lis, and it is upon this point that Christ, making contact only with the tip of one toe, is balancing. For the first time in the series he is enshrined within a full-length mandorla and, having completely overcome the ordeal of the storm, is standing erect. His arms are outstretched in order to help him balance, to acknowledge any applause which his achievement may evoke, and as a prefiguring of the Crucifixion position. As in the first illustration his hands, and here his feet as well, are displayed in a flattened position, as though already nailed to the Cross. Milton, who wished at this point in the poem to emphasize Christ's divinity, does not draw an explicit connection with the Crucifixion, but biblical commentators often did make such a comparison, seeing the pinnacle as a prefiguring of the Cross and Satan's words as foreshadowing the taunts of the crowd.

As regards design the illustration is itself a study in balance, a fulfilment of Christ's earlier warning to Satan: 'Know'st thou not that my rising is thy fall' (iii, 201). The Saviour on his spire commands the centre of the plate. To one side of him Satan is shown falling headlong through the air; to his other side, and balancing the figure of the Devil, are three hovering angels. The wingtips of two of them are raised and placed together in imitation of the holy Gothic spire; the third is kneeling over towards the pinnacle and holding his hands up to it, though without actually touching it—a detail which emphasizes that the angels, though willing and able to come to Christ's aid, have not found it necessary to do so. Ironically it was Satan

---

[23] Cf. Elizabeth Pope, *Paradise Lost: the Tradition and the Poem*, pp. 84–5.

who had earlier assured Christ that if he should happen to fall, 'in their hands/They [i.e. the angels] shall uplift thee' (iv, 557–8).

The Devil is depicted within a sheet of flame that, like the Serpent of *Paradise Regained* I, is coloured red, yellow, and blue. The angels' prophecy at iv, 618–20, contains a similar reference, though in the context of a later, more conclusive fall:

> But thou, infernal serpent, shalt not long
> Rule in the clouds; like an autumnal star
> Or lightning thou shalt fall from heaven

Satan's gesture, in which he grasps the strands of his beard in both hands and holds them to either side of his chest, is similar to that of Mohammed, one of the 'schismatics' depicted in plate 56 of Blake's Dante series—although in Mohammed's case the edges of a chest wound are also being opened. Both gestures may derive from that of Despair in Ripa's *Iconologia*,[24] which is glossed as

A sorrowful Man in Rags; with both Hands he opens his Breast, and looks upon his Heart encompass'd with Serpents; his Garment is blackish.

The Rags shew him to *undervalue* and *neglect himself*. His open Breast, and the Serpents, denote the *Trouble* and *Vexation* of Worldly Things, always gnawing the Heart.

PARADISE REGAINED XI: CHRIST MINISTERED TO BY THE ANGELS (90)

Blake celebrates Christ's victory over Satan by conflating several signs of glory to create a humanized mandorla that terminates in yet another Gothic peak—even though one that is not contained within the frame of the illustration. The Saviour is surrounded by four angels who are not only ministering to him but actually supporting him aloft—and in Satan's former dominion of the air. The arrangement evokes the spiritual majesty which resides in the purified Divine Humanity—a Christ from which the 'Satanic body' has lately been expelled.

Two of the angels, their wings and legs intertwined and their robe-swathed feet forming a decorative flourish, provide the 'foundation' on which Christ is standing. One is offering him bread, the other a goblet of wine—an enactment of Christ's earlier boast to Satan, here fulfilled without risk of sin:

> I can at will, doubt not, as soon as thou,
> Command a table in this wilderness,

[24] 1709, p. 2.

> And call swift flights of angels ministrant
> Arrayed in glory on my cup to attend
>
> (ii, 383–6)

The other two angels, their bodies swaying outwards but their wings bending back again to meet just outside the boundary of the illustration, forms a mandorla which encompasses Christ's body and his disc-halo, which is even larger than in previous illustrations. The harps of these angels are held in such a way as to harmonize with the full curve of their bodies.

Christ, his eyes raised heavenwards, is shown blessing the food which is being offered him. After the drama and the triumph of the temptation on the pinnacle he is enacting the solemn ritual of the priest celebrating communion—one aspect of the threefold role of prophet, priest, and king that is ascribed to him in *Paradise Regained*. Though by Milton the least emphasized of the three offices, the role of priest is the one which best accords with Christ's primary function as intercessor for man.

The picture's outlines are soft but clear, and its colours translucent. In his harmonious lines and solemn atmosphere it reflects the ordered nature of the Divine Vision, which has at last succeeded the turbulent era of Satan. It also manifests divinity by concentrating exclusively on the human form, where in the poem a pastoral setting was envisaged for the feast itself:

> a fiery globe
> Of angels on full sail of wing flew nigh,
> Who on their plumy vans received him soft
> From his uneasy station, and upbore
> As on a floating couch through the blithe air,
> Then in a flowery valley set him down
> On a green bank, and set before him spread
> A table of celestial food, divine,
> Ambrosial, fruits fetched from the tree of life,
> And from the fount of life ambrosial drink
>
> (iv, 581–90)

PARADISE REGAINED XII: CHRIST RETURNING HOME (91)

Blake's *Paradise Regained* series, like the poem, concludes with an abrupt change of focus from the public to the private and personal: 'he unobserved/Home to his mother's house private returned' (iv, 638–9). Conqueror in the tenth illustration and priest in the eleventh, Christ has here assumed his most enduring role—that of a humble, yet adored, member of the human family. Appropriately, his halo is less prominent than in previous illustrations.

Mary, in white robes and now with a white halo as well, has risen and raised her arms to welcome Christ as he, gazing intently up at her, approaches. She is still inside her house but her hands have now broken free of its confining shape. Her expression of heartfelt relief and Christ's look of clear-eyed devotion are skilfully rendered.

Signs of resolution reside also in the landscape: the palm trees—traditional emblems of redemption—are now bearing fruit and their fronds are stroking the roof of the house. An enormous sun is rising in the background. The meagre plants and the distaff, both present in the fourth illustration of the series, have disappeared.

To either side of the house stand the disciples Andrew and Simon Peter, who are also welcoming Christ. They are not mentioned at this point in the poem but their presence recalls the doubt-and-faith theme elaborated earlier. Their gestures are now identical with those made by their respective angels in *Paradise Regained* III —an indication that, their doubts overcome, they are now in harmony with the world of the spirit.

Blake has already identified Mary, both in *Paradise Regained* IV and in the first *Nativity Ode* illustration, as the earthly but not the spiritual mother of Christ. It is at least possible that the woman of the concluding *Paradise Regained* illustration, who is distinguished from the Mary of *Paradise Regained* IV by the colour of her halo, is intended to be a representation not of Mary but of Jerusalem, who in the Prophetic books is identified both as the spiritual mother[25] and as the bride[26] of Christ, as well as the human soul, and who unites with Christ in mystic marriage as the Jerusalem of Revelation unites with the Lamb. She may therefore be regarded as Christ's true Emanation, preparing to return to him after the vanquishing of his Spectre (depicted in the tenth illustration of the series) and breaking out of the 'house of mortality' as she does so.

If this identification is correct then Blake has concluded his *Paradise Regained* series with an allusion to the final union of the Church with Christ and of the soul with God—and incidentally of the Poetic Genius with 'the daughters of Inspiration, who in the aggregate are call'd Jerusalem' (*A Vision of the Last Judgment*, K 604). Despite the splendour of the conception, however, the image is one of humble and approachable humanity: for Blake Christ's divinity found its highest expression in his nature as a man.

[25] Cf. e.g. *Vala*, K 347; 259–62; and *Jerusalem*, K 695; pl. 61, 47–9.
[26] Cf. e.g. *Jerusalem*, K 649; pl. 27, 5–8.

VII PENCIL DRAWINGS

SEPARATE SKETCHES FOR COMPLETED ILLUSTRATIONS

All except one of Blake's surviving studies for his Milton designs are for *Paradise Lost*. Most of them show that the general arrangement, the positioning of figures, and the symbolic detail in the completed plates were normally part of the artist's design from an early stage.

The most detailed of the sketches for completed illustrations is the pen, pencil, and water-colour drawing for *Paradise Lost* II. It shows a Satan and Death whose postures identify it as a study for the larger of the two completed designs. Satan is fairly well finished, with a sculptured torso and a marked expression of grief on his face. Death's shape is not yet translucent but he is already wielding his fiery dart. The portcullis chain is suspended directly above his head—something which supports my earlier contention that it has a symbolic function. Sin's gesture is far less vigorous, though more symmetrical, than it was to become in the completed illustration. Her Medusa locks and snaky coils, and the hounds kennelling in her womb, are already discernible—though the serpent-heads have not yet appeared. The portcullis and stone arches behind the figures are also intimated.

Two preliminary drawings for *Paradise Lost* IV are known. One is a tiny sketch on the back of a letter, which depicts only the central figures and which is inscribed 'Adam and Eve'. The figures are embracing; a bower is adumbrated above them and scattered flowers to either side. The larger drawing is similar to the smaller except that a setting sun and a Satan in close colloquy with his Serpent, hovering above the human pair and pointing at Adam, have been added to it. Sir Geoffrey Keynes[1] claims that the sketch is for the Fogg version of 'Satan Spying on Adam and Eve', though the direction of Satan's figure is as in the Huntington version.

The figures in the sketch for 'Raphael Warning Adam' are arranged as they are in the Huntington version. The outline of the bower is visible; so too is the Serpent-entwined Tree in the centre of the Paradisal landscape. There is a hint of Gothic

[1] *Blake's Pencil Drawings*, 2nd ser., 1956, p. 43.

tracery among the 'stems' of the chairs in the foreground. Raphael's arms are raised but his eventual splendour is not foreshadowed, for his wings are down-turned and unobtrusive.

In the preliminary drawing for 'The Creation of Eve' a rectangular arrangement is formed from the vertical lines of Christ's body and of Eve's, and from the horizontals of Christ's outstretched arm and the central portion of Adam's body, from which Eve appears still to be emerging. A moon is drawn above the rectangle. Much of the charm of the completed version springs from the slight disturbances that were made in the geometrical symmetry of the drawing: Eve eventually comes to hover just clear of Adam's body, Christ's arm has been raised above the horizontal, and the moon has been shifted slightly away from the centre.

A full-frontal drawing of Eve with the Serpent coiled about her body and standing before the Tree, is thought by Sir Geoffrey Keynes and others to be an early sketch for *Paradise Lost* IX. The positions of Eve and the Serpent are less balanced in the finished versions but the suggestions of imprisonment and of sexual licence have been retained. No fruit is shown in the sketch and the Serpent appears to be kissing Eve on the mouth.

The only separate sketch for a completed design which is not based on *Paradise Lost*, is the drawing for the Huntington version of *Nativity Ode* I. It suggests most of the major details of the illustration—Peace descending with her olive branch through the spheres of heaven, the stable surmounted by a Gothic arch and with vegetation to either side, the Holy Family with Mary in a swoon and the Christ-child exultant, the oxen, and the figure of Nature beneath the stable. However, Nature is a little more alert than she is in the finished plate, and Zacharias, the husband of Elizabeth, is not included in the group within the stable.

SEPARATE SKETCHES NOT RELATED TO KNOWN ILLUSTRATIONS

A tentative sketch showing its protagonist apparently embedded in a liquid 'medium' and encircled by smaller and more insubstantial figures, is identified in an inscription as one for 'Return Alpheus' (from *Lycidas*, l. 132). The central figure must therefore be the river-god Alpheus, and the others are presumably the mud-daubed nymphs amongst whom Artemis concealed herself when fleeing from him. Alpheus's perplexity and the nymphs' taunting actions and ubiquitous presence are evident. The nymphs appear to be practising 'sports of cruelty' on a victim who is trapped in water, the element that to Blake represents materialism. It is perhaps because the subject of Alpheus's unsuccessful wooing of Artemis was susceptible to interpretation as a parable of life in the fallen world that Blake chose to render it, even though the river-god's pursuit of Arethusa was the origin of Milton's reference and is itself a better-known story. As it stands the design is rudimentary, and shows none of the complexities of the Alpheus reference in *Lycidas*.

Blake's pencil sketch for *Comus*, ll. 660–1—'as Daphne was/Rootbound, that fled Apollo'—shows the chaste nymph of Ovid's *Metamorphoses* being transformed into a bush. She is poised on one foot with arms outstretched and hair rising in a halo of petrified leaves. The emphasis is not on escape but on petrifaction. The greenery that is sprouting from her fingertips and round her ankles and elbows suggests fetters, and her open-mouthed expression and tilting head convey the distress that she feels as her fleeting essence is fixed in 'vegetable' form. Blake has made the episode serve his own vision of how the sexually timid woman becomes a prisoner of her own capricious self. A marking on Daphne's upper torso may represent the head of one of Apollo's sacred 'cattle of the sun'. Apollo himself is shown standing back from the nymph, though with his hand reaching out towards her (as in Ovid) as he gazes upon her transformation. (The extent of his responsibility for her fate is not indicated by Blake.) The massive figure recumbent on the ground between the nymph and the god must be Daphne's father Peneus, shown in the conventional posture of a river-god. He was in Ovid the agent—though a reluctant one—of the transformation. Although Blake's understanding of the myth appears to conform quite closely with his interpretation of its immediate context in *Comus*—the enchanter's 'immanacling' of the Lady—he omitted any rendering of the subject of the sketch from his *Comus* series. This may have been because it forms a picturesque digression and is not part of the main narrative line. At all events Blake's affection for the subject is evident in the fact that he repeated it twice with only slight variations in his Notebook,[2] though on these occasions he restricted himself to a portrayal of the tree-nymph.

A sketch for 'The Expulsion of the Rebel Angels' shows a central Christ standing erect and with right arm raised, and, about and below him, three descending devils. One is portrayed with a shield, the other is clasping his head. The work bears little resemblance to *Paradise Lost* III.

[2] On pp. 12 and 36. I have not repeated this discussion under the section, 'From the Notebook'.

FROM THE NOTEBOOK

Blake's Notebook originally belonged to his brother Robert. On Robert's death in
February 1787 Blake inherited it and himself used it as a work-book until it was
filled around 1818. In it he drew several sketches of Miltonic subjects, one or two
of which served as drafts for illustrations executed later. (Drawings of merely con-
jectural relevance to Milton have not been discussed below, nor has a pencil sketch
for 'God Creating the World'. The sketch on page 91 of the Notebook, which illus-
trates *Paradise Lost* i, 221–2, was treated after the discussion of 'Satan Rousing his
Legions'.)

A sketch on page 73 of the Notebook shows the profile figure of a woman in a long
robe or nightdress cradling a child in her arms. The child's coverings hang down
against the woman's body. The background appears to be one of draped hangings,
which strengthens the picture's emphasis on severely vertical forms. Blake's annotation for the sketch is:

> Yet can I not perswade
> me, thou art dead
> Milton

—line 29 from the juvenile poem *On the Death of a Fair Infant*. The drawing represents
the death of the body and exposes the morbidity of the view that death is the end
of life.

In Blake's *Comus* III the disguised enchanter is shown viewing the Lady's Brothers
at their grape-gathering; in Notebook, page 30, his description of them as

> a faëry vision
> Of some gay creatures of the element
> That in the colours of the rainbow live ...
> (ll. 297–9)

is noted down and sketched by Blake without any of the irony implied in the illustrative series. Four fairies of ethereal suppleness are shown pirouetting in the air before
a 'plighted', i.e. folded, cloud. Like the figures who form a humanized halo for the
Mirth of *L'Allegro* I and the related engravings, they presumably represent the 'joys'
of spiritual existence. As David Erdman[3] points out, they reappear on the title-page
to *Visions of the Daughters of Albion*, at the bottom of a rainbow, and their attitudes
are very similar to those of four airborne and ring-dancing fairies in Fuseli's 'Der

[3] *The Notebook of William Blake*, 1973, p. 19.

Traum des Schäfers' (1785), which Fuseli himself related to those lines in *Paradise Lost* comparing the devils at play to 'faerie elves' at their 'midnight revels' (i, 781–8). The Fuseli drawing may have served Blake as a model.

A sketch on page 27 of the Notebook is identified by its inscription as an illustration for the *Sonnet: to Sir Henry Vane the Younger*, line 6:

> The drift of hollow states hard to
> be spelld   Milton

Blake has transformed Milton's lofty tribute to Vane—a Treasurer of the British Navy, whose efficiency had helped to bring the war with Holland (punningly referred to by Milton as the 'hollow states') to a happy (for England) conclusion—into an impassioned indictment of violence. His sketch shows a prostrate figure, clearly a victim of war, being mourned by two other figures, also prostrate, at his side and by two with bent heads at his head. David Erdman,[4] who has examined the original Notebook closely, has also distinguished 'Lightning [striking] the neck of a tall woman at the left.' Part of a building is shown on the right.

The other Milton drawings in the Notebook are all related to *Paradise Lost*. The first is on page 90 and shows Satan

> With head uplift above the wave ...
>   ... his other parts besides
> Prone on the flood, extended long and large ...
>   (i, 193–5)

As David Erdman[5] observes, his 'ponderous shield ... like the moon', which Milton does not mention till lines 284–7, can be seen on his right. His head, with its rolled-up eyes and pouting mouth, is similar to a portrait by Fuseli, possibly of Satan, which Blake engraved in 1790. The head in the sketch is more grotesque than those in the completed *Paradise Lost* illustrations, perhaps as a result of Fuseli's influence.

On page 112 of the Notebook Blake sketched an airborne figure with arms outstretched, bearing a shield and sword. Three large circles are drawn above him and some smaller ones to either side. David Erdman[6] identifies the subject of the sketch as the Satan of Book II exhorting his Stygian council and adds: 'His mouth is open in speech; the circles sketched on each side of his track indicate his audience. The large circles above must be the "three folds" of the gates of Hell (*PL* II, 645–7).' However, the gates of Hell were not visible from Pandemonium, where the Infernal

---

[4] *The Notebook of William Blake*, p. 18.
[5] Ibid., p. 47.
[6] Ibid., opp. reproduction.

council was held, and the circles are anyway more suggestive of Satan's triple-barrelled 'engine' of war, which is described during the course of the celestial battle following a harangue of the Devil's to his vanguard:

> So scoffing in ambiguous words he scarce
> Had ended; when to right and left the front
> Divided, and to either flank retired.
> Which to our eyes discovered new and strange,
> A triple mounted row of pillars laid
> On wheels ...
>
> (vi, 568–73)

If this was the subject for the sketch then the smaller circles to either side of Satan must represent the newly divided vanguard. (In neither text does Milton suggest that Satan was airborne, as he is in the drawing.)

A sketch for the Trinity on page 104 of the Notebook shows the Father seated and with bent head, clasping the Son in a tight embrace. Christ's arms are outstretched in the Crucifixion position and his attenuated and airborne body is extended to one side. Above them hovers the Holy Ghost in the form of a gigantic bird with outspread wings that extend almost to the edges of the plate—more an eagle than a dove. The faces of all three are hidden. The Holy Ghost is related to the Jehovah-figure of *Paradise Lost* v (2), and the central pair are clearly a study for *Paradise Lost* III, although the finished versions lack the intensity of the sketch. The barely realized figure beneath the clouds must be that of Satan, who appears in this position in the finished drawings for *Paradise Lost*. Behind the Holy Ghost is the sun—or perhaps, as David Erdman suggests,[7] 'the sphere of "a blue heaven"'.

The drawing on the double page 110–11 also shows the Father, the Son, and Satan—the Father seated with hands on knees, the Son with bowed head and in profile at his side, and Satan recumbent below them and gazing upwards. David Erdman[8] suggests that it represents 'God the Father giving directions to the Son to save mankind from Satan ... (*PL* x, 55–84)'; but the isolation and upward gaze of Satan must surely indicate that the subject is again Book III, in which Satan catches a glimpse of heaven's gate on his solitary voyage through space, rather than Book x, in which he is associated first with Sin and Death and then with his cohorts in Pandemonium. The relationship between Father and Son that is suggested here is certainly different from that of the preceding sketch, but it is perhaps more suited to the loftiness and magisterial qualities of Milton's God.

[7] Ibid., p. 47.
[8] Ibid., opp. reproduction.

A drawing on page 102 of two full-frontal nudes walking hand-in-hand with heads held high, and placed between lightly drawn tree-trunks, suggests a reversal of the detail on the right-hand side of *Paradise Lost* v (2) and almost certainly owes something to Milton's description of Adam and Eve at iv, 288–92:

> Two of far nobler shape erect and tall,
> Godlike erect, with native honour clad
> In naked majesty seemed lords of all,
> And worthy seemed, for in their looks divine
> The image of their glorious maker shone ...

Lastly the sketch of Eve tempted by the Serpent on page 88 may be a preliminary drawing for the Tate tempera painting. David Erdman[9] justly observes that Eve's outstretched arms seem to rejoice at and direct [the Serpent's] 'circling spires, that on the grass/Floated redundant'; her right hand is drawn in two positions, one patting the serpent's head. In Blake's later tempera painting he makes more of Satan's 'rising folds, that towered', and shifts the indication of dominance: here Eve *seems* in·charge, there Satan.

[9] Ibid., below reproduction.

APPENDIX
A Statistical List of Blake's Milton Illustrations (excluding those in the Notebook)

(Acknowledgement for permission to reproduce illustrations listed below is gratefully made to the owners.)

Title	Basic medium	Size (to nearest cm)	Date	Present Ownership
'Milton' (head)	tempera and water-colour	91 × 40	c. 1800	Manchester City Art Gallery
'Comus with his Rout'	pen and water-colour	22 × 18	c. 1801	Huntington Library, San Marino, California
	pen and water-colour	15 × 12	c. 1801	Boston Museum of Fine Arts
'Comus Addressing the Lady'	pen and water-colour	22 × 18	c. 1801	Huntington
	pen and water-colour	15 × 12	c. 1801	Boston Museum
'The Brothers Plucking Grapes'	pen and water-colour	22 × 18	c. 1801	Huntington
	pen and water-colour	15 × 12	c. 1801	Boston Museum
'The Brothers with the Attendant Spirit'	pen and water-colour	22 × 18	c. 1801	Huntington
	pen and water-colour	15 × 12	c. 1801	Boston Museum
'Comus's Banquet'	pen and water-colour	22 × 18	c. 1801	Huntington
	pen and water-colour	16 × 12	c. 1801	Boston Museum
'As Daphne was Root-Bound'	pencil (sketch)	20 × 16	c. 1826	British Museum, London
'The Brothers Driving out Comus'	pen and water-colour	22 × 18	c. 1801	Huntington
	pen and water-colour	16 × 12	c. 1801	Boston Museum
'Sabrina Disenchanting the Lady'	pen and water-colour	22 × 18	c. 1801	Huntington
	pen and water-colour	15 × 12	c. 1801	Boston Museum
'The Lady Restored to her Parents'	pen and water-colour	23 × 18	c. 1801	Huntington
	pen and water-colour	16 × 12	c. 1801	Boston Museum

Title	Basic medium	Size (to nearest cm)	Date	Present Ownership
'Return Alpheus'	pencil (sketch)	20 × 16	n.d.	British Museum
'Satan Rousing his Legions'	pen and water-colour	25 × 21	1807	Huntington
	pen and water-colour	51 × 39	1808	Victoria & Albert Museum, London (Crown Copyright)
	tempera	53 × 41	c. 1808	Petworth House, Sussex (National Trust)
	tempera	55 × 42	c. 1809	Victoria & Albert
For Children: The Gates of Paradise, pl. 5	engraved plate	8 × 7	1793	British Museum, etc.
For the Sexes: The Gates of Paradise, pl. 5	engraved plate	8 × 7	1818	British Museum, etc.
'Satan, Sin, and Death at the Gates of Hell'	pen and water-colour	25 × 21	1807	Huntington
	pen and water-colour	50 × 40	1808	Huntington
	pencil, pen, and watercolour (sketch)	25 × 20	c. 1807	Johns Hopkins University, Baltimore
'Christ Offering to Redeem Mankind'	pen and water-colour	26 × 21	1807	Huntington
	pen and water-colour	49 × 39	1808	Boston Museum
	pencil (sketch)	20 × 16	c. 1793	British Museum
'Satan Spying on Adam and Eve'	pen and water-colour	26 × 21	1807	Huntington
	pen and water-colour	50 × 38	1808	Boston Museum
	pen, water-colour, and pencil	27 × 20	1806	Fogg Art Museum, Cambridge, Mass.
	pen and water-colour	52 × 40	1822	National Gallery of Victoria, Melbourne
	pencil (sketch)	14 × 13	c. 1807	British Museum
	pencil (sketch)	6 × 4	c. 1807	Coll. Geoffrey Keynes
'Satan as a Toad at the Ear of Eve'	pen and water-colour	49 × 38	1808	Boston Museum
'Raphael Descending to Paradise'	pen and water-colour	25 × 20	1807	Huntington
'The Expulsion of the Rebel Angels'	pen and water-colour	26 × 21	1807	Huntington

Title	Basic medium	Size (to nearest cm)	Date	Present Ownership
	pen and water-colour	49 × 38	1808	Boston Museum
	pencil (sketch)	50 × 43	n.d.	Tate Gallery, London
'Raphael Warning Adam'	pen and water-colour	26 × 21	1807	Huntington
	pen and water-colour	49 × 39	1808	Boston Museum
	pencil (sketch)	24 × 21	n.d.	British Museum
'The Creation of Eve'	pen and water-colour	25 × 21	1807	Huntington
	pen and water-colour	50 × 39	1808	Boston Museum
	pen and water-colour	51 × 41	c. 1822	National Gallery of Victoria
	pencil (sketch)	23 × 18	c. 1807	British Museum
'The Fall of Eve'	pen and water-colour	26 × 21	1807	Huntington
	pen and water-colour	49 × 38	1808	Boston Museum
'The Temptation of Eve' (differs radically from both the above)	tempera on copper	38 × 27	c. 1796	Victoria & Albert (Crown Copyright)
'The Temptation of Eve' (detail only)	pencil (sketch)	23 × 13	c. 1807	Victoria & Albert
'The Judgement of Adam and Eve'	pen and water-colour	25 × 20	1807	Huntington
	pen and water-colour	50 × 39	1808	Houghton Library, Harvard University
'The House of Death'	colour-print	60 × 48	1795	British Museum
	colour-print	60 × 48	1795	Tate Gallery
	colour-print	60 × 48	1795	Fitzwilliam Museum
(differs considerably from the above)	pen and wash	45 × 32	early 1790s	Tate Gallery
'Michael Foretelling the Crucifixion'	pen and water-colour	25 × 20	1807	Huntington
	pen and water-colour	50 × 38	1808	Boston Museum
	pen and water-colour	50 × 39	c. 1822	Fitzwilliam Museum
'The Expulsion'	pen and water-colour	25 × 20	1807	Huntington
	pen and water-colour	50 × 39	1808	Boston Museum
'The Descent of Peace'	pen and water-colour	16 × 13	c. 1808	Huntington
	pen and water-colour	25 × 19	1809	Whitworth Art Gallery, Manchester

Title	Basic medium	Size (to nearest cm)	Date	Present Ownership
	pencil (sketch)	24 × 19	1809	Coll. Lessing J. Rosenwald, Nat. Gall. of Art, Washington, D.C.
'The Choir of Angels'	pen and water-colour	16 × 12	c. 1808	Huntington
	pen and water-colour	26 × 19	1809	Whitworth
'The Devils in Hell'	pen and water-colour	16 × 12	c. 1808	Huntington
	pen and water-colour	25 × 19	1809	Whitworth
'Apollo and the Pagan Deities'	pen and water-colour	16 × 12	c. 1808	Huntington
	pen and water-colour	25 × 19	1809	Whitworth
'The Flight of Moloch'	pen and water-colour	16 × 12	c. 1808	Huntington
	pen and water-colour	26 × 20	1809	Whitworth
'The Star of Bethlehem'	pen and water-colour	16 × 12	c. 1808	Huntington
	pen and water-colour	26 × 19	1809	Whitworth
'Mirth'	pen and water-colour	16 × 12	c. 1816	Pierpont Morgan Library
	engraving (first state)	16 × 12	c. 1816	British Museum
	engraving (second state)	16 × 12	c. 1816	Coll. Geoffrey Keynes
'The Lark'	pen and water-colour	16 × 12	c. 1816	Pierpont Morgan Library
'The Sun at his Eastern Gate'	pen and water-colour	16 × 12	c. 1816	Pierpont Morgan Library
'A Sunshine Holiday'	pen and water-colour	16 × 12	c. 1816	Pierpont Morgan Library
'The Goblin'	pen and water-colour	16 × 12	c. 1816	Pierpont Morgan Library
'The Youthful Poet's Dream'	pen and water-colour	16 × 12	c. 1816	Pierpont Morgan Library
'Melancholy'	pen and water-colour	16 × 12	c. 1816	Pierpont Morgan Library
'The Wandering Moon'	pen and water-colour	16 × 12	c. 1816	Pierpont Morgan Library
'The Spirit of Plato'	pen and water-colour	16 × 12	c. 1816	Pierpont Morgan Library
'The Sun is his Wrath'	pen and water-colour	16 × 12	c. 1816	Pierpont Morgan Library
'Mysterious Dream'	pen and water-colour	16 × 12	c. 1816	Pierpont Morgan Library

'Milton: Old Age'	pen and water-colour	16 × 12	c. 1816	Pierpont Morgan Library
'The Baptism of Christ'	pen and water-colour	17 × 14	c. 1816	Fitzwilliam Museum
'The Temptation of Bread'	pen and water-colour	17 × 13	c. 1816	Fitzwilliam Museum
	pencil and water-colour	17 × 13	n.d.	Frick Collection, New York
'Andrew and Simon Peter Searching for Christ'	pen and water-colour	17 × 14	c. 1816	Fitzwilliam Museum
'Mary Lamenting Christ's Absence'	pen and water-colour	17 × 14	c. 1816	Fitzwilliam Museum
'Satan Addressing his Followers'	pen and water-colour	17 × 13	c. 1816	Fitzwilliam Museum
'Christ Rejecting Satan's Banquet'	pen and water-colour	17 × 14	c. 1816	Fitzwilliam Museum
'The Temptation of the Kingdoms'	pen and water-colour	17 × 13	c. 1816	Fitzwilliam Museum
'Christ's Troubled Dream'	pen and water-colour	17 × 13	c. 1816	Fitzwilliam Museum
'Morning Chasing Away the Phantoms'	pen and water-colour	17 × 13	c. 1816	Fitzwilliam Museum
'The Temptation of the Pinnacle'	pen and water-colour	17 × 13	c. 1816	Fitzwilliam Museum
'Christ Ministered to by Angels'	pen and water-colour	17 × 14	c. 1816	Fitzwilliam Museum
'Christ Returning Home'	pen and water-colour	17 × 13	c. 1816	Fitzwilliam Museum

Acknowledgement is also made to the British Library Board, London, for permission to reproduce 'Lot's Escape' from *The Protestant's Family Bible*, 1780.

SELECT BIBLIOGRAPHY

The place of publication is not given when it is London or Oxford

I. BIBLIOGRAPHIES ETC.

Bentley, G. E., Jr. and Nurmi, Martin K., *A Blake Bibliography*, Minneapolis and London, 1964.

Bentley, G. E., Jr., 'A Supplement to G. E. Bentley, Jr., and Martin K. Nurmi, *A Blake Bibliography* (1964)', *Blake Newsletter*, ii, iv, pt. 2 (April 1969).

Essick, Robert, 'A Finding List of Reproductions of Blake's Art', revised and expanded version, *Blake Newsletter*, v, i and ii (Summer and Fall 1971).

II. EDITIONS OF BLAKE'S WORKS

1. *Written Works*

Erdman, David V., ed., *The Poetry and Prose of William Blake*, New York, 1965.

Keynes, Geoffrey, ed., *The Complete Writings of William Blake*, 1966.

Stevenson, W. H., ed., *The Poems of William Blake*, 1971.

2. *Art Works*

The Gates of Paradise, 1793 and 1818, Trianon Press edn., 3 vols., with commentary by Sir Geoffrey Keynes, 1968.

Baker, C. H. Collins, *Catalogue of William Blake's Drawings and Paintings in the Huntington Library*, 2nd edn., enlarged and revised by R. R. Wark, San Marino, California, 1969.

Bindman, David, ed., *William Blake: Catalogue of the Collection in the Fitzwilliam Museum, Cambridge*, Cambridge, 1970.

Bunyan, John, *The Pilgrim's Progress*, ed. G. B. Harrison, introduction by Geoffrey Keynes, New York, 1941.

Butlin, Martin, ed., *William Blake: A Complete Catalogue of the Works in the Tate Gallery*, revised edn., 1971.

Erdman, David V., ed., *The Illuminated Blake*, New York, 1974.

——, *The Notebook of William Blake*, 1973.

Keynes, Geoffrey, ed., *Blake's Pencil Drawings*, 2nd ser., 1956.
——, *Drawings of William Blake: 92 Pencil Studies*, New York, 1970.
——, *Engravings by William Blake: The Separate Plates*, Dublin, 1956.
——, *Pencil Drawings by William Blake*, 1927.
Wells, William, ed., *William Blake's 'Heads of the Poets'*, Manchester, 1969.
Willard, Helen D., ed., *William Blake, Water-color Drawings*, Boston, 1957.

III. EDITIONS OF MILTON'S WORKS

Carey, John and Fowler, Alastair, eds., *The Poems of John Milton*, 1968.
Hayley, William, ed., *Latin and Italian Poems of Milton*, translated by William Cowper and
    with three line-engravings by A. Raimbach after J. Flaxman, 1808.
Warton, Thomas, ed., *Poems Upon Several Occasions*, 2nd revised edn., 1791.

IV. BLAKE CRITICISM ETC.

Adlard, John, *The Sports of Cruelty*, 1972.
Baker, C. H. Collins, 'William Blake, Painter', *Huntington Library Quarterly*, Cambridge,
    Mass., x (October 1936).
Beer, John, *Blake's Humanism*, Manchester, 1968.
——, *Blake's Visionary Universe*, Manchester, 1969.
Bentley, G. E., Jr., *Blake Records*, 1969.
Bloom, Harold, *Blake's Apocalypse*, 1963.
Blunt, Anthony, *The Art of William Blake*, New York, 1959.
——, 'Blake's "Ancient of Days": The Symbolism of the Compasses', *Journal of the Warburg
    and Courtauld Institutes*, II (1938–9).
——, 'Blake's "Brazen Serpent"', ibid., VI (1943).
Butlin, Martin, *William Blake*, 1978.
Cary, Elisabeth Luther, *The Art of William Blake*, New York, 1907.
Damon, S. Foster, *A Blake Dictionary*, Providence, Rhode Island, 1965.
Erdman, David V. and Grant, John E., eds., *Blake's Visionary Forms Dramatic*, Princeton,
    1970.
Frye, Northrop, *Fearful Symmetry*, Princeton, 1947.
Gilchrist, Alexander, *Life of William Blake*, 2nd edn. (new and enlarged), 2 vols., 1880.
Grant, John E., 'Blake's Designs for *L'Allegro* and *Il Penseroso*', *Blake Newsletter*, Albuquerque,
    New Mexico, IV, iv (Spring 1971).
——, 'The Meaning of Mirth and Her Companions in Blake's Designs for "L'Allegro" and
    "Il Penseroso"', *Blake Newsletter*, v, iii (Winter 1971–2).
Hagstrum, Jean H., *William Blake: Poet and Painter*, Chicago, 1964.
Harper, George Mills, *The Neoplatonism of William Blake*, Chapel Hill, North Carolina, 1961.

[Holmes, C. J.], 'The Creation of Eve', *The Burlington Magazine*, x, xlvii (February 1907).

Keynes, Geoffrey, *Blake Studies*, enlarged 2nd edn., 1971.

Mellor, Anne Kostelanetz, *Blake's Human Form Divine*, Berkeley, 1974.

Paley, Morton D., *Energy and the Imagination*, 1970.

Peckham, Morse, 'Blake, Milton, and Edward Burney', *Princeton University Library Chronicle*, xi, iii (Spring 1950).

Percival, Milton O., *William Blake's Circle of Destiny*, New York, 1938.

Pinto, Vivian de Sola, ed., *The Divine Vision*, 1957.

Raine, Kathleen, *Blake and Tradition*, 2 vols., 1969.

Roe, Albert S., *William Blake's Illustrations to the Divine Comedy*, Princeton, 1953.

Rose, Edward J., 'Blake's Illustrations for *Paradise Lost, L'Allegro*, and *Il Penseroso*: A Thematic Reading', *Hartford Studies in Literature*, West Hartford, Connecticut, ii, vii (1970).

Rosenfeld, Alvin H., ed., *William Blake: Essays for S. Foster Damon*, Providence, Rhode Island, 1969.

Tayler, Irene, *Blake's Illustrations to the Poems of Gray*, Princeton, 1971.

——, 'Say First! What Mov'd Blake? Blake's *Comus* Designs and *Milton*'; in *Blake's Sublime Allegory: Essays on 'The Four Zoas', 'Milton', 'Jerusalem'*, ed. Stuart Curran and Joseph Anthony Wittreich, Jr., Madison, Wisconsin, 1973.

Wittreich, Joseph A., *Angel of Apocalypse*, Madison, Wisconsin, 1975.

——, *Calm of Mind*, Cleveland and London, 1971.

Wright, Andrew, *Blake's Job: A Commentary*, 1972.

V. MISCELLANEOUS

Baker, C. H. Collins, 'Some Illustrators of Milton's *Paradise Lost*', *The Library*, 5th ser., iii, i (June 1948).

Bland, David, *The Illustration of Books*, enlarged 3rd edn., 1962.

Hagstrum, Jean H., *The Sister Arts*, Chicago, 1958.

Lewalski, Barbara Kiefer, *Milton's Brief Epic*, Providence, Rhode Island, and London, 1966.

Parker, William Riley, *Milton: A Biography*, 2 vols., 1968.

Patrides, C. A., ed., *Approaches to Paradise Lost*, 1968.

Pointon, Marcia, *Millon and English Art*, Manchester, 1970.

Pope, Elizabeth Marie, *Paradise Regained: the Tradition and the Poem*, Baltimore, 1947.

Réau, Louis, *Iconographis de l'art chrétien*, 6 vols., Paris, 1955–9.

Schiff, Gert, *Johann Heinrich Füsslis Milton-Galerie*, Zurich and Stuttgart, 1963.

INDEX

PLATES

1. Milton (head). City Art Gallery, Manchester.

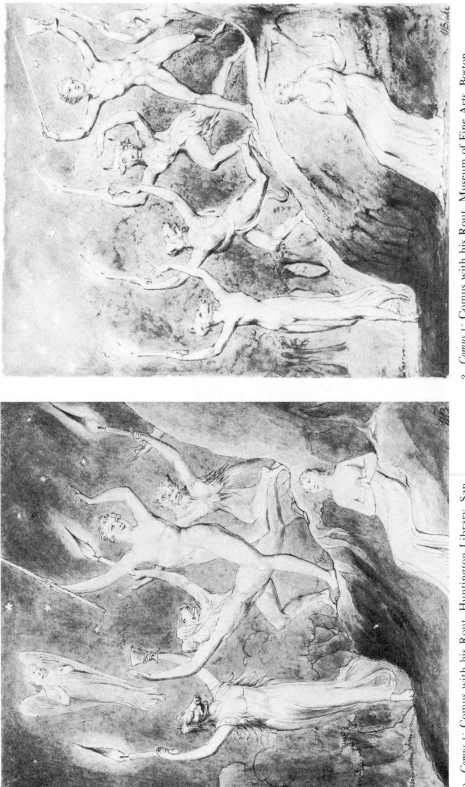

3. *Comus* I: Comus with his Rout. Museum of Fine Arts, Boston. Gift of Mrs John L. Gardner and George N. Black.

2. *Comus* I: Comus with his Rout. Huntington Library, San Marino, California.

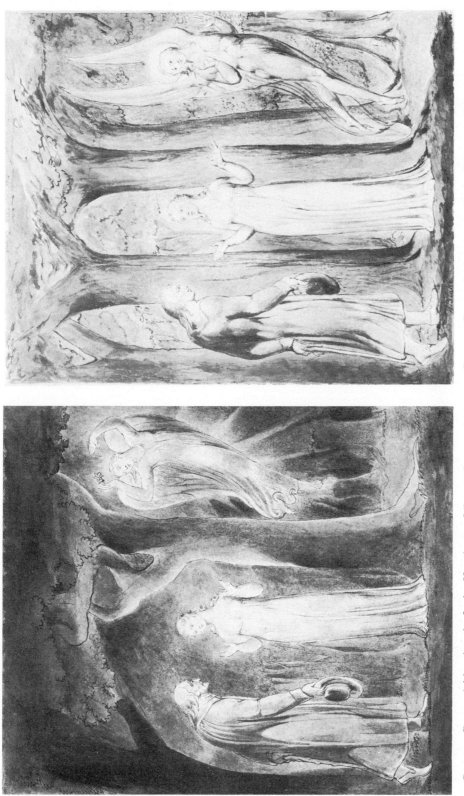

4. *Comus* II: Comus Addressing the Lady. Huntington Library, San Marino, California.

5. *Comus* II: Comus Addressing the Lady. Museum of Fine Arts, Boston.
Gift of Mrs. John L. Gardner and George N. Black.

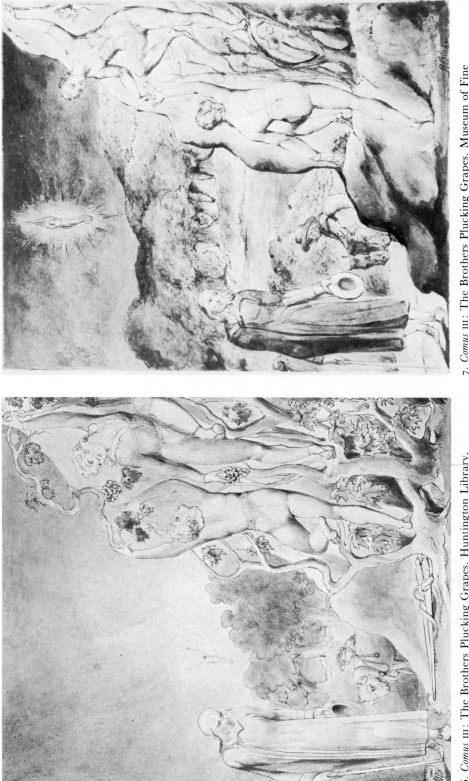

7. *Comus* III: The Brothers Plucking Grapes. Museum of Fine Arts, Boston. Gift of Mrs. John L. Gardner and George N. Black.

6. *Comus* III: The Brothers Plucking Grapes. Huntington Library, San Marino, California.

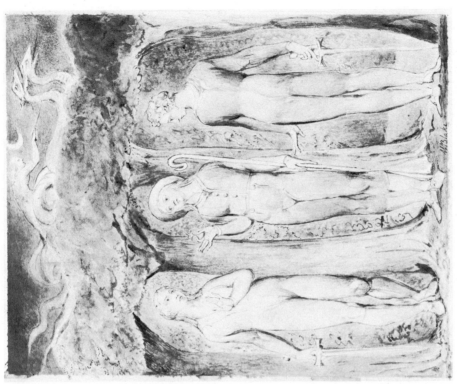

9. *Comus* IV: The Brothers with the Attendant Spirit. Museum of Fine Arts, Boston. Gift of Mrs. John L. Gardner and George N. Black.

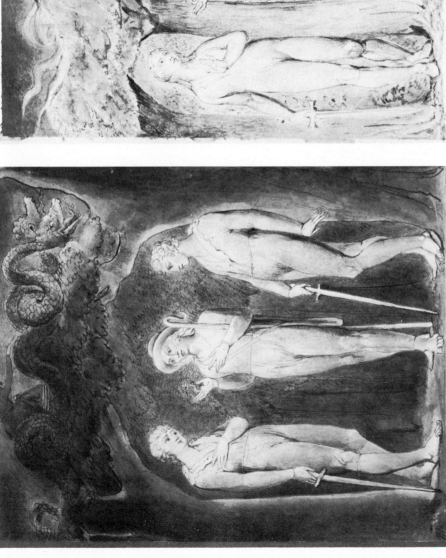

8. *Comus* IV: The Brothers with the Attendant Spirit. Huntington Library, San Marino, California.

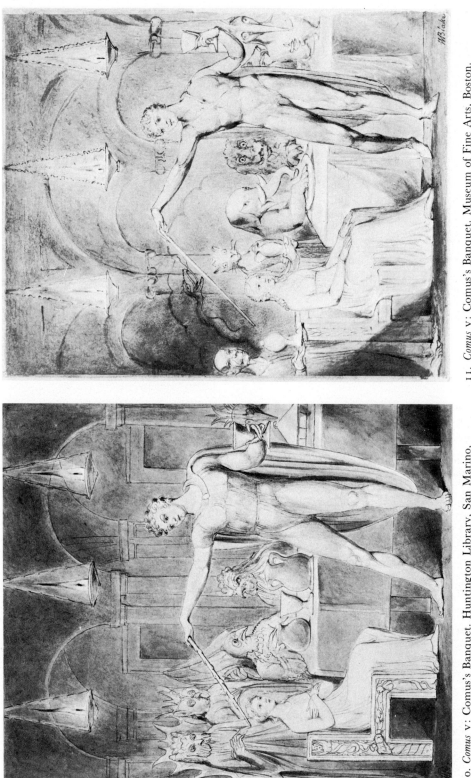

11. *Comus* v: Comus's Banquet. Museum of Fine Arts, Boston. Gift of Mrs. John L. Gardner and George N. Black.

10. *Comus* v: Comus's Banquet. Huntington Library, San Marino, California.

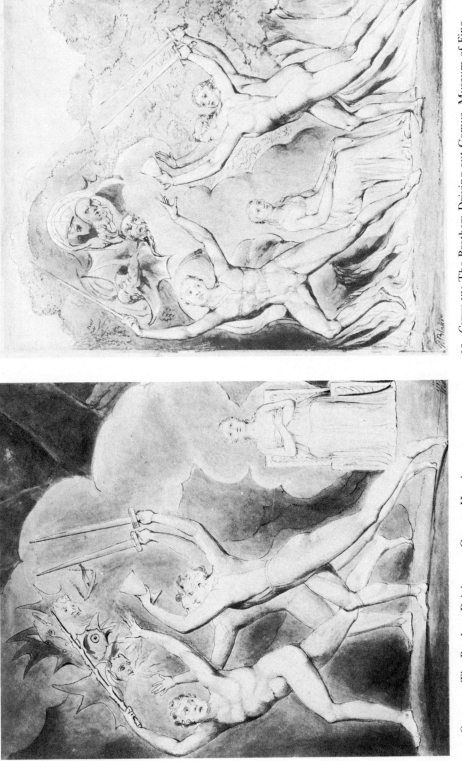

12. *Comus* vi: The Brothers Driving out Comus. Huntington Library, San Marino, California.

13. *Comus* vi: The Brothers Driving out Comus. Museum of Fine Arts, Boston. Gift of Mrs. John L. Gardner and George N. Black.

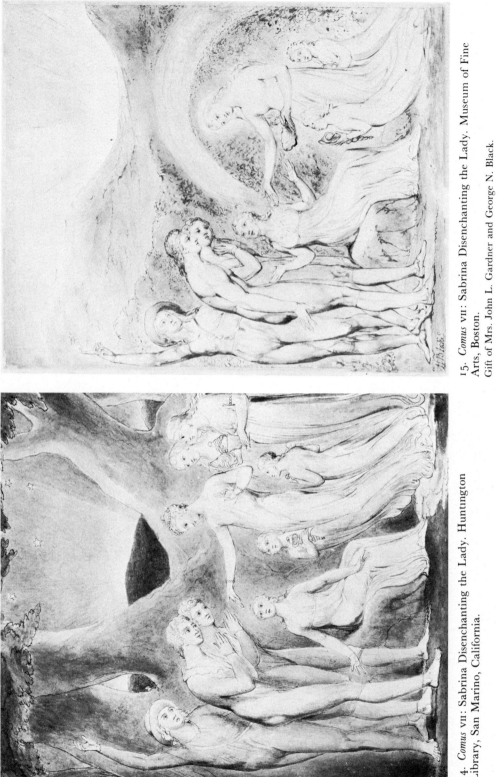

14. *Comus* VII: Sabrina Disenchanting the Lady. Huntington Library, San Marino, California.

15. *Comus* VII: Sabrina Disenchanting the Lady. Museum of Fine Arts, Boston. Gift of Mrs. John L. Gardner and George N. Black.

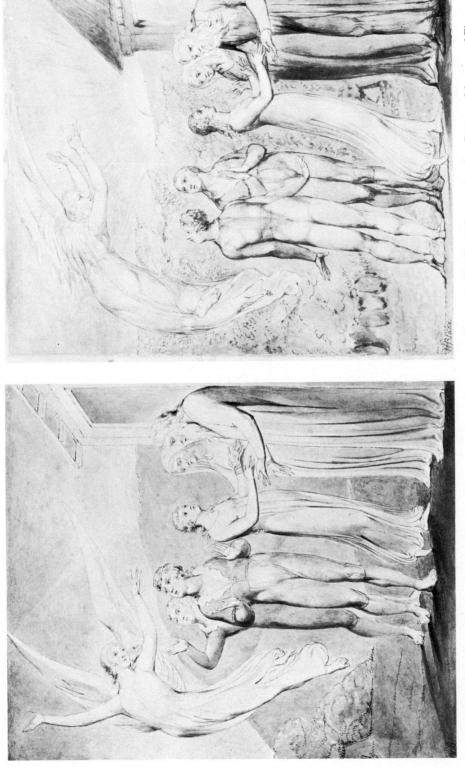

16. *Comus* VIII: The Lady Restored to her Parents. Huntington Library, San Marino, California.

17. *Comus* VIII: The Lady Restored to her Parents. Museum of Fine Arts, Boston.
Gift of Mrs. John L. Gardner and George N. Black.

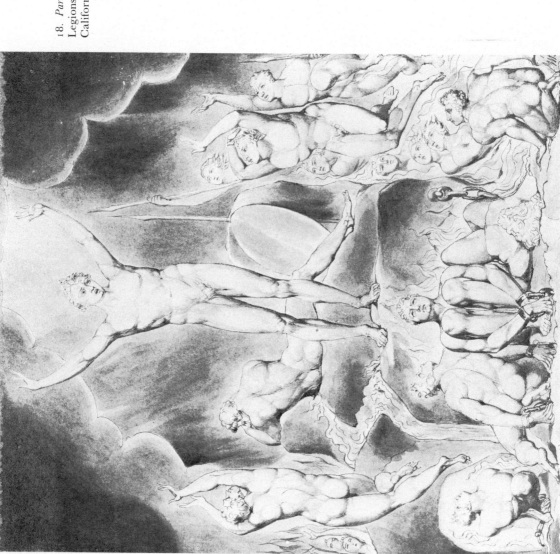

18. *Paradise Lost* I: Satan Rousing his Legions. Huntington Library, San Marino, California.

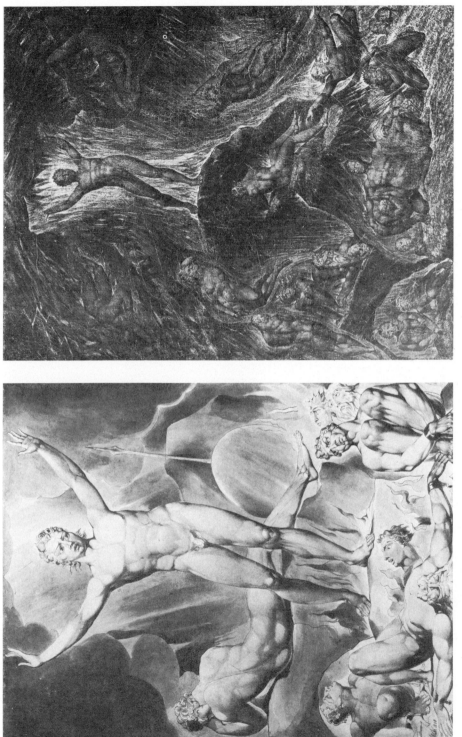

19. *Paradise Lost* 1: Satan Rousing his Legions. Victoria & Albert
Museum, London (water-colour).

20. Satan Rousing his Legions. Petworth House, Sussex.

21. 'For Children: The Gates of Paradise', plate 5. British Museum, London.

22. 'For the Sexes: The Gates of Paradise', plate 5. British Museum, London.

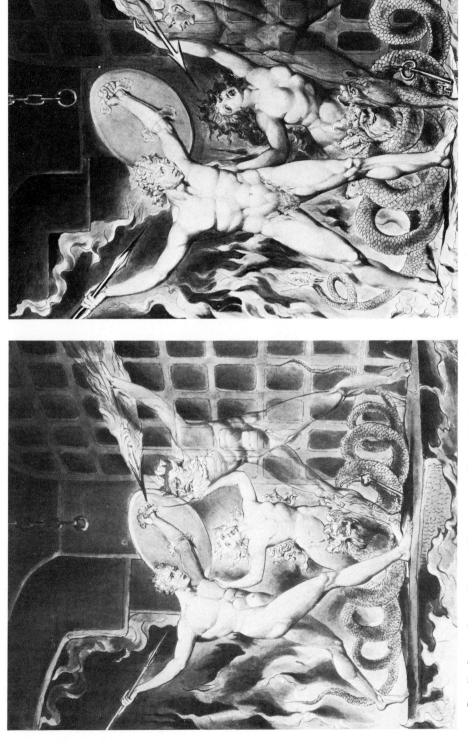

24. *Paradise Lost* II: Satan, Sin, and Death at the Gates of Hell. Huntington Library, San Marino, California (larger version).

23. *Paradise Lost* II: Satan, Sin, and Death at the Gates of Hell. Huntington Library, San Marino, California (smaller version).

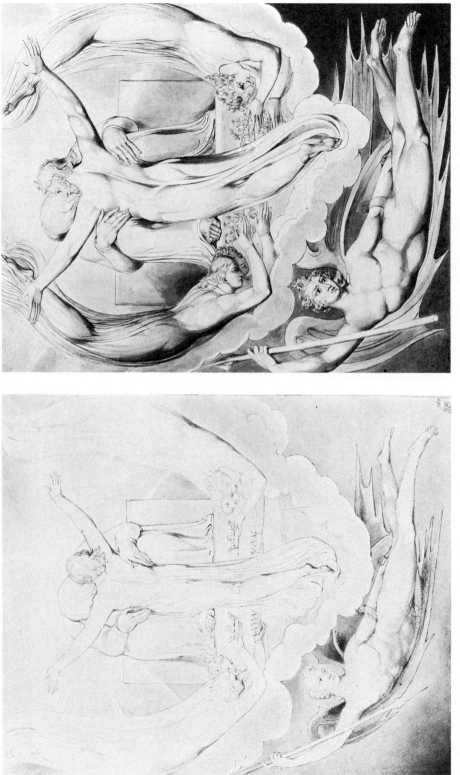

26. *Paradise Lost* III: Christ Offering to Redeem Mankind.
Museum of Fine Arts, Boston.
Gift by subscription, 1890.

25. *Paradise Lost* III: Christ Offering to Redeem Mankind.
Huntington Library, San Marino, California.

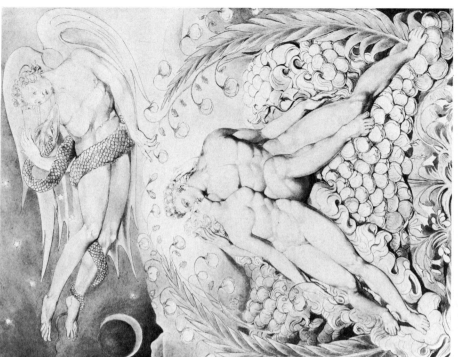

28. *Paradise Lost* IV: Satan Spying on Adam and Eve. Museum of Fine Arts, Boston. Gift by subscription, 1890.

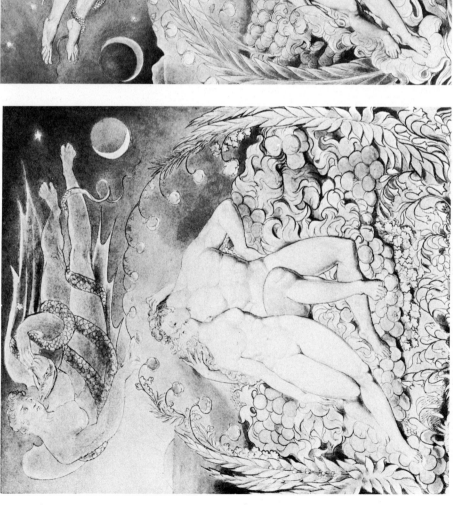

27. *Paradise Lost* IV: Satan Spying on Adam and Eve. Huntington Library, San Marino, California.

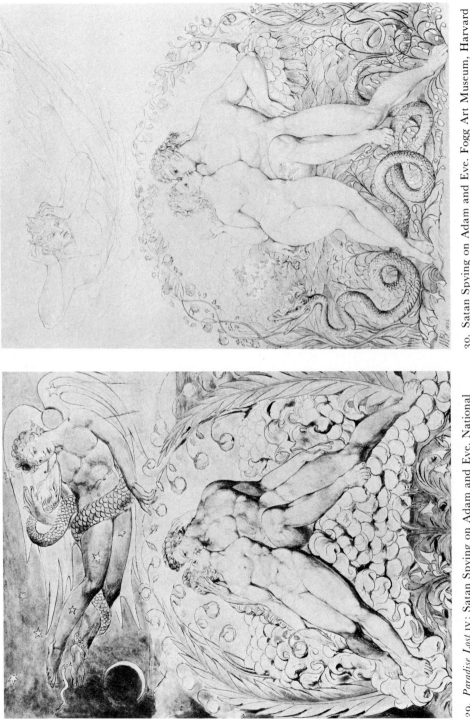

29. *Paradise Lost* IV: Satan Spying on Adam and Eve. National Gallery of Victoria, Melbourne.

30. Satan Spying on Adam and Eve. Fogg Art Museum, Harvard University. Grenville L. Winthrop Bequest.

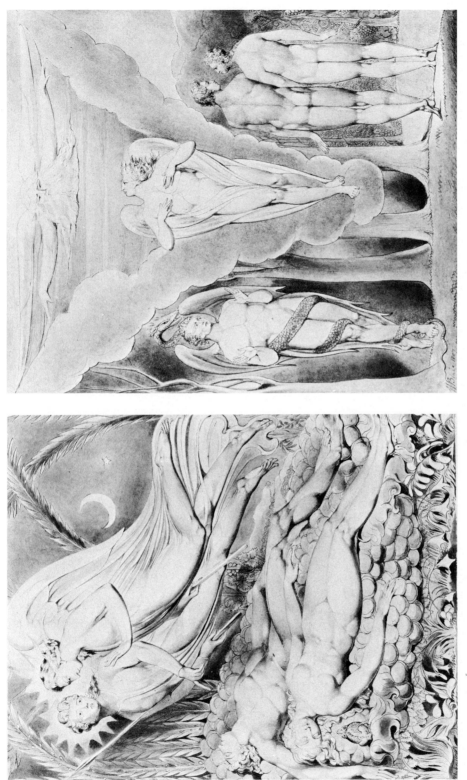

31. *Paradise Lost* v (1): Satan as a Toad at the Ear of Eve. Museum of Fine Arts, Boston. Gift by subscription, 1890.

32. *Paradise Lost* v (2): Raphael Descending to Paradise. Huntington Library, San Marino, California.

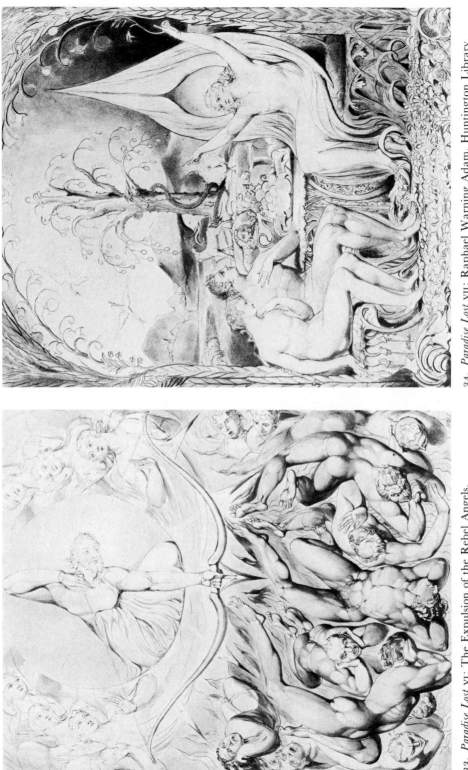

34. *Paradise Lost* VII: Raphael Warning Adam. Huntington Library, San Marino, California.

33. *Paradise Lost* VI: The Expulsion of the Rebel Angels. Museum of Fine Arts, Boston. Gift by subscription, 1890.

35. *Paradise Lost* VII: Raphael Warning Adam. Museum of Fine Arts, Boston. Gift by subscription, 1890.

36. *Paradise Lost* vɪɪ: The Creation of Eve.
Huntington Library, San Marino, California.

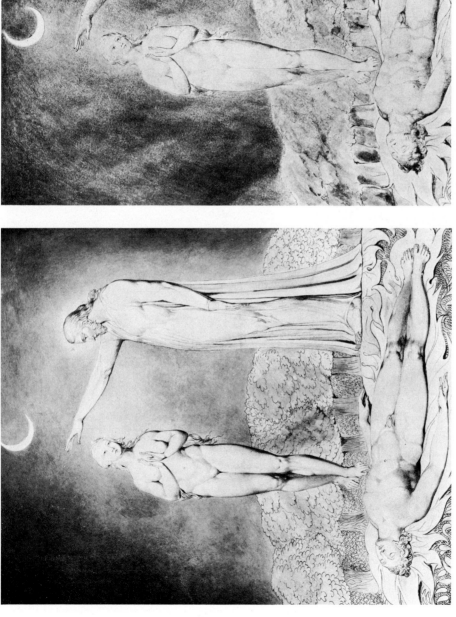

37. *Paradise Lost* VIII: The Creation of Eve. Museum of Fine Arts, Boston.
Gift by subscription 1890.

38. *Paradise Lost* VIII: The Creation of Eve. National Gallery of Victoria, Melbourne.

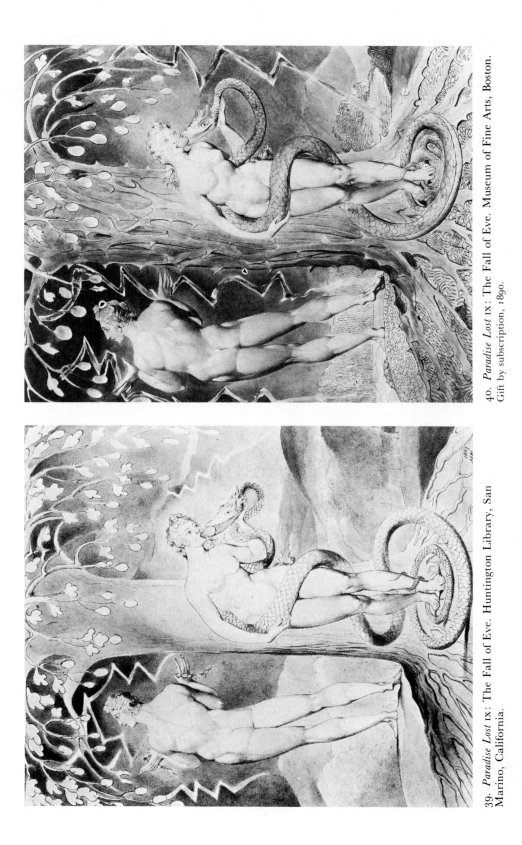

39. *Paradise Lost* IX: The Fall of Eve. Huntington Library, San Marino, California.

40. *Paradise Lost* IX: The Fall of Eve. Museum of Fine Arts, Boston. Gift by subscription, 1890.

41. The Temptation of Eve. Victoria & Albert Museum, London.

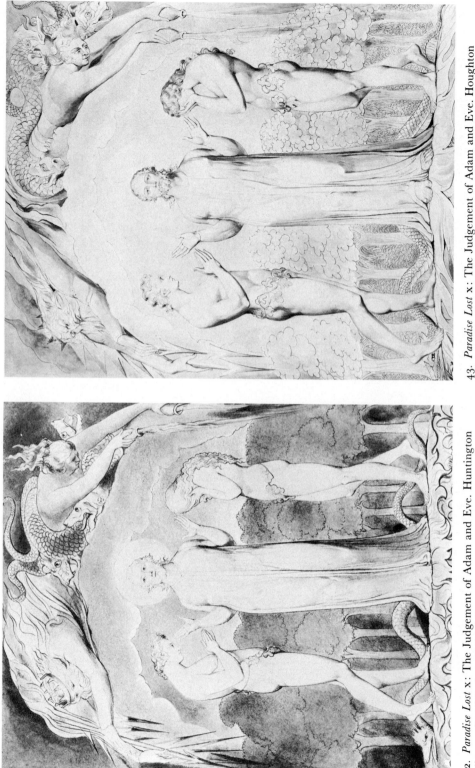

43. *Paradise Lost* x: The Judgement of Adam and Eve. Houghton Library, Harvard University.

42. *Paradise Lost* x: The Judgement of Adam and Eve. Huntington Library, San Marino, California.

44. The House of Death. British Museum, London.

45. The House of Death. Tate Gallery, London (pen-and-wash drawing).

46. The House of Death. Tate Gallery, London (colour-print).

47. *Paradise Lost* xi: Michael Foretelling the Crucifixion. Huntington Library, San Marino, California.

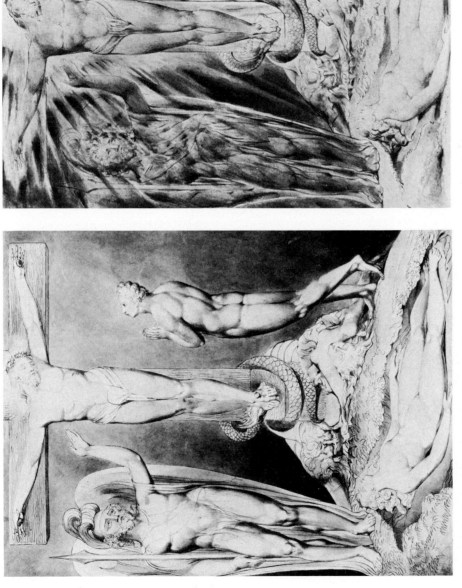

48. *Paradise Lost* XI: Michael Foretelling the Crucifixion. Museum of Fine Arts, Boston. Gift by subscription, 1890.

49. *Paradise Lost* XI: Michael Foretelling the Crucifixion. Fitzwilliam Museum, Cambridge.

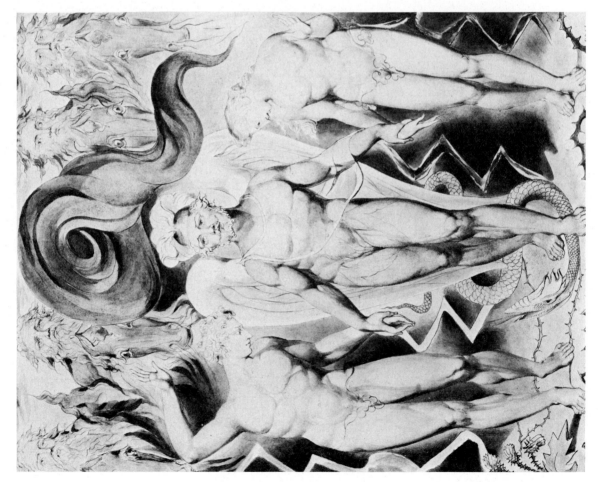

50. *Paradise Lost* XII: The Expulsion. Huntington Library, San Marino, California.

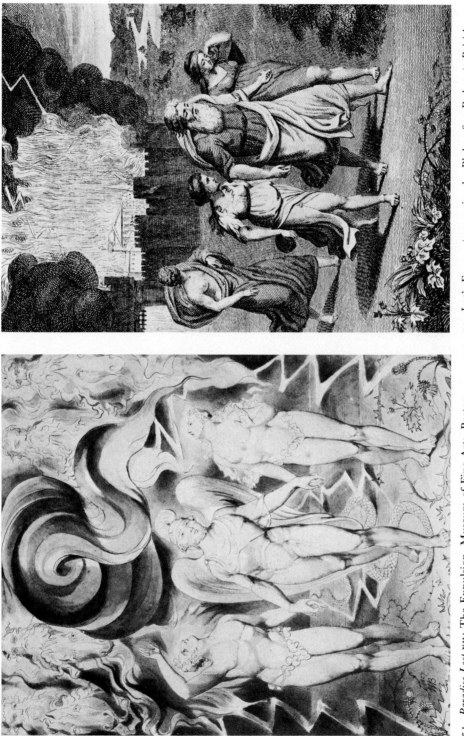

51. *Paradise Lost* XII: The Expulsion. Museum of Fine Arts, Boston.
Gift by subscription, 1890.

52. Lot's Escape (engraving by Blake after Rubens). British
Library, London.

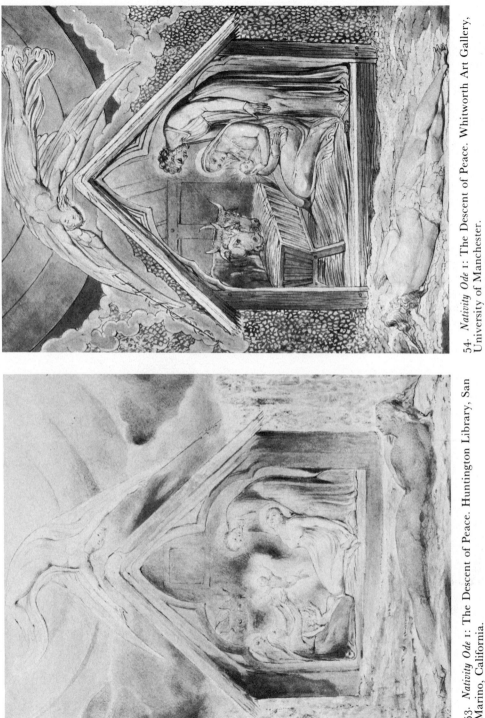

54. *Nativity Ode* 1: The Descent of Peace. Whitworth Art Gallery, University of Manchester.

53. *Nativity Ode* 1: The Descent of Peace. Huntington Library, San Marino, California.

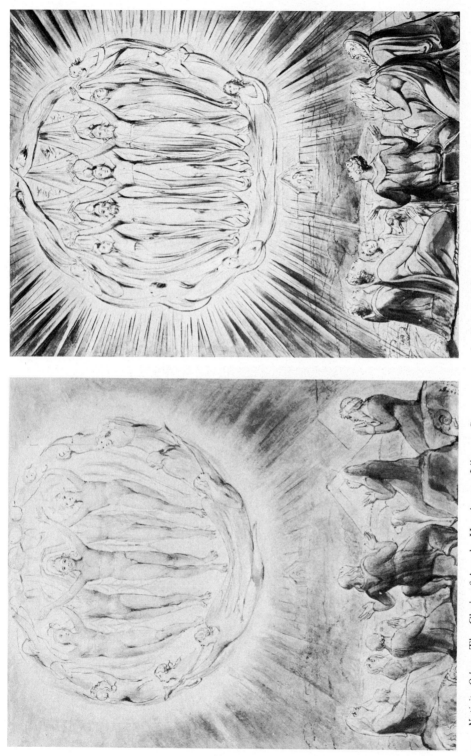

55. *Nativity Ode* II: The Choir of Angels. Huntington Library, San Marino, California.

56. *Nativity Ode* II: The Choir of Angels. Whitworth Art Gallery, University of Manchester.

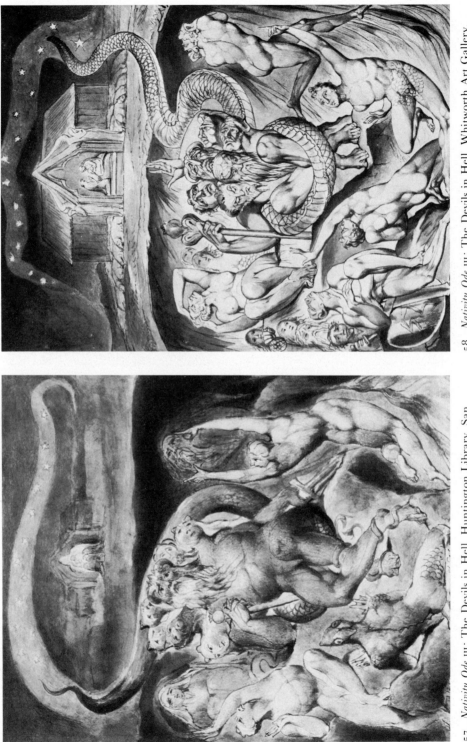

57. *Nativity Ode* III: The Devils in Hell. Huntington Library, San Marino, California.

58. *Nativity Ode* III: The Devils in Hell. Whitworth Art Gallery, University of Manchester.

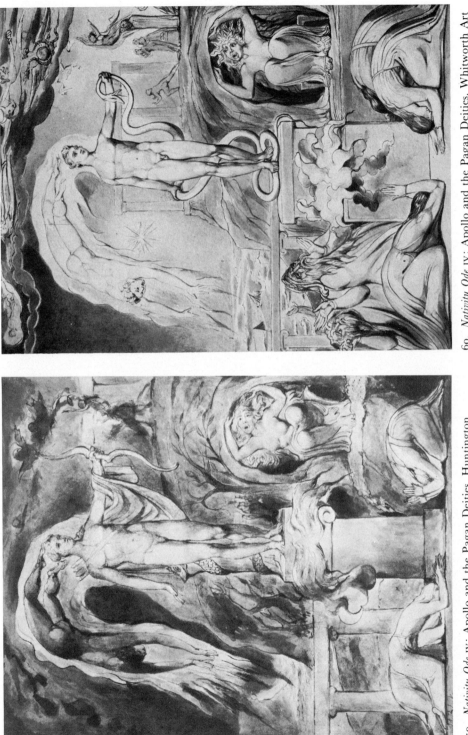

59. *Nativity Ode* IV: Apollo and the Pagan Deities. Huntington Library, San Marino, California.

60. *Nativity Ode* IV: Apollo and the Pagan Deities. Whitworth Art Gallery, University of Manchester.

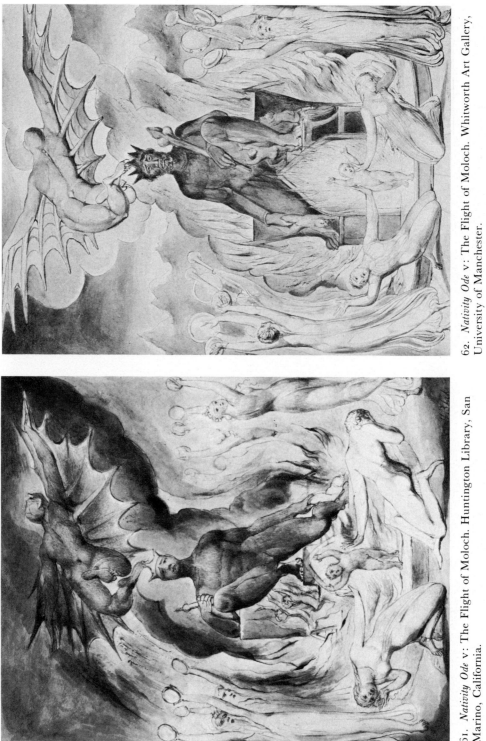

61. *Nativity Ode* v: The Flight of Moloch. Huntington Library, San Marino, California.

62. *Nativity Ode* v: The Flight of Moloch. Whitworth Art Gallery, University of Manchester.

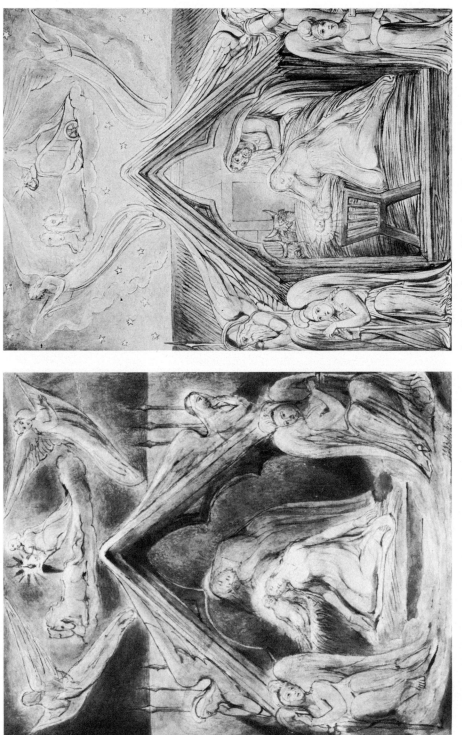

63. *Nativity Ode* vi: The Star of Bethlehem. Huntington Library, San Marino, California.

64. *Nativity Ode* vi: The Star of Bethlehem. Whitworth Art Gallery, University of Manchester.

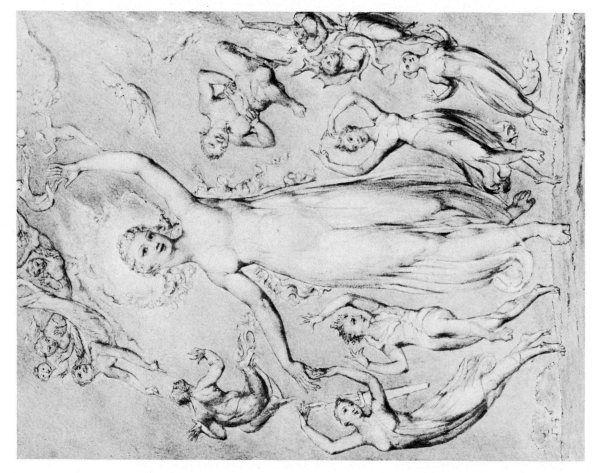

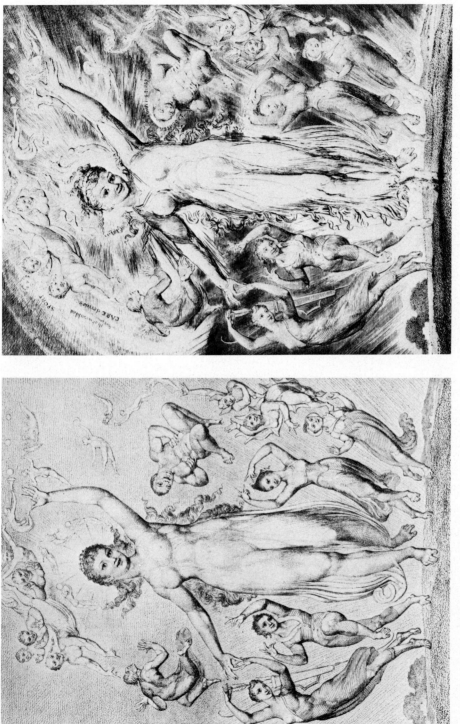

67. Mirth. Coll. Sir Geoffrey Keynes (engraving, second state).

66. Mirth. British Museum, London (engraving, first state).

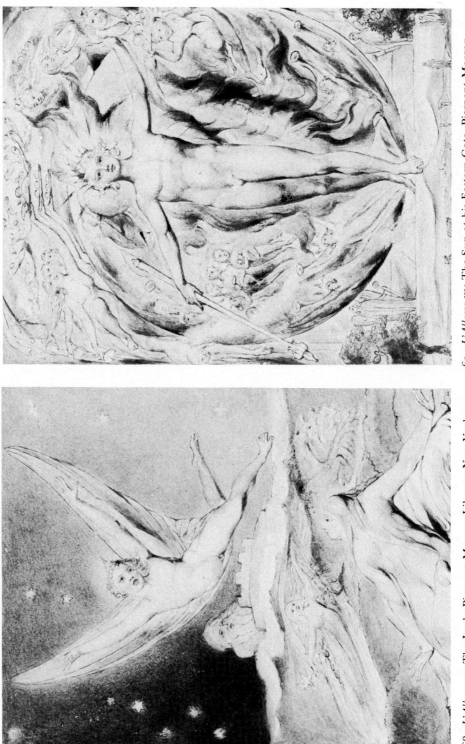

69. *L'Allegro* III: The Sun at his Eastern Gate. Pierpont Morgan Library, New York.

68. *L'Allegro* II: The Lark. Pierpont Morgan Library, New York.

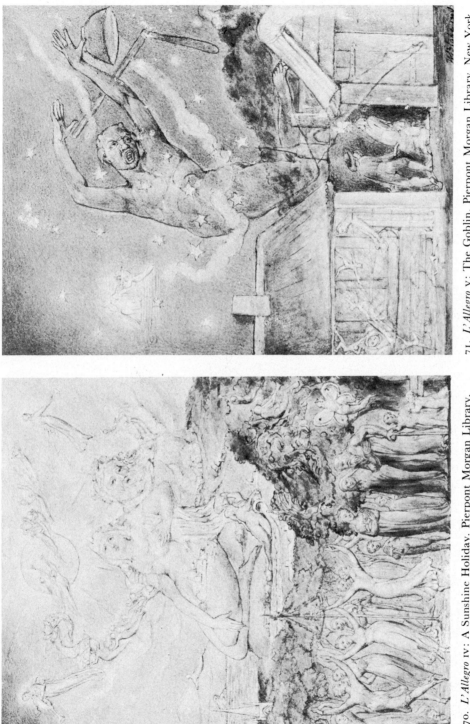
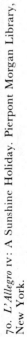

71. *L'Allegro* v: The Goblin. Pierpont Morgan Library, New York.

70. *L'Allegro* iv: A Sunshine Holiday. Pierpont Morgan Library, New York.

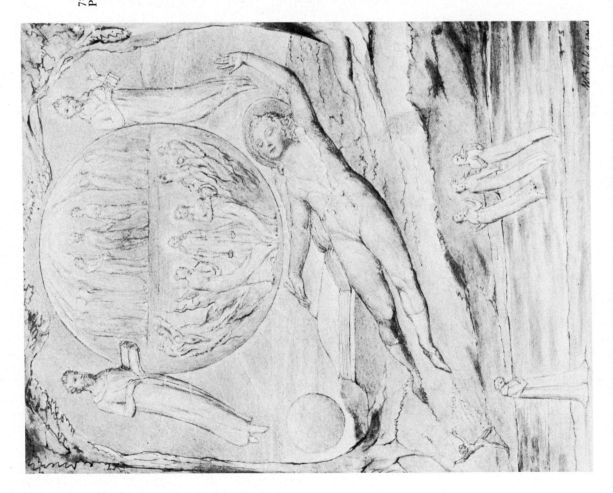

72. *L'Allegro* vi: The Youthful Poet's Dream. Pierpont Morgan Library, New York.

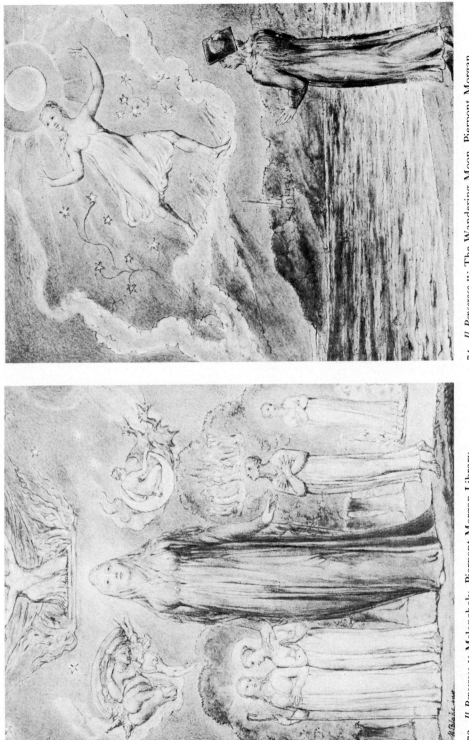

73. *Il Penseroso* 1: Melancholy. Pierpont Morgan Library, New York.

74. *Il Penseroso* ii: The Wandering Moon. Pierpont Morgan Library, New York.

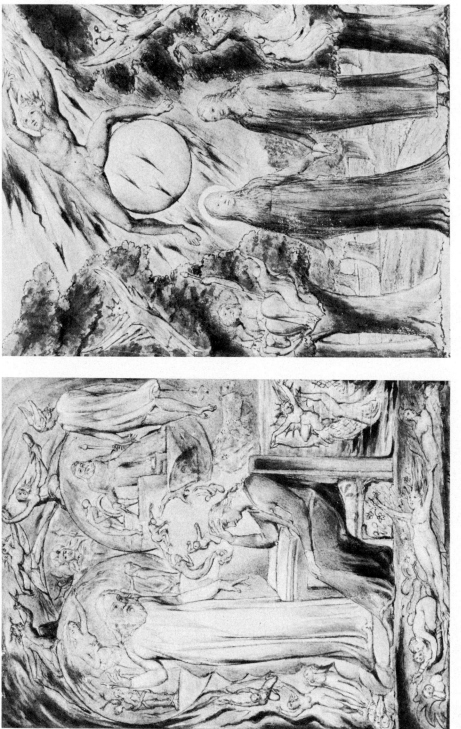

76. *Il Penseroso* IV: The Sun in his Wrath. Pierpont Morgan Library, New York.

75. *Il Penseroso* III: The Spirit of Plato. Pierpont Morgan Library, New York.

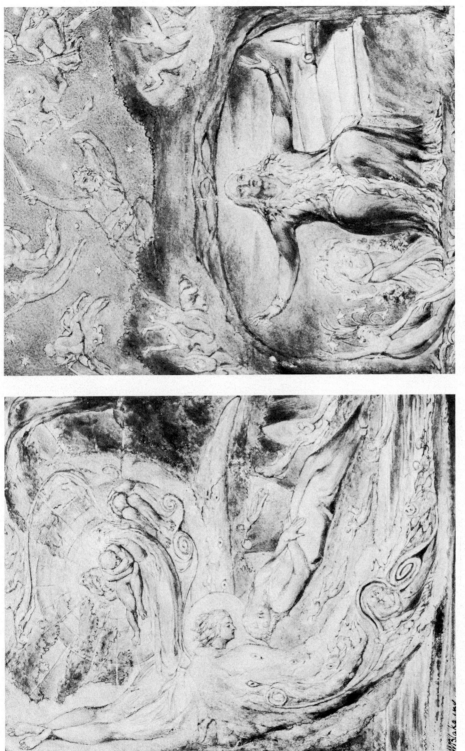

78. *Il Penseroso* vi: Milton: Old Age. Pierpont Morgan Library, New York.

77. *Il Penseroso* v: Mysterious Dream. Pierpont Morgan Library, New York.

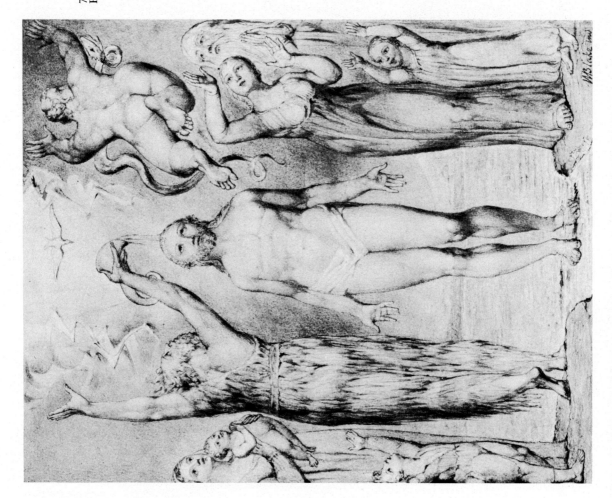

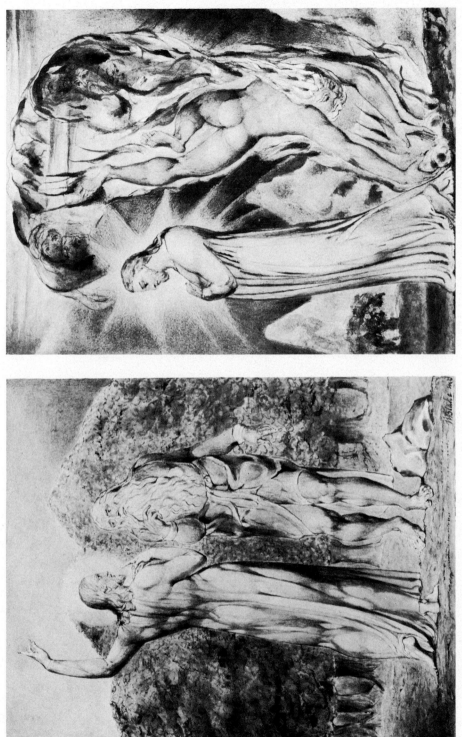

80. *Paradise Regained* II: The Temptation of Bread. Fitzwilliam Museum, Cambridge.

81. The Temptation of Bread. Frick Collection, New York.

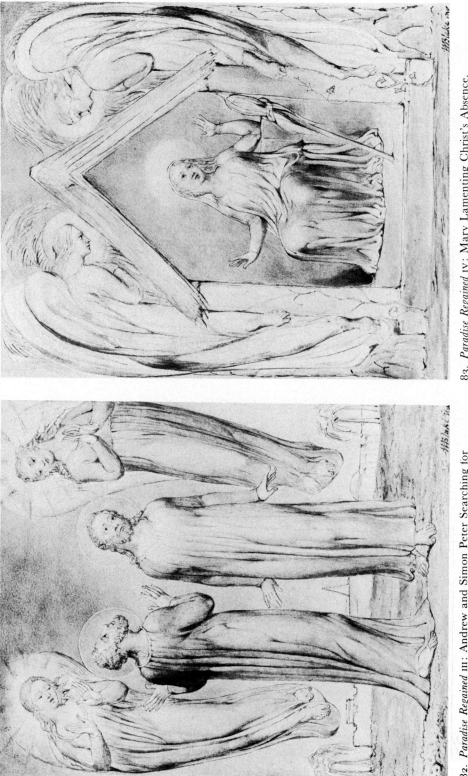

83. *Paradise Regained* IV: Mary Lamenting Christ's Absence. Fitzwilliam Museum, Cambridge.

82. *Paradise Regained* III: Andrew and Simon Peter Searching for Christ. Fitzwilliam Museum, Cambridge.

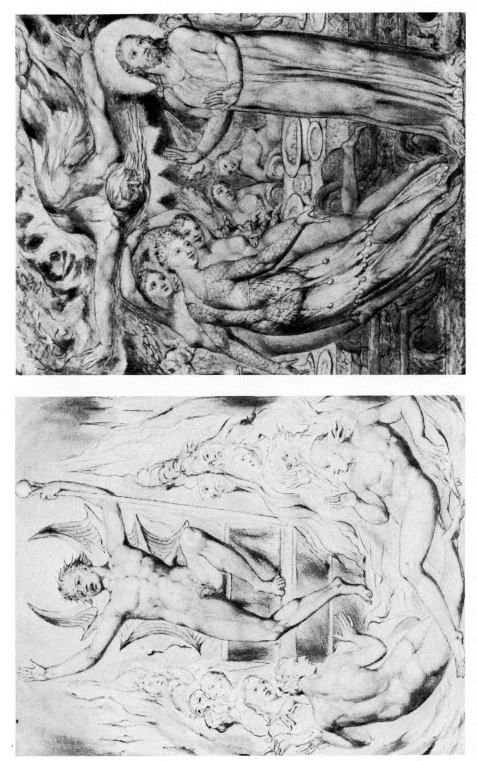

84. *Paradise Regained* v: Satan Addressing his Followers. Fitzwilliam Museum, Cambridge.

85. *Paradise Regained* vi: Christ Rejecting Satan's Banquet. Fitzwilliam Museum, Cambridge.

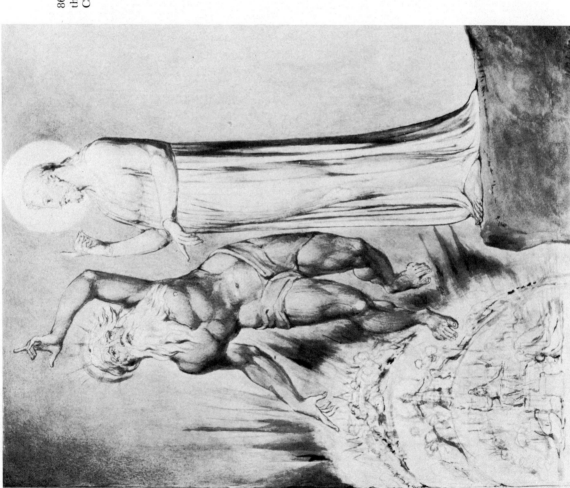

86. *Paradise Regained* VII: The Temptation of the Kingdoms. Fitzwilliam Museum, Cambridge.

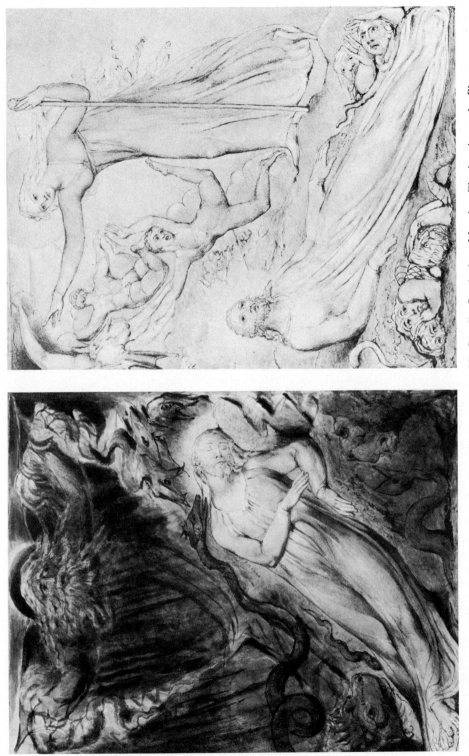

88. *Paradise Regained* IX: Morning Chasing Away the Phantoms. Fitzwilliam Museum, Cambridge.

87. *Paradise Regained* VIII: Christ's Troubled Dream. Fitzwilliam Museum, Cambridge.

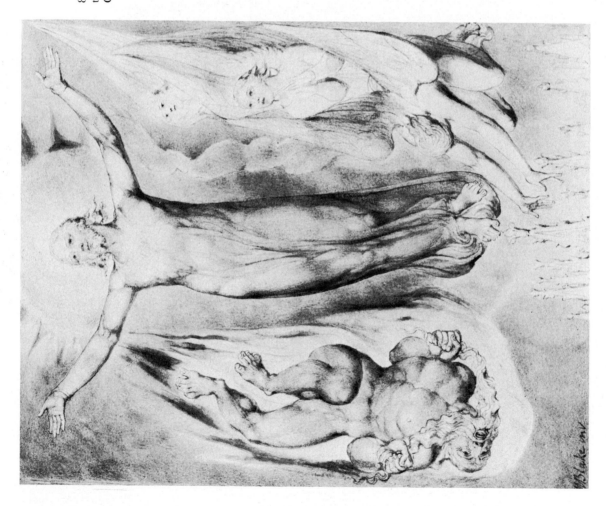

89. *Paradise Regained* x: The Temptation of the Pinnacle. Fitzwilliam Museum, Cambridge.

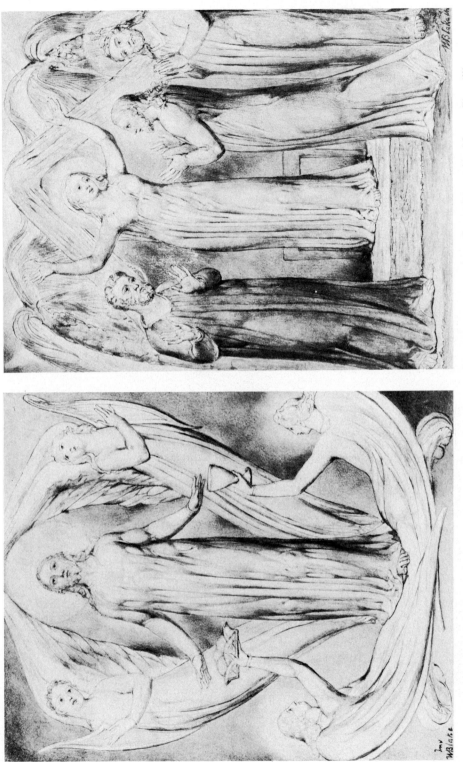

90. *Paradise Regained* XI: Christ Ministered to by Angels. Fitzwilliam Museum, Cambridge.

91. *Paradise Regained* XII: Christ Returning Home. Fitzwilliam Museum, Cambridge.

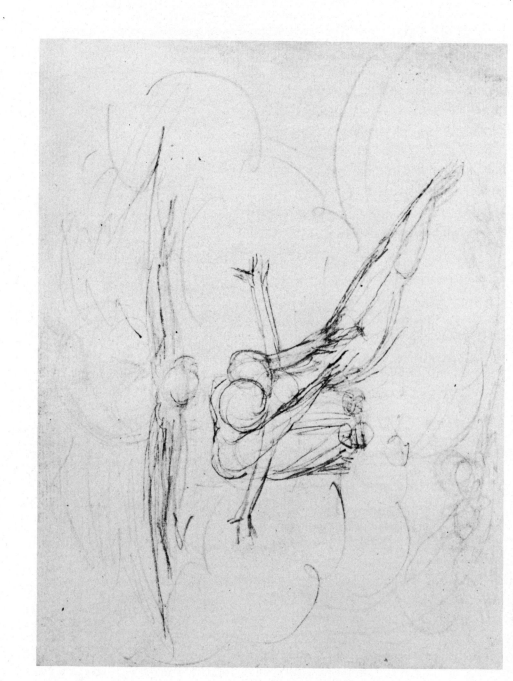

92. Christ Offering to Redeem Mankind. British Library (pencil sketch).